Power on the Move

Power on the Move
Adivasi and Roma Accessing Social Justice

Cristina-Ioana Dragomir

BLOOMSBURY ACADEMIC
LONDON • NEW YORK • OXFORD • NEW DELHI • SYDNEY

BLOOMSBURY ACADEMIC
Bloomsbury Publishing Plc
50 Bedford Square, London, WC1B 3DP, UK
1385 Broadway, New York, NY 10018, USA
29 Earlsfort Terrace, Dublin 2, Ireland

BLOOMSBURY, BLOOMSBURY ACADEMIC and the Diana logo
are trademarks of Bloomsbury Publishing Plc

First published in Great Britain 2024

Series design by Adriana Brioso
Cover image © AmitRane1975/iStock

A catalogue record for this book is available from the British Library.

A catalog record for this book is available from the Library of Congress.

ISBN: HB: 978-1-3502-2987-7
         PB: 978-1-3502-2991-4
       ePDF: 978-1-3502-2989-1
      eBook: 978-1-3502-2988-4

Typeset by RefineCatch Limited, Bungay, Suffolk

To find out more about our authors and books visit www.bloomsbury.com
and sign up for our newsletters.

This book is dedicated to:
My parents, Viorica and Lucian Andree, whose resilience in moving
impresses me every day.
Sadhguru Jaggi Vasudev, who inspired and pushed my limits beyond
anything I could ever imagine.
Aristide Zolberg whose life and generosity guided my path. Rest
in Power!

Contents

Acknowledgements

It is late evening in August 2021 in New York City. I get an alert on my phone; I set it up to alert me when anything is published about the Narikuravars, an Indian community. This time the alert reads that the Narikuravars have submitted a request for their legal status to be changed. I read it and then quickly send a text to Rajasekaran, asking for details. It is early in India, and I do not expect him to respond immediately. But he does. He sends me the information and the copy of the document submission, and asks me what else is needed.

The Narikuravars and the Roma people I have engaged with for this project have been working tirelessly for their communities, and they have been generous with their time, energy and knowledge. They have also been very patient with me, explaining in detail complex situations of their lives. I am grateful for their work and their time. I would like to thank Margareta Matache for her support, critical engagement, and challenging inquisitive thinking; Ciprian Necula – whose dedication and passion in fighting for the rights of Roma is unparalleled; and Doru Dima and Anca Dima for supporting my work in the community, and for always graciously hosting me.

In India, my work would have not been possible without the help of a myriad of people. Rajasekaran Selvam, Anuradha Jayashankar and Jayashankar Manikkam have been my guides, my friends and my support. Thank you very much. Translators and research assistants helped me every step of the way: Apoorva Trikannad, Partha, Bala Kumaran, Sukanya Janardhanan and Riyadhini Ravi have been wonderful in helping me navigate the Tamil language and more. Swarna Srininvarsan has impressed me with her maturity, intelligence, focus and dedication; the chapter 'Our Justice' would not have been possible without her help. Suzanne Boeters and Britta Peterson have been invaluable friends, and people who helped my work, supported me navigating logistics and, while challenging, continuously always heard me out.

In Romania, my work would not have been possible without the help of Georgeta Moarcaş, Cristian Pralea, Reika Szekely, Andras Istvan Popa, Levente Bodi and Ana Lacatuş. Special thanks to Iulia Salca, whose work and support in the field have been a blessing.

Over the years, different institutions and their representatives supported my work. Special thanks to the Isha Home School, which hosted me many times while in India and to the Rockefeller Institute at the State University of New York, Albany, where I started my project. Many thanks to the wonderful people from the Center for Advanced Study of India, University of Pennsylvania, and UPIASI in New Delhi where I was a fellow from 2016 to 2018. The support and love I received from Devesh Kapur, Juliana Di Giustini, Alan Atchinson and Georgette Rochlin were invaluable in my research and writing of this book. Many thanks to ZEIT- Stiftung Ebelin und Gerd Bucerius, especially to Anna Hofmann and Petra Borchard for their support on working on the project "Women Beyond Borders." Special thanks to the Global Liberal Studies Department at New York University, especially to Dean Julie Mostov, for their support to publish this book.

My work has been marked by two of my then professors – now friends – David Plotke and Terry Williams. Their mentoring, patience, encouragement, support and critical minds have guided my academic journey, and inspired my research.

The work of my friends, colleagues and partners in writing, Veronica Zebadua and Tal Correm, has been inspirational, academically powerful and caring. Thank you to my friends who were there for me when my research and my writing seem to be in disarray, but who never ceased to listen to me: Hadas Cohen, Ana Cristea and Dana Bucur. Warm thanks to Ryan Bhadlawala and Anushka Akhtar for their help in working their magic with the bibliography, and Ann Rostein, Arlene Ash, Florentina Rus and Alin Rus, whose nurture enabled me to finalize the manuscript.

For all their generosity, support and care I will always be grateful. You all have helped me greatly. Thank you.

1

Introduction

During one of my field visits in Ormeniș, Romania, I was walking the streets of the village with Doru, my key informant. Doru is in his early forties, tall, stout, with black hair and kind black eyes, who self-identifies as Roma. He is a teacher in the nearby village, mainly counselling Roma children. He is also completing a PhD in Sociology at Babeș-Bolyai University in Cluj, Romania, looking at the neo-Protestant religions' impact on Romanian Roma communities. His manner is soft, compassionate and gentle. He is married to one of the most achieved Romani language teachers, a beautiful tall woman, whose smile and candour are only suppressed by her calm and intelligent demeanor. They have a daughter, who was attending one of the best high schools in the country. Doru is always very busy with his work, his family and community life. In spite of his demanding schedule, he always has time to address with me matters that are pertinent in his community.

This summer day in 2016, we went to visit his uncle's house, situated next on the main village road. The house is big and imposing, with a large iron gate. His uncle and aunt received us well, and his uncle was eager to share with me his life story, a story of migration, of fleeing communism, of living in Italy and making a good life for himself and his family, and now retiring back in his home country. As he says it all in a charming and captivating manner, he refers to himself as 'Țigan' or 'Gypsy'. Not pejoratively – he just drops the name in conversation. After listening to him for a few minutes, Doru politely intervened: 'Uncle, but why do you say "Țigan", maybe Roma?' he softly suggested. His uncle turned around and with a loving, but dismissing gesture says: 'Eh . . . Roma . . . I am Țigan!' Doru does not quit: 'But uncle, this is a term that was given to us. It is not ours. And it is bad.' Doru's uncle continued unmoved: 'Well . . . I was born Țigan, this is who I am. Why change this name now? And I am proud to be "Țigan".'

I kept walking in the street listening to both of them. Their encounter brought to the fore the tender issues of today's ethnic politics: naming, self-identifying and labelling others. It is difficult to firmly take one side or the other without crossing ethical lines. Doru and his uncle represent two categories of identification of communities within Romania: Roma and 'Țigan'/'Gypsy'. In my fieldwork, I noticed that while the elites tend to predominantly identify as Roma, in communities the term 'Țigan'/'Gypsy' is still a prevalent form of self-identification. Moreover, this divide often follows both generational and educational lines. Put simply (while overlooking complexities on the ground), the more educated and younger a person is, the more likely they are to identify and publicly claim their identity as Roma. Thus, the identity debate between Doru and his uncle is neither surprising nor unknown, but one I often heard during my fieldwork, from Roma villages to city coffee shops and university venues.

Oceans away, in 2012, when I started my fieldwork in Tamil Nadu, south India, with the Narikuravar community, I was often asked how come I was there. Through translators, I tried to explain to the people greeting me that I was looking into how people who are nomadic fight for equality. To this, they asked how did I find out about them. I said that outsiders of the community told me that they are 'Gypsies' and I should talk to them. Whenever the word 'Gypsy' came into the conversation it produced a reaction from a few people. They pointed to themselves and proudly said: 'Gypsy'. The first time when I was visiting the community, one of the elderly men jumped up with joy, and he brought from his house a business-card and a stationery paper that were engraved (in English) with his name and title: 'President of the Gipsy'. The man neither spoke English, nor did he know how to read and write. His identity was one of prestige. 'Gypsy' is in Tamil Nadu an English term, and is a reference to a colonial hierarchy of power, in which the ones closer to the oppressor are in advantageous (hierarchical) positions. Thus, the self-identification as a 'Gypsy' (with various spellings) came from the powerful in the community, or from the young, educated people who usually speak and write in English, and who make use of this label when reaching outside of their community, and when claiming recognition internationally.

For example, one of my main participants, Rajasekaran, a Narikuravar man in his thirties, highly educated with two Masters degrees, speaking Vagriboli (his community's language), Tamil and English, posted on social media several photos of his community receiving supplies to help them overcome the COVID-19 crisis, saying: 'In order to meet our food and family requirement of Tamil Nadu Gypsies who lost their income due to this pandemic and lockdown we have been supporting them' (social media, 7 October 2020). Rajasekaran often posts on social media about the Narikuravar community, in English, using the 'Gypsy' label and hashtag, aiming to garner support and to receive donations for the Narikuravars in need.

Naming as a political endeavour: 'Gypsy', Roma, nomad or Adivasi/ Dalit

This book traces how people who find themselves in historically marginalized positions empower themselves to access social justice today. I showcase the fight of historically excluded communities, whose activism – when judged against that of mainstream communities – appears as minimal, negligible or completely absent. In other words, if struggle for justice is seen as lobbying, registering to vote, organizing boycotts and petition drives, etc., communities like the Narikuravar and the Roma might look passive or politically inarticulate. This book challenges this paradigm and offers a different perspective, a holistic understanding of the fight for justice, by looking at both formal and informal practices that expand in various areas of life and society.

In doing so, I reveal how structural violence and resistance manifests to address power inequality, while working through legacies and practices of mobility. In this process, following Rao (2018), I suggest we see resistance practices that Adivasi and Roma communities exhibit not as destructive forms of engagement, but as forms of social mobilization, as mechanisms aimed at 'ensuing changes in the society or asserting identity' (Rao, 2018: 19). These practices might not necessarily be fully developed into resistance movements, but are employed in various settings, at different levels of organization. They are tools of recognition in the eyes of power, ways to draw the state's attention towards their precarity, and as Mitchell (2012) says, ways to 'hail the state'. Thus, different from understanding these forms of struggle of the Roma and Adivasi/ Narikuravars as forms of resistance to the state, we should see them as forms of trying to access the state, in their own terms, in their own voices.[1]

Neither of the instances presented above were isolated occurrences, but ones that happened rather often, challenging the way I was to approach my research on access to justice. They revealed, the underpinnings of the politics of naming.[2] Naming creates a hierarchical taxonomy of power, where the terms of 'Gypsy', 'Roma', 'Adivasi' and 'Indigenous' place (and often lock) people in hierarchical positions that have reverberating economic, social and political consequences. Thus, while thousands of miles apart, my examples come together and bring to view how labels are changing depending on contexts, how they are transformed and re-invented by some users, and how naming can support the dignity of people and communities, or conversely infringe on their human rights. Following Iris Zavalla, Mignolo (2018: 22) argues that 'the heuristic code of naming is a form of political cartography or mapmaking that fixes the cultural image, subordinates differences, and radically destroys identities'. Mignolo, referring to Aimé Césaire, continues by explaining how naming was 'intended to annihilate all that existed before': 'I am talking about societies drained of their essence, cultures trampled underfoot, institutions undermined, lands confiscated, religions smashed, magnificent artistic creations destroyed, extraordinary possibilities wiped out, I am talking about millions of men [sic] torn from their gods, their land, their habits, their life—from life, from the dance, from wisdom' (Ibid.).

Naming and defining communities are not ahistorical, apolitical and amoral endeavours. Definitions presuppose impositions, self-identifications, hierarchies of power (i.e., on who does the naming of whom), and in doing so they impose a system of values. As such, the 'Gypsy' label has often been imposed as a synonym for mobile people, for those who are identified as nomadic. And because nomadism is perceived as a negative (even illegal) community and an individual characteristic, 'anti-nomadism contributes to explaining and justifying Roma [and other mobile communities'] exclusion' (Lauritzen, 2018: 59).

Referring to those often labelled (and at times self-labelling) as 'Gypsy' in a manner that is respectful, promoting a dignified approach is a political process. But to date, there is no consensus on the politics of naming, neither on the ground, nor among the elites. Many scholars and activists argue in favour of the use of the term Roma, because the names 'Gypsy' or 'Țigan' are loaded with negative connotations. For instance:

> The T-word holds heavy historical weight, along with its illegal and offensive nature. The 'Țigan' category connoted 'slave' for 500 years. There has been evidence that Romani leaders have demanded to replace the name Țigani with Roma since 1919, and there have been political efforts to officially recognize Roma as the umbrella term for Romani groups across the world since 1971 and even prior to that.
>
> Matache, 2017[3]

Alternatively, other scholars, like Yaron Matras, engage in historical analysis of the label, and conclude that:

> A confusion of terms has thus arisen in almost all European languages, on the one hand, 'Gypsy' refers to a very specific population – the people who call themselves, in their own language, Rom and who were referred to as 'Egyptians' in earlier documents; on the other hand, 'Gypsy' (and its various equivalent

terms in other languages) is taken as a way of describing certain social characteristics that were associated with Roms, but also with other populations: slaves, foreigners, and especially travelers and migrant nomads.

Matras: 2004: 19–20[4]

Furthermore, Matras, in *I Met Lucky People: The Story of the Romani Gypsies* (2014), still advocates for using the term 'Romani gypsies'. Similarly, the same name is used today to address diverse mobile Indian communities:

> The gypsies are indigenous people whose main occupation were hunting but are also considered as one of the greatest bandit communities in south India. The word gypsies is derived from Europe, which means nomadic people. Tamilnadu is a home to various categories of gypsies, and among them the nomadic tribes or gypsy named as Koravar (or) Narikoravan (or) Kuruvikaran stands in the forefront. The occupation of Narikoravar community is mostly hunting jackals and other wild animals.

Chandru and Thrimalaisamy, 2019

Differently, Matache draws our attention to the underpinnings of this designation: '*Gypsy* is a racialized and fixed construction that has fed Roma oppression through their steady representations as thieves, uneducated, nomads, and uncivilized' (Matache, 2017).[5] Matache further argues for using the name Roma as an alternative to the pejorative 'Gypsy' – and using the label of 'Gypsy' only in particular cases. Additionally, Matras' perspective that differentiates between the label 'Gypsy' and the Roma allows us to distinguish between communities named under the same definition (i.e., 'Gypsy') because of their social or economic traits, and ethnic communities (like the Roma or Adivasi) who have different histories, languages and traditions.

I contend that the label 'Gypsy' is primarily a social construction that enabled and reproduced systematized practices of injustice. This label subjected many communities for hundreds of years, and should be used with caution, mainly when people labelled as such prefer this self-identity. Throughout this book, I employ mostly the name Roma when I refer to European, mostly Romanian, communities.

'Gypsy' and Adivasi

However, the issue of naming is further complicated in other parts of the world, where the name Roma is not prevalent, neither employed by communities, nor by elites. In India for example, using the name 'Gypsy' to address people is yet again a marker of colonial labelling. For many Indian communities this label is predominately used by outsiders, but also by the members of the communities, while the Roma name is utterly unknown. Diverse communities labelled under 'Gypsy' category typically prefer the name of their unique community: Jogis, Yerukulas, etc., or the larger identification (recognized under law) of Adivasi, Scheduled Tribe or indigenous community. But their self-identification is not necessarily recognized within the mechanisms of the state. To date, the Narikuravars are not formally (i.e., by law) recognized as of yet (Dragomir, 2017, 2020b) as Adivasi, even though this is their preferred (larger) identity. Changing their official naming – as we will see in the following chapters – has been their main political struggle for decades.

To further the understanding of naming as a political process, the analysis of the Narikuravar's and Roma's process of accessing social justice will also be placed in conversation with literature on the Adivasi's historical and recent mobilization across India. Of course, the Adivasi community is not a simple identification in itself. Most groups that identify as such, claim their identity on the basis of belonging to the land, as being endogenous to a particular territory. The Narikuravars are a historically nomadic community and they do not have an ancestral claim to land. As such, they fall outside of the narrow definition of the Adivasi concept. Labelling them as Adivasi might seem inappropriate, but considering their voluntary self-identification, and their unwavering desire to be recognized as a Scheduele Tribe, I will refer to them as such.

Indigenous people and nomads

While for many indigeneity is intrinsically linked to claims to land, for Gandhi and Sundar (2019), being mobile and an early inhabitant of the South Asian land are co-existing traits:

> Nomads are one of the early inhabitants of the earth. They are of different types – nomadic tribal communities who are wedded to the nature; nomadic tribal communities who are traditionally involved in begging; and people who have become nomads owing to the demands of modern life. The term nomad stands for one who is always on the move. Anthropologists have earlier identified pastoralists as nomadic tribes. Nomadism is defined as a way of life.
>
> Gandhi and Sundar, 2019: 25

Gandhi and Sundar (2019) further define nomadism according to the *Cambridge International Dictionary of English* (1995) and the *Oxford Advanced Learner's Dictionary*, which define nomads and nomadism as a continuous state of movement, assuming lack of homes, and perpetual mobility of individuals and groups. These definitions are good tools to identify nomadic traits, but they fall short on several accounts. One is that historically nomadic communities have not moved continuously, but they had places of (temporary) settlement depending on the terrain and resources that they came across. Moreover, being nomadic does not mean to not have a 'home'. It might be that some nomadic people do not have a 'house', but to conflate the two is a misunderstanding and a mislabelling that underprivileges those who move. Many Narikuravars identify as nomadic, and some Roma refer to a history of their community's nomadism, but it is important to explain this characteristic further. In India, The National Commission on Denotified, Nomadic and Semi-nomadic Tribes (NCDNSNT), declared that nomads: 'May have a myth according to which they were settled at a place, but were constrained to move, and may consider that place as the one to which they would eternally belong, but this belief in an unchanging location where they emerged and, in some cases, to which they like to return, does not reduce their status as being nomadic.'

Thus, the NCDNSNT (2008)[6] refuses the artificial (and often inaccurate) differentiation nomadism and semi-nomadism,[7] as one that often causes a hierarchical value-based system, by highlighting that both communities and individuals could be mobile and have sedentary places as well.[8] Often those who are mobile have also been exoticized and essentialized:

> Nomadism had developed a much-valued sense of freedom, which meant 'not to be under the authority of an alien power'. Nomads saw the world without the 'roof' and the 'barricades', without 'barriers' and 'boundaries'. The entire world, for them, was one, and they moved in and around its niches in accordance with the demands of their lifestyle. The territorial frontiers and limits that the state had imposed upon its people were unknown to nomads, and they tried their best to escape from them.[9]

Their patterns of mobility have been counterposed to those of the settled communities, and from this juxtaposition further moral, ethical and political concepts were (precariously) drawn to reflect the differences between the communities, which often lead to them being seen as:

> Both a threat and a nuisance. They [i.e. nomads] could harm the settled people and disappear into the wilderness. (…) Thus, describing them as 'criminal' in many cases, to be dealt with severely, but also delineated stringent measures to force them to settle down. Once they sedentarized, it was thought that the law would be able to keep a vigil on them. Nomadism made them independent and unshackled, whilst sedentarization came hand in hand with surveillance. This

would explain why nomads have time and again opposed their settling down
that the state planned for them.

                                                            Gandhi and Sundar, 2019: 13

The legacy of caste: Adivasi and Dalits

To complicate matters even further, the Adivasi label is fluid, and it often
intersects that of the Dalits. Often Adivasi and Dalits are discussed under the
same term, and identified within the same label: Dalit/Adivasi (Yengde, 2019).
As a result of this naming-fluidity, to understand the systematic injustice
the Narikuravars encounter, as well as possible avenues for addressing it, the
Dalit scholarship revealing the struggle for justice for India's marginalized
communities is of help. While Adivasi literature is rather scarce, recent studies
engaging Dalits have been emerging. Both Dalits and Adivasi have been subjected
to systematic racism/'casteism' and practices of exclusion (Yengde, 2019) for
centuries, which underlines their commonality. In practice, the Narikuravars
distinguish themselves from Dalits, whom – Narikuravars have told me – 'spit on
us', highlighting the internal hierarchies and ethnic/social divides that exist
within and outside minority groups.

    In sum, the Roma, Adivasi and 'Gypsy' namings and definitions are far from
perfect, as they propose fixed and narrow identifications over a 'self-transforming,
multiple, ambiguous Romani [and Narikuravar] identity' (Matache, 2017). We
need to understand these processes as a part of political engagements that
stabilize hierarchies of power that are reinforced on the ground. While limited,
they are operational tools to allow for critical engagement and flexibility, as well
as to empower communities to force these meanings to their logical end, and to
reformulate them.

The Roma and Adivasi: myths of origins

While this study looks at the political process of communities that are often
labelled as 'Gypsy', the question of a closer link between Roma and Adivasi
often comes to the fore. Deeply grounded in fog and mystery, it is typically
assumed that the two communities share an Indian origin (Shashi, 1990;
Hancock, 1991; Crowe, 1996; Barany, 2002). They are described as 'Gypsy', which
refers to their ethnicity, assumed criminal behaviour, nomadic and mobile
traditions (Crowe, 1996: 129). In fact, the Roma and Adivasi labels overlap with

that of 'Gypsy', covering vastly diverse communities, present in both European and South Asian countries. The Roma and the Adivasi speak many languages. In Europe many speak a dialect of Romani, a language considered by many linguists to be similar to Sanskrit and Hindi. In South Asia, they might speak languages connected to Hindi and Sanskrit. Both groups typically observe the religion of the majority of people in the places where they live; thus, they are primarily Orthodox Christians in Romania, Muslims in Albania, Catholics in Hungary and Hindus and Muslims in India or Pakistan (Shashi, 1990). Nevertheless, they also observe distinctive religious traditions, such as worshiping a black virgin Mary, or goddess Meenashki, which reminds scholars of the Hindu goddess Kali. As we will see in detail in the next chapters, Roma and Adivasi people are diverse. While racist voices would argue that they are 'darker', even 'black' skinned, different from 'them' (whoever the 'them' is), they often have similar physical features to the local population, making them almost indistinguishable (at least for outsiders).

Mobility and criminality

The Roma and Adivasi peoples are often described as 'stranger' – they are the 'other' who came from somewhere else, and their historical nomadism is too often assumed and rarely investigated (Shashi, 1990; Fonseca, 1996). It is moreover an over-sweeping generalization that does not take into account different realities, in different geographical areas on the ground. Finally, it is also a categorization that has negative legal implications as nomadism has been historically associated with criminality, both in India and Europe, and those labelled as 'Gypsy' were thought to be both 'nomads' and 'criminals':

> Between the seventeenth and nineteenth century, nomadism and criminality became inter-linked and associated with the term "Gypsy". This connection has been perpetuated over centuries, leaving behind a strong social, legal, and political legacy that labels those considered "Gypsy" as criminals and nomads in need of rehabilitation. This intersection was facilitated by a legal system intimately connected with other literary discourses.
>
> Dragomir, 2019: 79

Thus, across Europe, especially in England, from the seventeenth century onwards those who moved came under the strict scrutiny of the state, and both their mobility and behaviour were criminalized. In pre-colonial India, nomads were overall better accommodated within the society, but nomadism was at times associated with criminal behaviour. However, once colonialist ruling brought its stereotypes and legal mechanisms, all nomadic communities of South Asia came under rigorous surveillance, and became severely criminalized (Dragomir, 2019).

Similarly in Europe, over centuries, state powers imposed their categorizations over mobile groups. They tightened control over those who moved, and criminalized them.[10] This labelling makes people suspicious and often reticent to the label 'nomad', and makes scholars (activists and others) interested in dissociating their community from mobility. In doing so, they also reveal a value-judgement that appropriates the hierarchy of the 'Gadje' (of the non-Roma), who always prefer the settled to the nomad, the sedentary to the mobile. In other words, reticence of describing the Roma people as traditionally nomadic reveals the imbedded, historically rooted issues that many have with nomadism and mobility. Once accepted and practiced, this aversion to those who move extends to the Roma and beyond. It not only leads to discrimination of traditionally mobile communities (such as Roma or Travellers), but it reflects on migrants, refugees and asylum seekers.

Theoretical engagements

'You know,' they say, 'the Tisgani are like your Negroes: foreign, lazy, shiftless, untrustworthy and black' (Bhabha, 2017: 1, citing Romanians in administrative positions). These appellatives are unfortunately not rare occurrences, but are often heard among European politicians, decision makers and the population at large. In India, the Narikuravar and other nomadic tribal communities are often called 'different', 'darker', 'dirty', 'lazy' and 'unruly'. On both continents, those labelled as 'Gypsy' are often over sexualized (Oprea, 2012), and considered a threat to the moral values. These patterns of discrimination, while an ocean apart, are strikingly similar as they follow the same lines of racist divide, producing and reproducing oppression and subordination.[11]

Roma studies typically take an ethnic perspective (Shashi, 1990; Crowe, 1996; Petcut, 2016). In recent years, scholarship has also been discussing the Roma as a category constructed by non-Roma (Surdu, 2016). At the same time, Nicolae Gheorghe (via Ciprian Necula, private correspondence, 2018) considered the possibility of understanding the Roma as an ethno-class, emphasizing that 'racism and racialization cannot be detached from the economic-political transformation of the last three to four decades, which is often described as the expansion of "neoliberalism"' (Bogdan et al., 2018: 6).

In India, Adivasi studies are typically categories used under ethnic research (Dube, 1977; Majumdar, 1937, 1961), which often brought along 'stereotypes of backwardness, nudity and isolation of tribes' (Ranendra, 2020), and more recently tribal studies (Behera, 2020), which challenges them. Similarly, the issue of economic precarity has been discussed over the past decade (Dubey, 2018; Muralidhar, 2018) as: limited access to education (Gupta and Padel, 2019) and health care (Chaudary, 2018; Dragomir and Zafiu, 2019); overall exclusion from developmental benefits (Gandhi, 2018; Rao, 2018); and facing hazardous situations (Das and Padel, 2010; Heidegger and Wiese, 2020). This turn in Adivasi scholarship led to a change in classification, which has been slowly contouring along the concepts of class and economic inequity.

Considering the complex and long-lasting structural forms of oppression the Roma or Adivasi have endured, it is important to analyse their process of marginalization considering their historical colonialization, racialization, class and mobility. Studying the overlapping categories of discrimination within the context of their occurrence, informs us about the crux of identities that these groups experience. Understanding the process of discrimination as 'further reinforced through liberalization and privatization allowing market forces to determine directions of production consumption and distribution' (Rao, 2018) allows for the analysis of the strategies of empowerment that these communities employ to tackle marginalization.

Thus, to properly address these forms of historical oppression, a mélange of analytical tools is necessary to understand, reflect upon, and dismantle forms of epistemic, practical and systemic oppression: critical race theory, decolonial perspective, theories of intersectionality, and feminist theories of power.

Critical Race Theory: dismantling structural discrimination based on race

Seeing the different treatment of Roma and Adivasi/Narikuravars through the lenses of structural and systemic oppression has been associated with racism and studies of race. The recognition that racism is structural and systematic, persisting within institutions and practices (rather than an individual and sporadic occurrence) is rooted in Critical Race Theory (CRT). CRT investigates the power structures, showing how they are based on white privilege and white supremacy; it furthermore brings into view that they systemetically perpetuate the marginalization of people of color (Brooks, 1994: 85, Soni-Sinha, 2012; Few-Demo, 2014). Furthermore, CRT's understanding that discrimination is structural, part of legal systems, allows for comparison to the studies of race in the United States (Chang, 2018) and beyond.

This engagement with CRT in recent years inspired the development of Critical Romani Studies,[12] and Critical Tribal Theory (Brayboy, 2005), which provide the theoretical framework necessary to address the complex relationship between Roma/indigenous communities and governments. Thus, we can now begin to understand these groups' 'liminality as both racial and legal/political groups (Brayboy, 2005: 425).

Decolonial perspectives: undoing power

The racialization of the Roma and Adivasi/Narikuravars is nevertheless different from the one taking place in the United States, where CRT has been developing. It has been a part of a double (concomitant) colonial process: one from outside powers (being the British in India, or Austro-Hapsburg/Turkish/Russian in Europe), and one from the internal elites (Lee, 2000) within their country. This is because, as Michael Hanchard (2010) argues, before the European colonial powers engaged in colonizing other parts of the world, they racially colonized others within the continent. Moreover, in the process of unifying disperse groups under one 'nation', majorities have often colonized minority communities, and exercised control over those who were declared unruly and disrupting to larger national projects. It is therefore important to understand the 'Gypsy' identity as a historical construction in which colonialism played an important role.

This process was based on the 'Western' European mindset:

> The colonial structure of power produced the specific social discriminations which later were codified as 'racial', 'ethnic', 'anthropological' or 'national', according to the times, agents, and populations involved. These intersubjective constructions, the product of Eurocentered colonial domination, were even assumed to be 'objective', 'scientific' categories, then of a historical significance. That is, as natural phenomena, not referring to the history of power. This power structure was, and still is, the framework within which operate the other social relations of classes or estates.
>
> Quijano, 2007: 168

In the same vein, those labelled as 'Gypsy' have been part of systems of discrimination, which in the name of science and objectivity they were assigned to marginal places for centuries, thus reinforcing their exploitation domination, and discrimination. These forms of power might not take the classical form of colonialization, which extracted land and resources from colonized communities, but it did systematically oppress the Roma and the Narikuravars by imposing:

> modes of knowing, of producing knowledge, of producing perspectives, images and systems of images, symbols, modes of signification, over the resources, patterns, and instruments of formalized and objectivised expression, intellectual or visual. It was followed by the imposition of the use of the rulers' own patterns of expression, and of their beliefs and images with reference to the supernatural. These beliefs and images served not only to impede the cultural production of the dominated, but also as a very efficient means of social and cultural control, when the immediate repression ceased to be constant and systematic.
>
> Ibid.: 169

Thus, it is important to distinguish between two forms of colonial power: a political/economic one and an epistemic one that recreates and reinforces the former (Mignolo, 2002). To address these injustices, we need to commit to a 'de-colonial turn', which:

> involves interventions at the level of power, knowledge, and being through varied actions of decolonization and 'desgener-accio'n'. It opposes the paradigm of war which has driven modernity for more than five hundred years, with a radical shift in the social and political agent, the attitude of the knower, and the position in regards to whatever threatens the preservation of being, particularly the actions of the damne's.
>
> Maldonado-Torres, 2007: 262

Specifically, to dismantle this colonial legacy we need to engage in decolonial work, exposing and dismantling gripping structures of power, to ensure that 'colonized and racialized subjects' are no longer pressed '*against* the colonial matrix of power in all of its dimensions, and *for* the possibilities of an otherwise' (Mignolo, 2018: 22). This is a minutious task that requires 'the recognition and undoing of the hierarchical structures of race, gender, heteropatriarchy, and class that continue to control life, knowledge, spirituality, and thought, structures that are clearly intertwined with and constitutive of global capitalism and Western modernity' (Mignolo, 2018: 22).

Supporting work on decolonialization within Eastern Europe, Boatca argues in favour of a different process of knowing that she names as 'counter-mapping', which 'can serve as a decolonial strategy to the essentialization of nation-states and world regions in social scientific and political discourse and propose a relational perspective capable of revealing the constitutive entanglements through which a global capitalism grounded in colonial expansion interlinked all areas of the world' (Boatca, 2021: 244).

These decolonial perspectives and tools challenge forms of oppression, especially those of epistemological and capitalist dominance, and are in turn empowering the analysis of the processes of accessing justice for the Roma and Narikuravars, in their own terms, without aiming to draw them closer to the colonizer's views.

Intersectionality and power

Structures of power, and epistemological articulations and practices of oppressions, do not create even systems, or treat every racialized and colonized body in the same way. Systems of colonialization are also interlinked to practices of oppression based on gender and class. As Patricia Hill Collins proposes, I argue that we need to investigate 'interlocking systems of oppression' (Collins, 2002) and examine race, sex, class, gender, ethnicity/tribal status, and analyse how their combination plays out in various settings to create, and reinforces hierarchies of domination. As Collins explains:

> [First] the notion of interlocking oppressions refers to the macro-level connections linking systems of oppression such as race, class, and gender. This is the model describing the social structures that create social positions. Second, the notion of intersectionality describes micro-level processes — namely, how each individual and group occupies a social position within interlocking structures of oppression described by the metaphor of intersectionality. Together they shape oppression.
>
> Collins, 2002: 82, in Clegg and Haugaard, 2009: 306

Likewise, Crenshaw (1991) shows how institutionalized discourses legitimize power dynamics that create and reinforce hierarchies and marginalization of racialized groups. However, when discourses seemingly resist racialization – such as feminism – but overlook race, they end up legitimatizing marginalization. Thus, she suggests, we need to investigate in tandem patriarchy and racism using the framework of intersectionality, which brings into view the interdependence of race and gender, but also that of class, in creating overlapping and interdependent systems of discrimination or disadvantage.[13] As we will see in Chapter 4, intersectionality allows us to understand what specific members of the two communities face and how they act against interconnected forms of oppression and discrimination. Particularly, this view furthers our recognition of the crux of injustice that Roma and Narikuravar women face, and how they have to undertake complex strategies to overcome injustice.

Feminist theories of power

To understand access to social justice for the Roma and Adivasi, I use Nancy Fraser's tripartite theory. Fraser wrote that different from previous theories, which argue that injustice is either cultural or economic, we need to investigate these two in tandem, and show that there are two dimensions associated with injustice: recognition and distribution. Therefore, 'injustice is misrecognition, a form of subordination rooted in institutionalized patterns of cultural values. And, injustice is maldistribution, meaning economic subordination, rooted in structural features of economic systems' (Fraser, 2000: 117[14]).

Fraser argues that: 'By understanding recognition as a question of status, and by examining its relations to economic class, one can take steps to mitigate, if not to fully solve, the displacement of struggles for redistribution; and by avoiding the identity model, one can begin to diminish, if not fully dispel, the dangerous tendency to reify the collective identities' (Ibid.: 120). She later on added another dimension, political representation:

> Participative parity is an interpretative ideal of social justice, and as such, does not exist. Instead, those who wish to live in the condition of participative parity should use the concept as a critical ideal to enable them, precisely, to reveal the existing disparities in participation, the asymmetries and the blocks placed by power, etc., and above all, to identify those obstacles that are rooted in social relations.
>
> Fraser, 2009[15]

While Fraser discusses the power dynamics of states, and the structural underpinning that facilitate one's access to justice, this tripartite approach is helpful as a tool in analysing the struggle for justice that communities employ. It allows us to analytically differentiate between aspects of justice that are interrelated in practice. In other words, it allows for an in-depth research and analysis of mechanisms that are in place when striving to access parity. Fraser's complex view takes into consideration questions of identity, economics and politics, arguing that only by looking at all three aspects could we reveal how mechanisms and dynamics of power operate. This approach also highlights the practices that both individuals and communities encounter in their specific contexts.

Moreover, Fraser's work (2000, 2010) shows how the twenty-first century brought to the fore 'the clash of rival conceptions of the substance of justice, each effectively equipped with its own scale' (Fraser, interview 2009: 4). This heterogeneity makes judging justice by one single measure, or scale, unfair. Therefore, rather than debating upon which scale of justice needs to be used, we need to focus on the process of accessing justice.

In the next pages, I employ these analytical tools to challenge the way in which we work with the Narikuravars/Adivasi and Roma, away from the Eurocentric/North-American-focused paradigm. In line with Mignolo and Walsh (2018), I place this book within the decolonial conversation, which (to date) has fallen short of integrating the Roma and Adivasi, 'and build understandings that both cross geopolitical locations and colonial differences, and contest the totalizing claims and political-epistemic violence of modernity' (Mignolo and Walsh, 2018: 1).

Creating research

In the summer of 2017, as I enter the Roma community on Strada Olt, Ormeniș, Romania, one of the young Roma women – who socialized with me a few days back – calls me over and says: 'I hope you will not put these videos on Facebook. My husband can see them, and then ... you know ...' She looks at me as if I understood, but I simply look back at her. She continues: 'He will ...' and she makes the gesture of being beaten. I empathically smile back, and we both nod as tacit gendered accomplices. I assure her that these videos will not be public. Years later, the memory of that comment stirs in me a wave of entangled feelings of sadness, anger, frustration and compassion.

My work in the field, both in Romania and India, has been intense. I had to be aware of my being, my vulnerabilities and privileges, and of how my presence influences my field of work. Throughout the time, I also learnt to pay attention to my translators and informants, and acknowledge their words even when their views actually differed from mine. As in the example above, more than once have I witnessed injustices towards women within Roma and Narikuravar communities, and I had to work my way through them, and come to terms with my limited role and power. I also often had to sit in tirades of racist discourses from the outsiders of the communities, about how I did not know (mainly because I was not a local) or how I 'forgot' how the Roma/Narikuravars 'really are'. I also had to justify my work as a non-Roma, non-Indian to those who challenged my work as an outsider. These are research complications that I have been acknowledging in my previous works (Dragomir 2017, 2018, 2019, 2020a), where I reflected on my positionality, and its impactions for this project. These are mostly engagements that highlight the dynamics of power that enabled, constructed, shaped and limited my work for this book.

Work on this project started in 2012, when I went to Tamil Nadu, south India, and began my work with communities that were labelled as 'Gypsy'. I was aware that there have been studies that provoke one into thinking about Roma communities in Europe as having their ethnic roots within the South Asian continent. I knew little beyond this; I knew little about Indian politics, about caste, or tribal hierarchies. And even less about Indian grassroots social movements. In spite of these lacunes of knowledge, it was rather easy to distinguish patterns of discrimination and marginalization that communities labelled as 'Gypsy' in India embodied. They were strikingly similar to the negative stereotyping of those labelled as 'Țigan' in Romania. It became quickly obvious that the term 'Gypsy' is mostly used to exoticize and to over-sexualize communities, and at the same time to impose one's power system and reinforce racial hierarchies. Pseudo-historical accounts, mostly referring to their historical mobility, are often used to invoke some unclear past that says they 'are not from here' (wherever 'here' is). This quickly employed perspective legitimizes strangeness and so-called 'inferiority', enabling people to condone practices of abuse.

While these patterns are visible in daily encounters, they can be spotted within institutions and structures, resulting in deeply-rooted political dimensions. For example, similar to the already familiar situations of many Roma living in Romania, I learned that communities labelled as 'Gypsy' in India live on the margins of the road, or in 'settlements' (i.e. housing typically given by the government in an attempt to sedentarize them), which are outside of the main lucrative land. Moreover, similar to the Roma groups, communities in India were considered resistant to inclusion, assimilation, civilization and overall progress. Their marginalization is made to be the 'Gypsy's' fault, overlooking hundreds of years of discrimination, abuse and systematic marginalization.

There are many differences between the two communities, and the contexts (both historical and contemporary) in which they live. A comparison between them will always be unequal, disproportioned and will always be forced within a limited centralized, Eurocentric/North American vocabulary. But when there are discriminatory patterns and terminologies/vocabularies present in political practices inflicted upon communities, a close investigation of forms of resisting discrimination and racism is essential. It is my aim in this book to engage and dismantle these transnational forms of racialization, colonialization and oppression, and in doing so to create bounds of solidarity. To me, these goals outweigh the possible comparative imperfections, as they speak to/about the life of peoples, and thus make this (imperfect) endeavour worthy of consideration.

Very often, work with Roma and Adivasi communities is a product of colonialization, as research is imposed on them. Their lives, struggles and processes are made to fit into the existent canons of various disciplines. Their quest for dignity and access to resources and mobility is often grasped through a neo-colonial gaze: it is confined into the struggle of other communities, their aims defined along the mainstream's standards, and their failure to reach these is intrinsically seen as their own fault.

To address these aspects, I have been committed to empowering their voices by 'naming one's own reality'. Following CRT methodological vision, using in-depth individual and community interviews,[16] I employ storytelling and counter-storytelling to showcase, explore and experience racial/caste oppression. Understanding that storytelling supersedes theory, I allow their narrative to challenge and reinvent theories of social justice.

Insider/outsider

Not being a part of the Narikuravar or Roma communities, conducting research from outside-in poses ethical and academic questions. Research with systematically marginalized, racialized and discriminated-against communities has been conducted, reinforcing structures of power and domination. As a result, the Narikuravar and Roma communities have been essentialized, exoticized and often further marginalized. Scholars may have had good intentions, but the results have been furthering oppression and domination of cultures, tribes and communities all over the world.

The present book aims to be different. It is not a study 'of' or 'about' the two communities, it is rather a study of the processes that communities with a long-lasting history of mobility, of living at the margins of nation-states, away from centralized power, engaged in accessing social justice. I present in the following pages the processes that they employed over the past thirty years. In doing so, I do not aim to dodge the ethical question of research with the Narikuravar and Roma communities, but to formulate strong ethical principles of engaging traditionally and/or historically nomadic communities in their own rights. I would like to stand firm about standards of fairness in research with communities, who – because of their mobility – have been typically excluded from 'the room where it [i.e. politics] happens'. Thus, I aim to address three interconnected concerns: (A) to challenge the notion of belonging to 'a land', as the necessary premise for political engagement; (B) to tackle pejorative negative association with nomadism and mobility; (C) to show how traditionally mobile communities have been politically active, engaging in social movements, organizing and making demands to the state. These processes, while not identical, or reproducible in their entirety, could also be used in understanding mobilization of migrants, including elite migrants, ex-pats, internally displaced people and refugees.

We need to discuss the limitations of this research in which the author is an 'outsider'. There are studies that claim that being an insider in the community is more of a valuable process, while others present being an outsider as a more objective manner of conducting research. These questions and doubts have permeated my fieldwork over the years, and I have reflected a great deal on these shortcomings and advantages. I have analysed my scintillating position in the field in a number of articles (see Dragomir, 2017, 2018, 2019). This is not even by far a resolved issue – it is a point that needs further investigation, and continuous reflection, because one's position as a researcher is not fixed, but ever changing, occupying simultaneous sites of power and of disentrancement. My work is thus a reflection of these ambivalences. And the way in which I address them is by being transparent about different aspects, stages and parts of the research process.

Engaging in an analysis of social movements is a complex endeavour that takes different forms, both informal and formal: at the elite and community level and in different political cultural, economic, social and political systems. To account for all these aspects while conducting comparative research is a gargantuan (and tiresome) task, which would take enormous efforts to complete. Facing obvious timing constraints and working with limited resources would therefore produce a schematic portrait of the social processes. In spite of these shortcomings, I found this work to be nevertheless an effort worthwhile undertaking, as it sets the basis for further research in this field.

Mixed methods

Each chapter in this book engages several methodological tools. While they often overlap, they are also separate, and create different discourses and different storytelling outcomes. Thus, every chapter reads differently. For example, the chapter about formal practices of access to justice presents the work of the elites, and therefore it follows their engagement with the issues, while detailing the historical context. Differently, the next chapter, which looks at the informal practices, is based on an ethnographical account, detailing the experiences of everyday life, and employs interviews and oral history, allowing for a more complex understanding of the striving for social justice.

Using this complex (and unorthodox) methodological undertaking creates a collage of the different ways in which the Narikuravar and Roma communities are striving to overcome discrimination, marginalization and historical neglect; in other words, to access social justice: redistribution, recognition and representation. Thus, in each chapter I use ethnography, include data from community and elite interviewing, and references to literature; I also engage in media analysis and visual feedback to reflect and analyse the patterns of access to justice of the Narikuravar and Roma people.

Ethnography

To address racial wrongs that have been historically cemented through the creation and practice of legal systems that perpetuated oppression and racism is an all-encompassing task that needs to be supported by close analysis of micro-aggressions, i.e. small acts of racism consciously or unconsciously perpetrated. Often the product of decades – even millennia – of cultural heritage, micro-aggressions are difficult to point to, and typically become visible once the context is minutely described through ethnographic approach.

As there is much mythology and legend, which in turn further essentializes and discriminates against those labelled as 'Gypsy' (including the Narikuravar and Roma people), describing communities is a necessary step in explaining their social processes, one that needs a careful and detailed undertaking. To address this, I have conducted ethnographic work in different settings in both Europe and South Asia. Since 2012, I have spent extended time on a regular basis with the Narikuravar and Roma communities in different settings in Romania and India. As these communities are part of larger groups, I have also conducted ethnographic work with adjacent communities labelled as 'Gypsy' in India (Lukmavar, Yogis) and in Europe with (mostly Romanian) Roma communities in Germany, Hungary, France and the UK.

My fieldwork took place in two main settings: Ormeniş/Transylvania, Romania, and Mettupalayam/Tamil Nadu in India. Here, over a period of three years in Romania, and five years in India, I have been engaging in in-depth fieldwork for three to four months a year. During this time, I undertook field trips in other parts of these two countries; in Sibiu, Romania I worked with Gabor Roma, and in Rajasthan, India I worked with Yogis. This work has been conducted at the level of the community, where I engaged in daily activities, as well as informal interviews (individual and community) with various members. I attended celebrations and other events, and I spent time in the houses of the people, who generously received my team and I.

Much description emerges from the detailed original quotations taken from the participants' own narratives. Moreover, as technology is widely used both in Europe and India, many of the photos and videos (not showcased directly in the book) I used for analysis in this work were taken by the participants themselves, and were much better than what I could have attained. This ethnography grows from seeing my role as being a co-generator of data, while assembling a multidimensional profile of my participants' lives. Seeing their experiences from different angles and assuming different perspectives helped me create 'ethnographic collages', (Terry Williams, correspondence, 2021) with narratives being supported by visual interventions and various vignettes.

Community and elite interviewing

Over the years, I have been conducting both formal and informal interviews with community members, and specialized interviews with elites. Unlike qualitative work that assumes individual interviews, this research exposed me to the life of the communities. The Adivasi/Narikuravars and the Roma are typically closely-knit communities. For example, in India often their houses do not have individual kitchens, and they cook and eat their food in common. Interviewing one person at a time was, therefore, not only impossible, but also inappropriate. This research challenge exposed me to the dynamics of the community, which rendered visible gender, class and age hierarchies.

As mentioned earlier, I have been conducting research with Narikuravar and Roma elites. As we will see next, this work is not perfectly balanced, as in the past thirty years the Roma communities in Romania have been developing an extensive network of Roma scholars, activists/politicians, creating a diverse and rather powerful elite. Similarly, the Narikuravar community, and Adivasi communities (more generally), have been striving to create a new generation of elites, who would be able to advocate and support their rights, but to this date (at least in the Narikuravar community) their number is very small.

Like any typical elites, most Narikuravars and Roma are busy pursuing their agenda, working around the clock for the benefit of their community, and often did not have time to engage in conversations with scholars and researchers. However, some of them did, they took their time, explained, engaged and furthered their thoughts even when time constraints were present, when language barriers seemed insurmountable.

Literature review

While the literature about/on the Roma communities is rather vast, it has also been seasoned (to say the least) with essentializing works, making it difficult to employ full-heartedly. However, in the past twenty years, new scholarship has been emerging – mainly conducted by, or in close relation with Roma scholars. As these works are rapidly growing, I tried to keep up and integrate new studies in my analysis. With respect to Adivasi communities in India, this is a new field of study, one that has been slowly developing, with many works created from outside the Adivasi communities. While they are faulty at times because of the same limitations as the old Roma scholarship, there are new works about Adivasi groups that have been developing recently. In spite of these new efforts, not many studies have been written specifically with/about the Narikuravars. To overcome this, I used general Adivasi literature to support (or challenge) my findings. Moreover, as the literature about Adivasi communities is still (to date) scarce, I engaged literature about Dalit people, and parallel their struggle for social justice within India.

Media analysis

While the Narikuravar and Roma communities have little visibility in the discipline of Social Sciences, they are very visible socially, with their tropes, stereotypes, etc. often present within the mass media. With the understanding that we are in the midst of a mass/social media overwhelming presence, the image of the 'Gypsy' often dominates the news, the minds and imagination of the general public. While I do not engage in a thorough research of the media and its tropes (as there are other scholars who have), I nevertheless have been paying close attention to the way in which the Roma and Narikuravars are described in the media, and this gave me an insight into the view that the majority holds about those labelled as 'Gypsy'. Also, tracking the media allows us to see how change is taking place, what voices emerge to the fore, and what is the language they use to address issues.

Historical analysis

Social justice issues, as well as the struggle to attain equity are not isolated incidents; they do not appear from nowhere, but are rooted in historical realities. Consequently, I have been analysing the historical development that led to the current conditions. This is not to say that I engage in a historical analysis, which would take a very different approach, and would lead to a different outcome, but that I consider that development and context are important in understanding the structures of power and hierarchies. It is therefore paramount in dismantling injustice to acknowledge the historical processes that the two communities underwent.

Visual feedback

Historically, minority communities have been mostly portrayed from outside. Photographs have shown communities as caught in time, old-world representatives of a by-gone era. The Narikuravars/Adivasi and the Roma have been visually objectified, as many other communities around the world, through colonizing lenses. For example, in the nineteenth century:

> The invention of the daguerreotype was announced in 1839. By the 1840s, photography had spread like wildfire and become a vital aspect of European colonialism. It played a role in administrative, missionary, scientific and commercial activities. As the Zimbabwean novelist Yvonne Vera put it: 'The camera has often been a dire instrument. In Africa, as in most parts of the dispossessed, the camera arrives as part of the colonial paraphernalia, together with the gun and the bible.'
>
> Teju Cole, 2019[17]

While visual analysis of the field is a powerful way of telling the story to further aspects of the community, the camera has been used as a tool of colonialization, of creating criteria of marginalization, instituting and reinforcing hierarchies. Aware of both sides of this matter, throughout the years, I have been documenting the Roma and Narikuravar processes and overall social movement, and I will use these data to further describe the work aiming to make these tools into ways of empowering the communities.[18]

For example, to dismantle photography and other visual analysis as a colonial tool[19], and to employ it as a feminist tool of resistance (Eileraas, 2003), I have been conducting a mixed media project titled 'Women Beyond Borders', working with women from Narikuravar and Roma communities, who have been engaged in the process of migration. The women in the project took ownership of their image, and took photos of themselves (or decided how to be photographed). This work was displayed accompanying their life stories, told in their own voices, uninterrupted, in their preferred language, forcing the audience to listen to their narratives, and to see them as the Narikuravar and Roma women would like to be portrayed. This work is visible here in the *Stories: Women on the Move, the Other Side of Gender* section (p. 93).

Similarly, throughout the years, I aimed at using visual analysis as a tool of empowerment, through which the community has agency over their image, over their overall story. Younger generations are more accustomed to visual immortalization and the uses of social media, they often exhibit agency over the mediatization process. However, older generations are at times shy, and not willing to take agency over their image. To overcome this, together with my team,[20] we would always check with participants and get their approval upon using their images, and always encouraged and welcomed their feedback. In spite of these photographs being powerful tools of immortalization, they risk objectification and exoticization of people. I decided against publicizing them, and used them solely as primary data of analysis.

It is important to say that times have also changed. While we were engaged in taking photographs and documenting our work in the field, very often the people in the community were filming and photographing us as well. While we are documenting them, they were also documenting us, thus creating their own forms of knowledge and memorialization.

What is next: overview of chapters

Chapter 2. Being Adivasi: The Narikuravars in Tamil Nadu

Who are the Narikuravars? This question does not aim to reveal an existential or anthropological answer, but to contour the community's identity using the political categorizations of nomadism, criminality, 'tribal' identity or denotified community. Using a historical perspective, the chapter introduces the Indian community of Adivasi people – the Narikuravars – mainly located in the state of

Tamil Nadu. Using ethnographic depictions, historical analysis, visual reflections and interviews with Adivasi/Narikuravar activists, as well as the community, this chapter describes the conditions under which the community has been living over the past fifty years. It ends by discussing the contemporary implications of their traditional patterns of mobility.

Chapter 3. Being a Roma in Romania

Who are the Roma? In this chapter, the second community is introduced: the Roma from Transylvania, Romania. Aiming to contour the community's identity using the political categorizations of mobility/nomadism, assumed criminality, racialization and discrimination, the chapter presents a critical assessment of how the community has been imagined. Using ethnographic depictions, historical analysis, visual reflections and interviews with Roma activists, as well as the community, this chapter describes the conditions under which the community has been living over the past fifty years. It ends by discussing the contemporary implications of their traditional patterns of mobility.

Chapter 4. Power: Internal and External Dynamics

This chapter comparatively describes the internal dynamics of the Roma and Adivasi communities. It asks: How is power constructed internally and what type of markers create axis of authority? It exposes the diversity of these groups and, while it acknowledges the history of nomadism that often blurs gender divides, and it critically engages with the hierarchies of power that the Roma and the Narikuravars inhabit, particularly aligned along the gender and class nexus.

Chapter 5. 'Our Justice'

This book is about access to justice, but when we are articulating paths for justice, what are we referring to? Whose version of justice do we employ, and to what ends? Starting from the perspective that justice needs to be articulated within one's own voice, and inside their community, this chapter comparatively analyses the traditional forms of justice in the forms of the Kriss and Panchayat, and their nowadays legacies. Based on extensive (100+) formal and informal interviews with both community members and Adivasi/Roma elites, the chapter links their history of mobility with their traditional forms of justice, while presenting the Adivasi/Roma's complex views and practices. It ends by stating how these visions are visible, and how they could be understood and accommodated in current (national and international) systems of justice.

Chapter 6. Discrimination and the Politics of Denial

What are these two communities battling in terms of discrimination? How do they see and understand these practices? To further understand the struggle for justice, this chapter uses the voices of the Roma and Narikuravars to expose the systematic and structural injustices they have been facing, along the lines of recognition, redistribution and representation. In this chapter, I further reflect on a puzzling finding that was highlighted by field research: many members of communities labelled as 'Gypsy', in spite of the blatant racism and discrimination they face, often deny these experiences. The chapter continues by outlining different ways in which marginalized mobile communities react to such injustices, thus introducing the upcoming chapters.

Chapter 7. Formal Practices of Aiming for Justice

Contrary to many views that deem historically mobile communities as absent from the political sphere of struggle for justice, this chapter – following Nancy Fraser's (2009) tripartite justice theory (i.e. recognition, redistribution and representation) – analyses the formal political activities of the Narikuravar and Roma communities. It comparatively presents the political activities of the Roma and Adivasi, including their marches, petitions, voting patterns and interviews with the press. The chapter ends by outlining how Roma/Adivasi groups (might) attempt to obtain political recognition, while preserving their legacy of mobility.

Chapter 8. Informal Practices of Aiming for Justice

Continuing the same path of questioning commenced in the previous chapter, here I show how – when formal struggles to achieve justice (described in the previous chapter) fail – Roma and Adivasi people often engage in informal struggles. In doing so, I ponder on alternative means for addressing injustices, such as taking over land that is not formally recognized as theirs, migrating, employing their traditional skills or practicing the community's laws.

Chapter 9. Conclusions

How does all this impact our understanding of how those who move access power? While summarizing the main points presented in the previous chapters, this final chapter further shows Roma and Adivasi's contemporary mobility, daily lives and obstacles, their dreams and aspirations. It also creates a possible theoretical normative framework that could better describe, and integrate mobile communities, such as those labelled as 'Gypsies' – but also refugees and migrants in general. Furthermore, it outlines possible normative pathways to understanding their struggles to attain justice.

Those who move

A study that invokes a comparison between historically mobile Roma and Adivasi communities from India and Romania is (of course) raising suspicion. Previous research often treated people as objects of the study, thus risking a rapid spiralling down into racist perspectives, typically reinforcing the outsiders' view as "normal" and valuable. Differently, in this work, I analyse the Roma and Narikuravars' processes of accessing justice. Let me be more specific. While historically grounded, this book highlights recent developments of social movements, political activity and a history of discrimination, while bringing it forward for analysis in the current geo-political-social-economic contexts. This work also exposes the dynamics of change that traditional nomadic communities go through, highlighting the ambivalence of accessing power on the move.

It is my firm belief that only when we stand together in solidarity are we able to confront racism and discrimination. Facing marginalizing and racism is painful. Facing it alone is devastating. Working in solidarity, overcoming limits and cultural barriers is important, not only for us to develop a human bond, but also to be successful in our struggle. I am neither Roma nor am I Adivasi, but I am a Romanian migrant, and I am a woman – and I face discrimination in my daily life from the streets of London to those of small American towns. These experiences help me tell their story of access to justice, to lift up their voices, and stand in solidarity if or when needed.

I hope this book will be part of the larger contemporary narrative of decolonial struggles for justice of those who move. This is a story of empowerment and survival, of resistance. And it is also a cry for inclusion. One that I hope will inspire other mobile people (refugees, internally displaced people, asylum seekers or migrants), in their yearning for a more just life.

Being Adivasi: The Narikuravar in Tamil Nadu

Fox and Vaghiri (a Narikurava tribe)

It was a dense forest. All the animals and birds in the forest, living in harmony came to assist. The forest was filled with joy, bee's music and colourful flowers.

Without the horrific animals, such as lion and tiger, the forest was filled with rabbits, goats, foxes and birds. One day, a Lion visited the forest. The advent of a lion in the jungle was a threat to all animals and birds. That day, the Lion as the king of all the animals of the forest was formerly proclaimed. The Lion was happy to become a lazy lion once he settled in the forest. He planned to take advantage of these animals to find food, and to provide other services for him. He made it known to everyone, with his roar.

The Lion instructed the other animals: he wants everyday life his prey, an animal or bird from a given species. Otherwise, he threatened to kill everyone. But the Lion also offered a way out. He said that he was a meat lover, and if anyone could correctly identify the smell coming from his mouth as good or bad, he will spare all of them and he will leave the forest forever.

Next day, it was the rabbits' turn to provide the Lion's meal. They were full of worry and fear. It was very hard to choose the one rabbit from the whole specie to be sacrificed. But one aged rabbit raised his hand, and offered to become a prey to the lion. The Rabbit went to the Lion and asked permission to smell its mouth. With great confusion and fear, the Rabbit said that the smell was good. But the Lion refused his answer and killed that Rabbit for his lunch.

Then next came the goats. A goat was chosen to meet the Lion. The Goat had a little more courage than the rabbit. When she met the Lion, she asked him to come forward. The Lion got tensed, but he moved forward towards the Goat. The Goat smelled the lion's mouth, and immediately replied that the smell was bad. The Lion showed his very angry face, and took the Goat as prey.

And the next turn went to the foxes. The foxes were trying to find a way to save their lives. Worried, the boss of foxes was walking around trying to get help. He found a Vaghiri (Narikuravar) under a tree. The Vaghiri seemed tired after a day of hunting and catching birds. The Fox decided to ask the Vaghiri for help. So, the Fox requested the Vaghiri to save its life. The Vaghiri had a condition to save the lives of foxes. The foxes should help him to catch the birds and animals. The Fox agreed to the condition, and in return got a wonderful idea from the Vaghiri.

Still very confused, fearful and all, the Fox left, thinking about the big day when he was meeting the Lion. When he stood before the Lion, he played a very good act saying that he was sick. He got very close to the Lion and smelled his breath. He did not say anything, he just sniffed the mouth of the Lion again and again. The Lion got irritated, and lost his patience. He asked with an angry voice: 'Well, how do you find the smell?' Still the Fox was smelling the Lion's mouth and said nothing. After a while, the Fox said in a very confused and fearful voice: 'Sorry sir, I felt sick over the past four days. I am having severe running nose and nose block. So, I could not identify the smell that comes from your mouth.' The Lion was confused and disappointed – but could not eat the fox. Tricked and ashamed, the Lion conveyed that he will leave the forest next day. Hearing this news, all the birds and animals were pleased and joyful. They kept celebrating and praising the Fox.

After a while, the Fox met with the Vaghiri, and they shook hands. In gratitude, the Fox offered his help to the Vaghiri. He said: 'I can be helpful to you when you catch the birds and animals.' The Vaghiri agreed. But after some days, the Fox stepped back from his promise, and the Vaghiri was upset. So, the angry Vaghiri decided then to kill foxes for his food, and use them whenever he could for other occupational purposes.

The moral of the story is that: Children should not be like the fox. They need to keep their promises all the time. Don't become lazy, and don't satisfy personal needs by using others. Work hard.

Anuradha, personal correspondence 2019

Introduction

My name is K. Sugan and I am 34 years old. I am Narikuravar born, and grew up in the 'settlement', where officially there are about 300 to 400 people, but many are always on the road for business. I got married here. I have one son, 10 years old, and a 3 years old baby girl. Before these times, we are Raja Singh generation – we were hunting people from Punjab. Step by step, we came here, and we didn't have homes to stay. Hunting is our job. We hunted wild animals for kings. We came like that. And then we separated into groups of people. We used to live in hills, rivers, and forest. In the past, we never come to town area. We didn't have any assets. So, we hunt and eat.

We all moved here from Punjab two to three hundred years ago. Because, kings kept on wars like that. And stayed where we could hunt animals, so, we chose the hill area. Because we only know hunting. But we stayed in the area where wild animals were. We eat animals for hunger.

Then we separated into groups of people and came to Thiruvannamalai, Sengam, Kunchankarai. Some people are in Mysur and Bangalore.

I'm Most Backward Class (MBC). From the beginning we are MBC. We are requesting the government to make us Scheduled Tribes (ST). Because they give good salary for Scheduled Tribes. They are giving job opportunities to them only. We are MBC, so we don't have any assets; our parents left us nothing. So, we have to earn our own money and eat.

I am proud to be a Narikuravar, of course, I'm proud. We never do bad things; we never go for terrorist activities. We get girls for marriages in our community only. Our gods – Kaaliamma and Chennamma – don't like us getting married to a girl in another community. We don't get from other communities and we don't give too. We are controlling in these matters. For that I'm proud. We have full control about their living, and also about their community. We won't cross the borders.

Sugan interview, 2016

K. Sugan is one of the Narikuravar people I met in 2012, in the small 'settlement' near Mettupalayam, Tamil Nadu. The Narikuravar are a small community that predominantly lives in south India, in the state of Tamil Nadu. There are about 30,000 inhabitants who identify as Narikuravar. While they are proud to be Narikuravars, and hope to be recognized as Adivasi and as a Scheduled Tribe, others mostly refer to them as 'Gypsy'. Outsiders often have a racialized image of them, one painfully resembling the stereotype of those labelled as 'Gypsy' in Europe:

Around 1980, the Narikuravars were called Vagharis. These people temporarily stayed in my village. That is the path through which we got acquainted with them. They used to be near the Thanjai District, and lived in a very low manner. They used to eat things on the street, beg for a little money, and run away from anything that scared them. They used to live like tribals in a modernizing society. Their children wouldn't study and would get married very young.

R. Vijayasundaram interview, November 2020[1]

Members of other communities describe them as nomadic, as people without permanent settlements, whom they got used to seeing at the margins of the roads, or passing through their villages. Like Vijayasundaram, the non-Narikuravars in Tamil Nadu, with a smile on their face, share memories of their childhood when Narikuravars come to their villages: 'My mom would tell me to run outside and bring the pots and pans in', one of my Tamil translators shared with me after a trip into one of the Narikuravar 'settlements'. I looked at her questioningly. Amused by my curiosity, she explained: 'We were afraid they will steal them. Everybody knew you can't leave your dogs and cats out if the Narikuravars were nearby.' Responding to my visible puzzlement, she continued: 'We knew that they eat them!' In the Tamilian society, where many are vegetarian, this presumed consumption of domestic animals seems beastly and makes the Narikuravars to be seen as subhuman.

Like the colonizers before them, the prevalent attitude is one of assimilation, of saving the Narikuravars by making them 'similar' to others:

> Most of us kids grew up wanting to do something for them, seeing how bad their situation was. When we got older, a few friends and I tried to discipline them and tame them to fit in with society to help them. We had to sometimes be harsh because their view of them would not make them survive for long. It was a very embarrassing situation. We sometimes had to scream at them, or be kind and slowly we got them citizenship and a little recognition.
>
> R. Vijayasundaram interview, 2020

The Narikuravars are a diverse community who live (while not permanently settled) in several sites. Rajasekaran of the Narikuravar community shared a study conducted by the Tribal Society in 2008, which shows that they are present in 28 Tamilian districts, with a total taluk of 90, spread across 168 villages, with 7,647 families composing a population of 28,253 (male: 14,736 and female 13,517). In terms of education, out of 8,241 children aged 1–14 (male 4,397 and female 3,844), 2,518 go to school (male 1,395 and female 1,123). The community's school dropout rate is high, with 1,074 children (male 613 and female 461) stopping attending school. However, the number of children never attending school is even higher: 4,649 (male 2,389 and female 2,260):

> Regarding our history, research shows that we have different origins. Some people are from places like Gujrat and Rajasthan. Because we have a gypsy background, they named us differently in different states. For example, in TN, we are called the Narikuravars, in Andhra Pradesh, we are called Nakuluvalas, and Hakki Bikki in Karnataka. In other central states, we are called Vagaries. This was based on the research that showed that we had similar characteristics and

the language. Our language is Vagriboli. This is based on the regional language plus Gujarathi, Marathi, and Hindi. This is the major mixture of languages that we speak. There is also no script for our language. However, the people also speak their local language well.

Rajasekaran interview/correspondence, 2020

Thus, the Narikuravars mostly speak their community language Vagriboli, which until recently had no written script. The Narikuravars I spoke with describe the language as a mixture of Sanskrit, Hindi, Mahrati and other local languages. As they have been living within the state of Tamil Nadu, around other Tamilian families, they often speak Tamil in their vernacular. As the community has a very low education rate, and a medium English education is typically private and expensive, most Narikuravars do not speak English. Their low rates of literacy make government programmes and schemes hard to access, as they are often not known by the Narikuravar.

While still rather dire, their situation has been slowly changing over the past decade, as Vijayasundaram - a Tamilian man working with the Narikuravars has shared:

We have more than 20 kids that are degree holders. In the three districts – Thanjavur, Thiruvarur and Nagapattinam, we work in 22 quarters. We started this accidentally, questioning why these people are like this. The situations changed without considering them, and they didn't adapt to anything. They got scared of the change though. This is the truth. The day when this gap disappears, the day when the politicians will notice us, will be when the situation changes.

R. Vijayasundaram interview, 2020

Anuradha, who is a Narikuravar woman, activist and teacher, highlights the main obstacles encountered by the community as follows:

The majority of our kids only study till the 8th grade. Mostly everyone works in selling products, jewellery. Recently, the range of products has increased to more types of jewellery, toys, long hair pins, and herbal oil. In other districts, the focus is on jewellery. This community is big on child marriages and labour, but we are hoping that educating them will drastically reduce this. One of the main reasons to get their daughters married is because when they go out on their own for long trips to sell their products, the girl will be alone at home and because this is dangerous, [so] it would be better to get her married. They value social security a lot. When the families are big, children are made to work to support the family.

Anuradha interview, 2020

Story of origins

In a world that traces origins as an emblem of honour, establishing one's position within the society and legitimizing hierarchies, relies on defining where one comes from. Thus, one's origin is paramount in explaining their existence, and in constructing their narrative (or counter-narrative) of belonging. Hence, even if the Narikuravar identify as a mobile group, not tied to any land, they have to tell their story of a place of origin.[2] They often tell the story of their beginnings in line with those of describing a mythological past, grounded in oral history. The Narikuravars traditionally have been warriors, who lived in forests, and were skilled in weaponry and war. They lived and moved through the northern part of India, and were employed in the royal court as guards. In this role, they were treated well and esteemed by those in power. But as politics have changed, so has their position. They had to flee the courts and retreat (once more) into the forests. There, the Narikuravars survived as a community because they know the forests well and could hunt. Hunting provided the community with necessary nourishment, and also engaged them in commerce with other (settled) populations, who treated the wild game meat as a delicacy. So, over the years and under different systems, including colonial ruling, the Narikuravars were 'roaming around', as they often told me, and – about 500 years ago – they migrated into the southern part of the Indian peninsula, and established their mobile dwellings in the state of Tamil Nadu, typically in government allocated 'settlements'.

Housing or 'settlements'

On a warm winter day, as we were spending time with the Narikuravars, together with my translator, and accompanied by children and elderly folk, we took another stroll into their 'settlement'. The small dwellings, one-room houses with no bathroom, close to one another, washed out by monsoons and hot South Asian sun, accommodate a large number of people. As we talked, we got pulled towards a group of women in the common yard who were washing clothes on a pedestal with a stone and soap. The process is labour intensive, and the women confirm it: 'Yes, it is hard work', one of them agreed, and then she added: 'We don't have a washing machine.'

Knowing that water is scarce in the community, I ask her where does she get it from. She says there is a common tank, and she points to the other side of the settlement. She explains that they do not have running water, and it is hard for Narikuravars, like many other low-income communities, to access water resources. The Narikuravars are dependent on the government water that is delivered for free in tanks once a week. It is a common tank, where they go and they take their rations in large big blue plastic bins, which they then portion in their own homes: for washing, for cooking, for brushing teeth and for drinking. While the situation was dire, the Narikuravars in Mettuplayam never complained about it.[3]

The small houses have no toilet inside. The only place that looks like a toilet – even though it is not always used as such, I am told – is a building with two rooms right outside their "settlement", after crossing the road. However, the wash room does not actually have a place to wash one's hands, and does not have running water either, which makes the situation – especially for women menstruating – even more difficult to navigate.

To others, the Narikuravars in Mettupalayam are always on the road, 'roaming around', and sleeping at the margins of the roads. However, in reality they have been allocated to 'settlements' on government land,[4] which was promised to the Narikuravars as property. Sugan shared with us the complicated and uncertain situation of the Narikuravars owning land within his 'settlement': 'Government gave us permission to stay here 50 years ago, and we can sell it within our community. Before, we stayed in the road sides, because we didn't have a home. They migrated here and stayed here. They stayed here for 15 years, before the government gave the ownership to the stay area' (Sugan interview, 2016). Thus, while the Narikuravars have been living on this land for more than fifty years, I was told that the 'settlement' was officially created about thirty to fifty years ago, and their land ownership is still uncertain, further leading to their marginalization.

Ambiguity of identity

The Narikuravars' past and present (as those of others) are ambiguous and complex, to say the least. They partially inhabit social and political categories, and refuse/resist assimilation, misrecognition into categories, which they deem not feasible. They make demands to the state based on these particular and partial identities, and ask for respect in the name of who they are – as full communities and individuals. In other words, they are irreverent towards the meek, feeble, incomplete political categories operating in the organization and distribution of power. In what follows, I will analytically separate these identities, that of course on the ground exist in tandem. Moreover, as we will see, these categories are also fluid, blending into one another and interdependent. These categories are: hunting and criminality, Adivasi, nomadism, 'Gypsy', Dalit/'untouchable' and Scheduled Tribe. And what links all these different aspects is the Narikuravar identity.

Hunting and criminality

As we have seen in the myth about the origins of their community, the Narikuravars identify by tradition with jackal hunters. However, once invaders took over the territories they inhabited, Narrikurovars, like many others, became nomadic and retreated into forests, where they preserved their traditions and freedoms (Dragomir, 2017).[5] They are typically described in the media as: 'The Narikuravas (literally, jackal-hunters), also known as kuruvikaras (bird-hunters), are among the poorest of the poor, barely making out a living hawking beads, bangles, sea-shells and assorted trinkets' (Srinivasan, 2018):[6]

> Majorly preferring isolation and limited contact with modern life style of living, the society and life processes of the Hill Korwas got influenced and subsequently changed with the contact of the outside world or the mainstream society. With the changing forest laws and development of communication facilities, their daily life and ways of living are slowly influenced. Depletion of forests, decline in forest catches and lack of forest produce to meet the subsistence for them, gradually made them dependent on the farm produce and local markets for their food and day to day living.
>
> Das, 2020: 92

Rajasekaran (interview, February 2017) further explained: 'Hunting is banned by the government of India. So, we had to be seeking other opportunities; we were seeking help for our family to survive and meet the expenses.' Thus, 'when hunting became illegal, so did their forefathers' tradition. Since then, the Narrikurovars have lived at the margins of the society in dire poverty, making and selling beads and other small ornaments in local markets and temples' (Dragomir, 2017).[7] This change in the legality of livelihood has been abrupt, but it does not mean that the legacy of their traditional professions disappeared overnight. As the Narikuravar are typically allocated marginal places, at the end of roads and within forests, they still employ hunting to make ends meet.

Historic criminalization

Their gunmanship traditions and their hunting skills make others fear them, and also create space for (mis)interpretations. When discussing with the Narikuravars, most of them argue that their community needs to be understood as different from other neighbouring, or similar ones. However, there are some Narikuravars (like the Roma in Romania) and authors who voice a different view, and argue that they are a part of a bigger group, the Kuravars (or Kuravers): 'Kuraver in Tamil Nadu is a blanket term of reference for nomadic tribes, with each being differentiated on the basis of its traditional occupation. The Narikuravas were traditionally hunters and even today every hut [is] in the Narikurava settlement in Kalmedu village near Madurai' (Doval, 2019).[8]

As the Kuravar category is larger, there have been more studies and official acknowledgements of the community. Moreover, they also came more often under the scrutiny of the state, including under colonial eyes, which criminalized them under the Criminal Tribes Act of 1871:[9]

'The Kuraver belongs to one of the great robber castes of India ... they are systematic thieves ... they are hereditary (criminals), habitual and incorrigible' (*The Land Pirates of India* by WJ Hatch, 1928). In 1871, Imperial Britain passed the Criminal Tribes Act that declared many of India's nomadic tribes, including hunters and forest dwellers, to be criminals. These tribes, as is obvious from the extracts of Hatch's book quoted above, were a subject of equal parts fascination and equal parts contempt. It's been nearly a century and a half since the Act was passed: it was repealed by the Indian government in 1952. And while the fascination with the country's nomadic tribes may have waned, the distrust still lingers, as do the prejudices.

Doval, 2019[10]

The Kuravars criminalization was part of a larger colonial project to control the diverse communities of the sub-Indian continent:

Major changes for the Adivasis began with the arrival of the British colonial power. The expressed purpose in coming to India was to take control of the most profitable type of trade. Therefore, the British wanted to take control of the Adivasi territories – which were abundant in natural and mineral resources. Control of Adivasi lands was effected through various laws, and the transformation of Adivasis into a labouring class for the industrial and market-led system began.

Minority Rights Group International, 1998: 6

While the grip of the colonial power was strong, it was also met with the resistance of communities on the ground, who refused to be brought to heel:[11]

The British began exporting finished products and raw materials from India – these exports were one of the contributing factors in the rise of the Industrial Revolution in Britain. Colonization led to unrest among the Adivasis, and more than 75 major revolts beginning with the Mal Paharia uprising in 1772. The suppression, however, continued.

Minority Rights Group International, 1998: 6

To exert their control, in the state of Tamil Nadu, communities like 'Koravars, Kallars, Yenadis, Agambadyas, Valayars, etc., the British registered them as Criminal Tribes through the Criminal Tribes Act of 1871' (Neela and Ambrosia, 2015: 44). The criminality of the community, as well as the labels/names of the communities have been rather ambiguous:

> In the Census Report of 1891, Mr. J.A. Bains, the Commission of Census classified the castes on the basis of the traditional occupations namely as 'Forest Tribes', Animists, etc. They lived with their hereditary nature, illiteracy, poverty and slavery. At that time legal protection was not totally given to these communities. The economic condition of these people were mainly based on the hereditary occupations like salt trade, basket making, kaval work under local chieftains.
>
> Neela and Ambrosia, 2015: 44

The Narikuravars often want to separate themselves from this view and from the label of criminality, and claim that their use of weaponry has been limited to hunting birds and animals, not employed in criminal social contexts. And they further claim it is this very confusion that is partially responsible for the 'backwardness' of their community. Thus, the British taxonomy[12] of indigenous communities, done in haste and with colonial narrow views, disregarded much of the diversity of the sub-Indian continent, and led to massive misrepresentations still impacting today's politics.[13]

Modern forms of criminalization

The Criminal Tribes Act (CTA) was repealed in 1952, and thus the 'notified' tribal communities became 'de-notified'. The CTA was replaced by the Habitual Offenders Act,[14] which aimed to investigate 'suspect' and 'criminal tendencies' and decide whether traditional occupations are 'conducive to a settled way of life'. According to this Act, a habitual offender is one who manifested a set of criminal practices, who presents a danger to the society. While aiming at 'denotified' communities, in effect it actually re-stigmatized them:

> According to the recent survey reports, 'India has 198 groups belonging to nomadic and denotified tribes: unorganized, scattered and utter nobodies. Social justice is alien to them and economic disempowerment eventually resulted in

slavery, bonded labour and poverty. Public welfare measures pay scant attention to the issue of reform and rehabilitation of these sections and they are made to suffer from an identity crisis today. Most of these communities are split under reserved categories: Scheduled Castes and Other Backward Classes.'

Gandhi and Sundar, 2019

As a result of this partial or unfinished 'denotification', in the era of globalization, 'with the neo-liberal market also playing a key role compounding Adivasi exclusion' (Rao, 2018: 2), most of the formally criminalized tribes live in dire socioeconomic conditions. Most live 'a faceless existence' (Gandhi and Sundar, 2019: 28), which often leads to systematic marginalization.

More recently, another layer of criminalization was created and inflicted on communities like the Narikuravars, due to their traditional professions. In 1972 the Wildlife Law was passed,[15] which made hunting illegal (Dragomir, 2017).[16] The Narikuravars, struggling to make ends meet, sometimes venture into the nearby forests and hunt. The caught wild life is then sold on the market as a delicacy, and birds are kept for breeding and eggs. When I was visiting the community next to Mettupalayam, the folks often brought their birds in their palms, and – showing them with pride – they smacked their lips in delight. They also shared with me the complicated relationship they have with the police. While according to the Wild Life Act their hunting is forbidden, everyone in the surroundings know that Narikuravars sometimes hunt. So, at times, the police venture into the Narikuravar "settlement", raid it, and either ask for bribes or make arrests, putting them in jail for a few days. The Narikuravars tell me that this is mostly a form of intimidation and harassment by the police, that in effect their practices are mostly silently tolerated, while everyone in search of delicatessen meat reaches out to them.

In 2016, while in the 'settlement' next to Mettupalayam, a few Narikuravar men shared with me: 'We are still interested in hunting. Even, we do have licensed guns. But we can only shoot small birds like Kaadei, Kavuthari. Not wild animals. We don't teach our children how to hunt; now they go to school. Hunting stopped with us', they said referring to generational changes. 'Two or three people in the community still have their guns and hunt rabbits and hens. But the forest department people does not allow it; they say we have to use nets to catch them.'

This tense relationship with the police and its practices have been taking place for years. For example, in 2016, according to *The Hindu*, in a raid of the Narikuravar Colony by the Forest Department, two men were arrested as they were trafficking Monitor Lizards, which were 'sourced from Narikuravars (. . .), and the live reptiles were transported through buses'. This, the report continues, is an 'illegal trade on a scheduled animal', which led the Forest Department officials to go on 'a five-hour checking spree of over 63 vehicles' and which discovered the 'possession of Monitor Lizard'.[17]

At times, the arrests become public, and the stigma of criminality of the Narikuravars is publicly endorsed, as we see in the *Times of India* report of early 2021:

> Forest department officials arrested a member of the narikuravar community on Saturday for poaching two spotted deer at Nellithurai beat of the Mettupalayam forest range on January 23[2021]. The arrested person was identified as J Arul of narikuravar colony at Thimmampalayam, Karamadai. Arul and a relative used country-made guns to kill the deer, range officer Palaniraja said. He was booked under the Wild Life Protection Act, 1972 and remanded in judicial custody.[18]

Facing these dire consequences, most Narikuravars adapted, and transformed their traditional skills, while they continued to live 'at the margins of the society in dire poverty, making and selling beads and other small ornaments in local markets and temples' (Dragomir, 2017).[19] Nowadays, 'the Narikuravas are better known for selling beads or hawking their tattoo-inking skills (a traditional art they refer to as pachai kuthu) in exchange for a day's living' (Doval, 2019).[20]

The Narikuravars' skill for making beads are revered, as they are thought to be picking up raw, natural materials from the forests and crafting them into 'malas' and necklaces. Their skills are believed to be transmitted to the youth, who often accompany their parents to the markets.

The talk of the past: traditions

Today, the Narikuravars' traditions are more visible in their religious and cultural practices. In a country with millions of gods, the Narikuravars have theirs. While they are not officially Hindu, living in the proximity of Hindu communities, the religious osmosis is rather expected. However, their religious beliefs are also different; they worship several goddesses: 'How this works is that the two main ones are the people that worship Meenakshi and those that worship Kali. The Meenakshi cut goat and the Kalis cut buffalo. These two exchange men and women so they can marry from different clans. I pray to Madurai Meenakshi' (Arun interview, 2020).

Anuradha further explains referring to the internal structures of the community: 'Every clan has a leader. Or maybe we can call these sub-clans. These can also be separated by the goddesses. Meenakshi, Maariyamma, and Kali. I used to worship Kali, but I married into the Meenakshi clan. These sub-clan leaders take care of around ten families each' (Anuradha interview, 2020).

Rajasekaran also describes his identity along the same traditional spiritual lines: 'My subdivision is called Behawala. We sacrifice the buffalo. These are clans. There are 2–3 clans. Some people sacrifice buffalos and are called Behawalas, people who sacrifice goats are called Bokudawala. On this basis, we marry. The people that sacrifice buffaloes worship goddess Kali or Durga. The other clan worships goddess Meenakshi' (Rajasekaran interview, 2021).

To appraise their goddesses, the Narikuravar sacrifice animals and ingurgitate their blood. Depending on the goddess they worship, the sacrificed animal is either a buffalo or a goat. The Narikuravars know that their traditions are different from those of other communities, so once they felt comfortable with me, they were eager to show me photographs from past traditional events. On glossy faded paper was the image of an older man with long white hair and beard, surrounded by younger men with red turbans (the symbol of the Narikuravars). His hands touch his face, and blood drips from them on his chin and bare chest. The other men support him, by holding the bowls filled with the blood of the sacrificed animal. The next photo shows the same elderly man in front of a basin full of the internal organs of the sacrificed animal, as the Narikuravars eagerly explained. In spite of their low quality, the pictures are graphic and descriptive, immortalizing traditions that happen often behind closed doors, only among men.

The pictures also tell the story of the community. The vision of blood and dead animals sits uncomfortably with other Tamilian communities, who are mostly vegetarians, and see bloodshed and animal eating as a sign of the 'low caste', of a community that is 'polluted' and able to 'pollute' others by their simple presence and contact. But these traditions are nevertheless the pride of the Narikuravars:

The traditions we still keep are music and dancing for marriages, child ear piercing, puberty ceremony or sacrificing buffalos for god (Kaali). During the functions they will offer the buffalos and drink their blood too. We enjoy these a lot and we drink (alcohol) too. We think that when we drink that blood, we get Kaali's blessing and power. The energy of Kaali comes inside us. And during that time, we drink and are very happy too. For Kovil Festivals we invite everyone. They come and eat. But for Sacrificing buffalos (Kaali function) we don't call anyone, only our people.

Sugan interview, 2016

The people who conduct the rituals are men (not women),[21] and the one that drinks the blood of the animal is the leader (most respected) in the community. He now impersonates the goddess. When taking part in the offerings, in the blood and meat of the sacrificed animal he embodies the goddess, and blesses the community. Not all traditions, which may be controversial by modern standards, come at odds with those of other communities of Tamil Nadu. For example, Narikuravars support the practice of Jalikath celebrated by Tamilians in January during Pongal times: 'A tradition over 2,000 years old, Jallikattu is a competitive sport as well as an event to honour bull owners who rear them for mating. It is a violent sport in which contestants try to tame a bull for a prize; if they fail, the bull owner wins the prize' (Janarhanan, 2021).[22]

While these traditions are viewed with suspicion by outsiders, and with contempt by animal rights activists, they are customs that the Narikuravars share with other communities in Tamil Nadu:

> Precinct of India agreed to have jalikath! Definitely support it because it is about the engagement; when we practice the bull traditions, the bull gives the power to the cow; transfers the genes. This continues the energy of the gene. They train the bull in a good manner – [give] healthy foods etc. make them practice. They are very strong, healthy and this is just transferred to the cow. So, the cows also more healthy [and have] power. The milk is also more hygenic. I had participated in the streets [to protest the legislation against Jalikath].
>
> Rajasekaran interview, 2017

Narikuravars as Adivasi

When I met the Narikuravar community in the vicinity of Mettupalayam in the winter of 2012, and I asked them to tell me more about who they are, they proudly said in strong voices: 'Adivasi!' As typically they are referred to as 'Gypsy' or as nomads, and they are not officially recognized as Adivasi, their response was puzzling. When I got to spend time with them and understand their struggle, their demand for this recognition became clear. Based on their 'needs and backward status', as Rajasekaran always reminds me, the Narikuravars ask the state (as we will see in detail over the next chapters) to recognize them as 'Adivasi', or indigenous people of India. Out of respect for their choice and because the Narikuravars' life-conditions are similar to many Adivasi communities, in what follows I will present them in the larger Adivasi context. As said earlier, while studies about Narikuravar are scarce, recently the field of Adivasi studies has been developing,[23] and definitions have been emerging: 'The word "Adivasi" means original inhabitants or indigenous peoples in Sanskrit. The Adivasis are thought to be the earliest settlers in and the original inhabitants of the Indian peninsula. It is believed that the Adivasis were already present in the Indian subcontinent at the time of the Aryan invasion' (Minority Rights Group International, 1998: 5).

Nevertheless, like many other terms (i.e., 'Roma'), 'Adivasi' is a term[24] that refers to very diverse[25] indigenous peoples, and tribal communities.[26] Adivasis[27] are a part of the Indian hierarchical system, which has been historically rooted and systemically reinforced, placing Adivasis at the bottom, struggling for overcoming injustice and oppression:[28]

> The term Adivasi is commonly translated as 'indigenous people' or 'original inhabitants', and literally means 'Adi or earliest time', and 'vasi or resident of'. The state and discourse in India, however, reject the term 'indigenous peoples' as it is considered 'divisive, undermining the unity of the Indian nation'.
>
> Das and Mehta, 2012: 1

To date, the Indian government recognizes most Adivasis under the Constitutional term 'Scheduled Tribes' derived from a schedule in the Constitution Order of 1950 (Das and Mehta, 2012),[29] and declares that Adivasis have been systematically marginalized through social-economic exclusionary and land-encroaching practices, often being characterized as 'underdeveloped' (Rao, 2018).

According to Minority Rights Group International (1998),[30] over all, the situation of the Adivasis is dire. They have been facing:

> Expulsion from their ancestral lands, with over 90 per cent of India's coal mines, 72 per cent of the forest and other natural resources, 80 per cent of India's minerals, and over 3,000 hydro-electric dams currently existing on their lands, but they rarely beneficiate from these developments. Thus, 85 per cent of Adivasis live below the official 'poverty line', and 83 per cent of the total bonded laborers are Adivasi.
>
> Minority Rights Group International, 1998: 5

There are multiple, interrelated factors that contribute to the Adivasis' historic deprivation, which pushed them 'to the margins of vulnerability' (Kannabiran et al., 2018: 81), including physical segregation, dispossession from the land and forests, exploitation by the mainstream society and various forms of *internal colonialism* (World Bank, 2011). The World Bank suggests that Adivasis rank among the twenty-five most-deprived communities of the world, along with inhabitants of Sub-Saharan Africa.

Identification with the Adivasi is a perilous one, as the Narikuravar, due to their nomadic traditions (and like the Roma), do not make claims to ancestral land. However, they find that 'Adivasi' is the term that best describes their living conditions, as well as their historical marginalization. They also hope (as we will see in the next chapters) that this identification will give them access to rights and resources.

Narikuravars and Nomadism

One of the reasons for criminalizing tribes has been their mobile lifestyle. Nomadic communities have been facing historic and systematic criminalization and marginalization (Dragomir, 2019), but in India not all have been included in the list for denotified communities, i.e. Scheduled Caste or Scheduled Tribes. The Narikuravar is one such community, which has been nomadic/semi-nomadic, but has not been legally classified in any 'recognised categories for positive discrimination' (National Commission for Denotified, Nomadic and Semi-nomadic Tribes, Ministry of Social Justice and Empowerment Government of India, 2008: 8).[31] While many traditional nomadic communities have been shifting from nomadism to settled residence, moving to 'non-agricultural labour' (Kannabiran, 2017: 1), the Narikuravars are slow to settle and proud of their nomadic ways. Thus, in spite of having state identifications (Aadhaar cards)[32] that specify their permanent address, the Narikuravars I engaged with proudly state that they are nomadic, that they 'roam around' and often 'go for business'. Because their mobility is well-known, it often interferes with the request and assumption of the state for their permanent sedentarization, and puts them at odds with the local police and other state institutions, who often harass them especially when they are 'going for business'.

Their nomadism is neither absolute nor perfect. Many of the Narikuravars I worked with have in effect been living in state-given houses, i.e. 'settlements'. They use these dwellings as their base and their main living quarters, but they still claim their nomadic lifestyle, and argue that these dwellings are just temporary as practical houses that support their 'roaming around'. Moreover, not all Narikuravars feel the same way about their mobility. The younger generation, which is exposed via the media and internet to other lifestyles, also shared with me their desire for a settled urban life.

Labelled as 'Gypsy'

The term 'Gypsy' has been imported to India by the British colonizers, and in common usage it typically refers to nomadism in general, a category covering many communities. As the Narikuravars are nomads, they are often named 'Gypsies':

> The gypsies are indigenous people whose main occupation were hunting but are also considered as one of the greatest bandit communities in south India. The word gypsies is derived from Europe, which means nomadic people. Tamilnadu is a home to various categories of gypsies, and among them the nomadic tribes of gypsy named as Koravar (or) Narikoravan (or) Kuruvikaran stands in the forefront. The occupation of Narikoravar community is mostly hunting jackals and other wild animals.
>
> Chandru and Thrimalaisamy, 2019

The Narikuravars have limited access to education, especially to (often expensive) English medium education, and as a result the (colonial) English word is not widely known. Furthermore, seldom are its historical/colonial roots understood. They accept the 'Gypsy' label, as they assume the reference is to their mobility, but they refuse the criminality label that is quickly associated with it. This is a difficult endeavour as nomadism and criminality have been historically thought in tandem (Dragomir, 2020), and this legacy is still powerfully employed:

> The Criminal Tribes Inquiry Committee, 1947, was constituted in the United Province. In its report, this Committee felt that till the Gypsies settled down, they would continue with criminal tendencies. It proposed that 'efforts should be made under sanction of law (suitable provision may be made in the Habitual Offenders and Vagrants Act) to settle them and teach them a life of industry and honest calling as against idleness, prostitution and crime to which their conditions of existence make them prone'.
>
> National Commission for Denotified, Nomadic and Semi-nomadic Tribes,
> Ministry of Social Justice and Empowerment Government of India, 2008: 2–3

Thus:

> the nomadic groups included the *gypsy-like* [my emphasis] tribes such as Sansis, Kanjars, etc., and 'Had an innate preference for a life of adventure.' The settled and semi-settled groups were deemed to have descended from irregular fighting men or persons uprooted from their original homes due to invasions and political upheavals.[33]

Moreover, according to the National Advisory Council Working Group on Denotified and Nomadic Tribes: 'All *gypsies* [my emphasis] are criminals, and following that logic, all Indian nomadic communities were also believed to be potential criminals. For this reason, there is a large overlap between communities that were declared criminal tribes and those that were nomadic.'[34]

The name 'Gypsy' has also been unreflectively adopted by outsiders referring to the Narikuravars: 'When the Gypsies Settle: The Narikuravar are an indigenous community in Tamil Nadu, who are also considered Gypsies and Dalits (Untouchables)' (Yamuna Flaherty, 2018).[35] Moreover, the 'Gypsy' identification has been officially employed by the Narikuravars as well, typically to denote their mobility. For example, the mission statement of the Narikuravar Education and Welfare Society (NEWS) stated their activity focus: 'To bring about the social, economic, political and cultural enhancement of Narikuravar *Gypsies* [my emphasis], with focus on children, youth and women' (NEWS, social media, 2017). Also in 2017, Narikuravars developed the 'Gipzys Development Society/Tribal Society', establishing residential schools for the community. As we will see in the following chapters, the Narikuravars employ this label, which is globally known, for practical reasons, mainly to raise awareness abroad and garner international support.

Adivasi–Dalit alliance

Those labelled as 'Gypsy' are often associated with the Dalits. Specifically, while the Narikuravars want to be recognized as Adivasi, and are typically referred to as 'Gypsies', often the Roma are associated with Dalits. This parallel is discussed along the lines of marginalization:

> Both European Roma and the Dalits of India who continue to suffer acute marginalisation. Present day marginality for Dalits continues despite the outlawing of caste-based discrimination, which is one of the most pernicious causal factors of contemporary exclusion in India. As with the Roma, for the Dalits, age-old prejudice and forms of institutional racism interact with poverty to create profound forms of marginality.
>
> Dunajeva et al., 2017: 1

While the field of Adivasi studies is in its incipient phase, Dalit studies have been developing for the past decades,[36] and thus the scholarly liaison between these two communities has been feeble. However, the connection between Dalits and Adivasi exists at the Indian national political level, where placed next to women, they are considered vulnerable populations: 'The present prime minister, Narendra Modi, has stated that his government's StandUp India initiative will transform the lives of Adivasis along with the Dalits and women in the country and noted that the "job seekers" will become "job creators" in this scheme (IANS 2016)' (Rao, 2018: 1).

However, the connection on the ground and at the scholarly level is yet to develop. The Narikuravars tell me that the Dalits disrespect them because they are Adivasi, and thus out of the caste system, and see them lower than Dalits. When I asked Anuradha about a possible Adivasi and Dalit alliance, she looked at me and said: 'Dalits spit on us' (Anuradha interview, 2017). It is not surprising that communities struggling to make ends meet compete with one another for the limited resources allotted to them by the state, and as a result they do not build coalitions, but further their rivalry. Nevertheless, in building partnerships, Dalits could support the Adivasi struggle for justice and political transformation. In doing so, Adivasis 'need to delineate today its markers, methods, and agenda, its possibilities for dialogue with other fields like Dalit Studies' (Dasgupta, 2018: 7).

As mentioned in the previous chapter, while this connection is still to be explored, the Dalit literature is important and could stand as a reference to the Adivasis and Narikuravars' struggle for justice, and in the next chapters it will be (gently) mentioned here, when and if opportunity arises.

Narikuravars as Scheduled Tribe

The next identification, and the most important one to the Narikuravars – as mentioned above – is Scheduled Tribe (ST). Their struggle for recognition, for economic access, and for political representation revolves around their ST status. As we will see in the next chapters, the Narikuravars are tirelessly fighting for this recognition, employing a variety of means, hoping to resolve this matter soon. They would like to be recognized under a large umbrella (like Dalits), next to different and diverse communities. As per the Minority Rights Group International (1998): 'Approximately 8.08 per cent of India's population has been designated as "Scheduled Tribes" (STs). The term indicates those communities specified by the President of India under Article 342 of the Constitution. It is an administrative term, which is area-specific and envisaged to reflect the level of socio-economic development rather than a distinct ethnic status.'

To be recognized as ST, the communities need to meet rather unclear criteria, which – as we will see in the next chapters – the Narikuravars do not perfectly meet: 'The criteria of "geographical isolation, distinctive culture, primitive traits [sic], shyness of contact with [the] community at large and economic backwardness [sic]" are generally considered relevant in the definition of such a tribe' (Minority Rights Group International, 1998: 5).

The ST term is typically used as a synonym to 'Adivasi' as 'Indians generally call most of the STs "Adivasis", and the terms are used interchangeably' (Ibid.). However, there is an important distinction: the legality of the term. Under the ST status, one is legally recognized as a beneficiary of rights and reservations according to the schemes and rules in place. Thus, ST status is of paramount importance in practical aspects of everyday life of both individuals and communities.

Many stories of a community

These multiple identities are often seemingly blended within the lives of the Narikuravar people. The Narikuravars are also further embodying identifications along lines of class and gender (explored in detail in Chapter 4). The people I worked with for the past years were always eager to share their stories of their complex identities. Of course, who gets to have a voice in any given community is stratified by numerous accounts, and many are still silenced, in spite of one's efforts of inclusion. However, among those who came to the fore was Rajasekaran Silvam (whom I mentioned earlier), who became my 'key-informant'. He is the person who worked locally with me, helped and shaped my research. Here is his story and that of his community in his own words:

> My name is Rajasekaran Silvam. I'm very happy to share my story with you. My father's name is Selvam and my mother's name is Vijaya. I have a little brother who is married too. My wife's name is Swetha and I have a one-and-a-half-year-old baby. This is a family and we are all a part of the Narikuravar community. Actually, I belong to the Narukruvas community, a 'Gypsy' community.
>
> About my background, I have been working as an administrator and running two residential schools as a part of the Tribal Society. This is a part of a special scheme by the central government. It used to be called Sarva Shiksha Abhiyan and now it is called Samugara Shisha. There are approximately fifty students in each centre and most of these kids are from the Narikuravar community. As a part of this scheme, the children get three meals and the education they need.
>
> The community people are very backward in education, employment and economic status. The people are really facing hard times without a proper support to get education, employment opportunities. 'Till today, only 10% of the community has access to education, and very few people have reached college level education. I am one of them. I'm really proud. I got this opportunity with the help of my parents, my cousins and some sponsors. I used the opportunity. I have completed my schooling in my nearby native place. The school name is Nehru Higher Secondary School, and I completed first to twelfth standard there

and I started my college. I completed Bachelor of Business Administration; later with the help of some donors, my parents and my cousin, my uncle, I joined my Master of Business Administration MBA in Loyola Institute of Technology, Chennai. And later, I got one more degree from St. Joseph's College, Trichy where I did my MPhil in human resource management. Soon after that I became the assistant professor in the MBA department, from our community at St. Joseph, College of Engineering, Chennai. I worked there for almost four years, but due to the condition of my community, I returned back to my home, and joined hands with my community's pioneers: my uncle and my aunty: Mr. Jaishankar and Mrs. Anuradha Jaishankar and my parents Mr. Silvam, and my mom Vijaya with my brother to run back as president in school for our children.

I do not come from a[n economically] good, comfortable family. Even my mom still is selling beads and strings for almost 30 years. She cooks for children of our community. She motivated us to get good education. She still involves herself in providing education to the Narikuravar community children. I'm really grateful to them, and grateful for the donors and my uncle and aunt. To stand, [as] who I am. This is my little story. Thank you.

Rajasekaran interview, 2021

Conclusion: trends on change

As we will see throughout this book, the Narikuravars are traditionally mobile people, and are seen by others as nomadic, but their ways of life have been dramatically transformed in the past thirty years. This transformation is not linear, and not all in the community are changing at the same pace.[37] But, as the community is changing, the world around them is also shifting, and some are proudly seeing the Narikuravar people transforming: 'In the past we were called Nadodigal, migrating people. We have a good name among people. Because, we don't rob, lie, and betray people. We don't migrate anymore; the time has changed. Hunting is not legal anywhere now. So, we started doing business now, and we have to educate our children' (Sugan interview, 2016).

Most of the Narikuravars are also engaged in a rapid modernization process. While two generations ago the Narikuravars lived a secluded life, inhabiting forests and making do with the fruits of the land, now their world is different. These days, their life is dependent both on the state programmes (such as education, health, employment, schemes.), and on larger communities with which they interreact for business. Like many other indigenous, traditional communities today, some of the younger members keep some of their ancestral traditions, while they adapt many of their behaviours to modern life. While their grandparents might dress traditionally, men wear red turbans and women long skirts, the younger generation wears jeans (for men) and sarees for women.

The Narikuravars have been distinguished in the past by their clothes. Men used to tie a red turban around their heads, 'but the culture had changed enough, so now we are not tying', said Sugan. 'Now we only can tell who is Narikuravar by language. Because, now fashion has changed. So, they are dressing like the others' (Sugan interview, 2016). While in the Mettupalayam 'settlement', talking to Sugan and other members of the community, I directly asked them if they like the changes that took place over the past few decades.[38] Sugan promptly replied: 'Now it's more freedom than past. We love it.'

'How about the traditions? How do you feel about them?' I asked, trying to understand their legacy:

> We left the traditions with our parents. Now we started studying, using cell phones, watching TV, going to films like other people. So, we are interested in these things now. Before, we stayed in forest, so when our dad was hunting, I was interested in hunting. Now dad is doing business, building homes, educating children. So, we got interested to this now. We want some standard[s].
>
>   Sugan interview, 2016

Their inclusion in the globalized, technologically advanced market has been inevitable. The Narikuravars have cell phones and access to internet (in addition to some having computers, tablets and TVs) and they are much immersed into the global realities. The young folks share the same aspirations as many others around the world: travel abroad, prosper economically, dress like their peers.

They understand the need for education, but also disdain being kept at arm's length, and resent not receiving employment because of their ethnic belonging. Typically, they are also political – as we will see next – striving to assert themselves in their own terms in the social, economic and political life. At the community level, the Narikuravars are not looking to be simply assimilated into the larger culture, but to be included with due dignity.

3

Being a Roma in Romania[1]

In June 2017, together with a colleague from the University of Bucharest and a friend who was also a social worker, I went into a southern part of Romania into the ethnically mixed community of Cetate. Here, we met Bratu Vergenica – a 31 years old, vivacious and well-spoken Roma woman who invited us to her house. She told us that she 'can read letter by letter', as she studied until 4th standard: 'My grand-mother did not allow me to go to school because she was afraid that I would meet boys. I told her: "if it wanted to have boys, I will also find them here",' she explained on a whim the cause of her limited schooling.

Vergenica now has four kids – 'only boys. I really wanted a girl, but if God did not want ... This is who I am. Come sit next to us', she gestures me to sit on the small bed, in a house with a low ceiling, with old furniture, covered with worn-out clothes, all creating a homey and well-kept room. 'Make sure you get a soda', Vergenica tells one of her kids, who rushes out the door with money in his hands. Vergenica watches the kid go, and turns to us: 'I get along with my children.'

Her house, like the others in the village, does not have direct access to gas or water. The electricity is taken through an unsafe connection to the public pole. Vergenica explains all this as a matter of fact, not complaining or asking for anything different. It is just how things are. She grew up in the village; after her parents split up, her paternal grandmother took her in. Then 'I got married at 15 years old, I wanted to get married earlier, but I was too little. To get married you should know how to cook and wash. Not before', she proudly explains.

We asked her about her community ties, and she says: 'We are not those Țigani with gold in in their hair', referring to traditional Roma who are often becoming the stereotypical Romani figures. 'We are Țigani who wear trousers, and short skirts, while other Țigani do not wear these types of clothes.' 'How come', I asked. Vergenica shrugs: 'I do not know, here in our village, all are wearing modern clothing. I am the kind that goes in the water, and even swims in a bathing suit. Which other Țigani women do not do', she says, referring to the conservative clothing within traditional Roma communities. 'Even though I am coloured', she says, showing off her arm, 'I still like to sun bathe. I also work the field in shorts and T-Shirt. I work as daily-labourer. I like to work – anywhere. Even in the men's job – to unload or something– I am strong', she says confidently.

I wanted to understand more about how come she was using the word 'Țigan' to identify. So I asked: 'Are you Roma? Or are you "Țigan"?' She promptly replied: 'We are Roma, and this is how we are called. I heard this on TV when I listened to the news! Even late in the night', she says laughing, and pointing out the difference between modes of formal and informal identity recognition currently used in Romania.

She then explains the situation of her family: 'My husband left for a "season".' I look at her confused. She explains that he is a seasonal worker: 'He is in Spain. He went to work in agriculture. He picks up garlic. I miss him. But I have the kids and I can't go to Spain with him, especially because the older one . . . he is not healthy – he has issues with his heart.'

All her children go to the local school, but their experiences differ, she explains: 'There are some teachers who care. For example, the kid who is in the 3rd grade, he does not know how to read and write. But my younger one, in 1st grade works a lot, as his teacher cares. For the older one, I went to school, and the teacher blamed the kid; she said he was not paying attention. The principal of the school is really nice and wants to help. But there are mothers who do not wash their kids. I pay attention so my kids are clean', she says proudly, breaking away from the often-encountered stereotypes of Roma's assumed lack of willingness to send their children to school and poor hygiene. 'We have water here, but only cold water; we warm it, and pour the water in a small basin. And that is how we wash ourselves. It is difficult, but we need to do it. Sometimes the water supply is short, and then we save water in the bottles. And we will still do it.'

Vergenica further explains to us her identity: 'We are Ursari – we are different from Căldărari [Roma]. They go and steal. We are not like that. On TV we see the weddings of the Căldărari, and they say they are Roma, but it is not like that. Our weddings are similar to the Romanians. We make sarmale [i.e. traditional Romanian dish of cabbage and red meat], and steak, but we do not grill the entire pig!' she says referring to the lavish banquets showcased in the media from the Roma weddings. 'We do not show off our wealth – we also do not have this gold, like the Căldărari. How do they get to have all this? They steal, and they murder! We are of a different kind. The truth is that in Spain they steal so much. Women go to stores and steal perfumes, everything. Me, I would not even steal a chewing gum.'

I nod, and then ask: 'You were in Spain? When?'

'Last year I went', she responds. 'I went to work. I wanted to give my kids what they need, so they do not look over the fence and yearn for what others have. I went,

and worked in agriculture. There, we lived in tents in the field. We bought the tents, and we placed them on the owner's land; but we had no access to water. We had to go with 5-litre canteens, and we carried them into the village, and then we will carry them back full to the tents and wash ourselves.'

I look at her trying to imagine these hardships that seasonal migrant workers face, so I followed with: 'How did you feed yourself?' She replied: 'We bought propane, and we cooked in the tents. When I came back, we left them there for those who are coming next.'

'Will you join your husband, and go back?' I asked.

'No!' she firmly replied, 'I will not go back. When I went, I had to leave my four children with some relatives. But the authorities from the child protection, from the town hall came to take my children away. They said that I was not allowed to abandon my children, and because they were minors, I could not leave. They did not say that I left to get work. They said I abandoned my children! Before I left, I went and declared that I am leaving for work and that I leave my children with my mother-in-law. At relatives . . . but they did it . . .'

We then also talked about the difference between Roma and Romanians: 'Not much [difference],' Vergenica said nonchalantly, 'we talk to one another. We are treated well. We all communicate – when we have something to talk. Romanians call me by my name; but they sometimes say "Țigani".'

Considering the daily tensions between Roma elites and Roma communities, we discussed the leadership in the village: 'We used to have a Roma leader here in the village. But he did not care about us. He did not know that my oldest child was sick. He did not help me apply for state programmes for him. A Romanian helped me. Now, there is no one else. Here, we go straight to the town hall [if we need anything].'

She shared with us that she voted, and that before the elections the former Roma leader came to her door. 'This Țigan I mentioned came to me. But, because he did not help me in the past, I told him: "if you want to mess with my signature, I will send you to jail!" I do not want to sign it, because he wanted to collect votes ahead of time. I told him: "You said you will help me pay for social support, and you did not. You said you will put electricity in the village – you did not. You promised to fix the fountains – you didn't keep your word. How do you dare to come to me with this notebook? Do not dare to do something with my name",' Vergenica recalls passionately.

Lacking Roma leadership, I wonder how she accesses here rights. She replied that she turns to the village officials: 'The mayor is the one who could help. But this was a [Roma] leader who was the one to go and talk to the mayor. But once he occupied this place and he did not care for us.'

Vergenica was clearly the leader of her house, even more now that her husband was in Spain, so we wanted to know what are their dynamics. 'I make the decisions *in this family – I saw a few times that my husband did not do things properly, so I said: if I say it is black, it is black. I give him money to pay the bills. Now that he is in Spain, he sends money home. When he sends money, I put them aside.'*

The story of Vergenica is not unusual, but one that I heard throughout the years of fieldwork in different Romanian Roma communities. It is a story that captures many aspects of what it means to be a Roma today; it encapsulates the struggle for a better life, for the dignity of the people, their ambivalence about them being named 'Roma' and/or 'Țigan', the diversity of their community, the complex gender relationship, the early marriages and the resentment they provoke. It also outlines today's mobility/migration process and their hopes for a better life for themselves and their children.

Introduction

Compared to the Narikuravar/Adivasi studies, which are in an incipient scholarly phase, Romani studies have been developing for decades.[2] From this scholarly perspective, Romani studies/works have generated a large palette of political conceptualizations. Here, I will give an insight into the conceptualization of the identity of the Roma communities, showing their taxonomy and underpinnings within their political context.

Like the Narikuravars, the Roma in Romania, inhabit many identities simultaneously, battle to be recognized and demand respect for their own community, while struggling with gross mis-recognition. Just like many Adivasi communities across India, the Roma in Romania are highly diverse (as we will see in the next chapters), and not all agree with the identification proposed by others, being that of their fellow community members or of the Roma elites, and this leads to an ambiguous and polysemic identity.

Origins and history

Similar to the Adivasi, and especially to the Narikuravar, the idea of the Roma origin is imprecise. Roma folks, not unlike many others, often trace their personal histories only two to three generations back, making ancestral research the realm of historians and other social scientific inquiries. However, as the narrative of one's beginning is part of political legitimation, their origin is quickly and quite confidently assumed to be the north-west of South Asia: 'The migration of the ancestors of the Roma from what is now modern India and Pakistan, that took place around or after 1000 CE, was military in character because all migrations in that Eurasian feudal era had to be military in character' (Acton, *Roma Archive*).[3] Similarly, Crowe declares: 'The Gypsies, or Roma entered Eastern Europe and parts of the former Russian Empire and the Soviet Union during the Middle Ages from Northern India' (Crowe, 1996: XI).

Over the past seventy years, this Roma–India connection has been explored and exploited left and right for political outcomes (Trehan, 2017). To fit their political agenda, often scholars and political figures do not use clear historical references to support these claims, but rely on circular scholarly references when mentioning the Roma's South Asian roots (Wogg, 2006). For example, in *Bury Me Standing*, Isabel Fonseca declares that: 'The Gypsy migration has been likened to a fishbone spread over the map of Europe, from India to Persia – and then a fork, to Armenia to Syria and Iraq in one direction, and in the other Byzantine Greece, the Balkans, and into Western Europe and the New World' (Fonseca, 1996: 84).

Furthermore, Fonseca, without any precise reference, declares that 'most scholars believe that the Gypsies left India sometime in the tenth century' (Ibid., 94). At times, the Roma's Indian origin is assumed (Lal, 1962):

> Probably nobody among you is expecting from me a speech proving the Rroms' Indian origin. This point is obvious for all of us, since we are gathered in New Delhi and not somewhere in Egypt, Romania, Bohemia, Israel or any other country. We are all convinced of this origin and I feel free to stress, that, beyond our group, the Rromani people are now aware and proud of it in its overwhelming majority.
>
> Courthiade, 2017: 4[4]

Similarly, Tcherenkov and Laederich (2004) also reiterate the traditional explanation of Romani origins: '[It] is but a small step to support the hypothesis that these Indian Dom are the ancestors of the European Rroma. The professions exercised by the Dom in the Indian subcontinent—musicians, dancers, smiths, basket weavers, sieve makers, even woodworkers, are transmitted from father to son' (Tcherenkov and Laederich, 2004: 13, cited by Hancock, 2002).[5]

To cement the Roma's Indian origin, linguistic arguments are typically presented as:

> Romani is a language of Indian origin. It remains closely related to the languages of India, as a comparison of basic vocabulary can easily demonstrate: Romani words such as pani "water", sap "snake," kan "ear," pandz "five," rat "night," macho 'fish," and countless others are practically identical to the corresponding words in Hundi, Punjabi, Guajarati, and other languages of India. Linguists have also been able to analyze the grammatical structures of Romani and to point out the way in which they derive directly from the grammar of older languages of medieval India.

The fascination with discovering a tangible connection between diverse communities labelled as 'Gypsy' is explored in genetics (Morar et al., 2004; Nagy et al., 2007). Using DNA data from six Roma groups, Moorjani et al. (2013), estimate that 'the Roma harbor about 80% West Eurasian ancestry—derived from a combination of European and South Asian sources—and that the date of admixture of South Asian and European ancestry was about 850 years before present'. The study concludes that Eastern Europe is a major source of the Roma ancestry, and north-west India is the other major source. In a similar vein, using molecular studies, Rai et al. argue that:

> The presence of Indian-specific Y-chromosome haplogroup H1a1a-M82 and mtDNA haplogroups M5a1, M18 and M35b among Roma has corroborated that their South Asian origins and later admixture with Near Eastern and European populations (...). Here we present a detailed phylogeographical study of Y-chromosomal haplogroup H1a1a-M82 in a data set of more than 10,000 global samples to discern a more precise ancestral source of European Romani populations. The phylogeographical patterns and diversity estimates indicate an early origin of this haplogroup in the Indian subcontinent and its further expansion to other regions.
>
> Rai et al., 2012: 1

Understanding the limited resolution of most genetic studies, Martínez-Cruz et al. 'performed a high-resolution study of the uniparental genomes of 753 Roma and 984 non-Roma hosting European individuals' and argued that 'Roma groups show lower genetic diversity and high heterogeneity compared with non-Roma samples as a result of lower effective population size and extensive drift, consistent with a series of bottlenecks during their diaspora' (Martínez-Cruz et al., 2016: 937).

Their study 'points to a Northwestern origin of the proto-Roma population within the Indian subcontinent' (Ibid.). While this is notable progress in determining the Roma–India connection, precise origin within the diverse South Asia pool is not revealed, as 'previous studies have left unanswered questions about the exact parental population groups in South Asia' (Rai et al., 2012).

However, the enthusiasm for establishing the Roma–India connection is not shared by everyone. Thus, while emerging studies are looking at the Indian liaison, on the grounds the connection is not so obvious. For example, in an interview with Dr. Ciprian Necula, the Roma scholar and activist, he charged this connection as precarious and problematic, often used for political gains:

> In my fieldwork, never in my experience have I met a Roma who really thought they have Indian origins. It appears as a cartoonish remark; or it is used when someone wants to look smart. Actually, the news about the 'Roma origin' had become a new public label given to the Roma. Roma-Indians [connection] has a negative connotation, referring to their foreign, Asian, inferior – compared to the Dacs [the presumed Romanians forefathers] origin. So, when you call someone in Romania 'Indian', you do not pay a compliment, quite the contrary. Roma are Roma, even though 1000+ were throughout India. What we know for sure is that they left, and never went back.
>
> Necula, 2018, personal correspondence

He adds sarcastically, thinking about the day-to-day relevance of these connections: 'I would be curious to see which Roma traditions are of Indian heritage. Blah-blah about respecting the elder, and alike are commonalities that are generally applicable, and function just like "palm reading", meaning: you hear what makes sense in any circumstance, such as: you are hurt, something is weighing you down etc.' (Ibid.).

In his view, this connection is invisible at the level of the overall community, and mostly used by elites and politicians as political tools and manipulation mechanisms:

> Well, the Roma have all the reasons in the world to smile when hearing about their possible Indian origin, and they accept it as possible, but they do not care about India, and about the grand Indian culture (beyond their curiosity for the exotic) because the European pressure and experience weighs more than a faraway possible origin, which is stereotypical and for many Roma is demeaning.
>
> Ibid.

Necula's fierce opposition to this connection seems relevant to the experience that I have encountered during my fieldwork in Ormeniş. Here, most of the people shrug their shoulders and smile when asked if they are aware of the possible Indian ancestry. Some people watch the new Indian TV series broadcast in Romania, and say that they enjoy watching them, and that they find their values similar. Others simply did not engage with this idea whatsoever. And a few Roma from Ormeniş fervently expressed their ideas, and took pride in this possible connection:

> We are part of the India nation. And I am quite proud of it. India is a country where people philosophise, where they respect religions; it is a country where all kind of people are known as being valuable. This [i.e., India] is a country which generated the Roma, and this is why I am very proud of where I come from. There is a connection between the Roma and India. Absolutely! And this isn't believed only by us, the Roma people, but it was proven scientifically that Roma come from India and this is their native place.
>
> Yosua interview, 2017

And Yosua continued to explain eloquently that in his view there is a connection in the origins of the language and traditions. And 'we can see that the Roma identify as Indians from a spiritual point of view, through their desire to grow spiritually', he said, referring to his own personal journey of conversion to the Pentecostal church, like many other Roma in Ormeniş. For Yosua, this connection needs to be officialized and the Roma should be offered Indian citizenship: 'It is the normal thing to do'. And he explains: 'I watched on Youtube how Roma go to India to research their native place. And you can see that Indians have a great compassion towards them and are welcoming.' He emphasizes the connection, and imagines a different understanding of his community, one that is actually well received: 'This is a great thing to know that you belong somewhere, you have a people, and they really want you.'

The India–Roma ethnic connection is still up for investigation. While there are grounds to assume it, it also furthers a political process that might empower certain stereotypes about the community, and (re)articulate the strangeness of those labelled as 'Gypsy'. My work does not aim at further investigation into this connection, or to settle this debate. Differently, it aims to pose the question of Romani (and Adivasi) taxonomy vis-à-vis its political underpinnings, to trace how these identifications become a part of the process of making claims to access justice.

Nomadism and criminality

The point of Roma origin is not the only sensitive, unsettled or politicized issue. While the Roma are typically referred to in connection to their mobility and to traditional forms of nomadism, many Roma activists and scholars insist in separating the two identifications: nomad and Roma/ 'Gypsy'. Most traditionally, nomadic communities labelled as 'Gypsy', both in India and Romania, are currently officially settled. Nevertheless, the assumption of mobility as part of the 'Gypsy' label persists. According to Matras, there have been numerous migration waves in the European Roma history: 'A large wave of migrants in the fourteenth and early fifteen centuries brought the Roms into various parts of Europe from the Balkans, Roms from Germany migrated to German colonies in Russia, Hungary and Romania during the eighteen century' (Matras, 2015: 33).

The Roma mobility is often declared without contextual (historical/political etc.) references. For example, referring to Papusza as 'one of the greatest Gypsy singers and poets ever', Fonseca (1996) describes her as a Roma woman from Poland whose family 'was nomadic – part of a great *kumpania*, or band of families, traveling with horses and in caravans, with the men at the front and the women and children following behind open carts' (Fonseca, 1996: 3).

However, Necula (work in progress) cautions against Romanian Roma nomadic characterization, and argues that researchers, such as Okley in 1983, use the *nomadic* label to exoticize the Roma communities. Thus, he recommends that nomadism is not used as a criteria for analysis of Roma issues. His view follows Nicholae Gheorghe's critical position towards Andras Biro, who in 2013 considered the Roma to be the 'eternal nomads'. Differently, Gheorghe argued that to find 'the marker of Roma uniqueness in nomadism is a wrong approach, although it was the most used concept in solving the Roma dilemma and their relation to land and territory' (Gheorghe, 2013: 41, cited by Necula, work in progress).

Over-generalizing nomadism exoticizes the Roma, creating the assumption of their romantic movement. This furthermore disregards geographical, political and historical contexts in which different Roma communities live. For example, 'in Western Europe it is commonly thought that nomadism is an essential feature of the Gypsies. But in Eastern Europe, where most of the world's Gypsies live, far fewer than one percent of the gypsies travel' (Stewart, 1997: 13). The assumption of Roma mobility was often addressed legally, creating a system of 'prohibition of Roma nomadism, perceived as a social, hygienic danger – the spread of diseases, cultural and, last but not least, military' (Necula, work in progress).

This further reflects different historical contexts. Starting in the fifteenth century and for the next few hundred years, the institution of slavery in Romania tied Roma to the land, and in the twentieth century communist regimes controlled and limited the mobility of the Roma (and others).

> The issue of Roma nomads in Romania has not become a problem for the authorities during the communist regime, but much earlier, starting at least with the period of slavery/dismantling of the Roma in the Romanian Principalities. The way the Roma have reached the present Romanian territory is still a topic in the debate of the historians. It is certain that they reached the two Principalities as nomads (or travelers perceived as nomads). (...) In fact, elsewhere in Europe, the "nomad issue" has been a continuing concern of the states in relation to the Roma. Regretfully, [for the] Roma (and not only) nomadism was given both positive attributes (freedom, magic, exotism, etc.) and negative (anarchy, imbalance, illegality, disease transmission, poverty, witchcraft, savage, primitivism).
>
> Necula, 'Studiu de Diversitate', work in progress

Roma's nomadism, while geographically, politically, community and historically specific, is difficult to totally declare absent or simply as a tradition of the past, as there are Roma communities and individuals who even today recall their nomadic lives: 'Until 1981 we lived in tents, we were nomads, we were moving around from one village to the next, wherever we had work', recalled Isoc Căldărar, from Brăteiu, during an interview at Radio Romania Târgu Mureș in 2016. 'Well, when we saw that our relatives settled here in Brăteiu, we also did.' Like Sugan and other Narikuravars I met, Isoc also describes the hardships of nomadic life: 'It was really hard to live a nomadic life in the tents. We lived during summers and winters.'[6]

While Isoc was referring to internal nomadism of his community, for the various Roma communities in Romania movement usually involves crossing international borders:

> Currently, most of the inhabitants of Toflea (Brăhășești, jud. Galați): there are children, teenagers and the elderly, [and] mostly, adults being gone to western countries (England and Germany are the most popular destinations), most working in agriculture, slaughterhouses or factories. (...) Most of the Toflea community members live today in Germany or England. (...) Although many keep in touch with their native village, parents are increasingly skeptical about

the prospect of their return: 'At least I'm still sending money home', young people declared referring to their remittances.

Necula, 'Studiu de Diversitate', work in progress

The Roma I spoke with in Ormeniș did not recall a personal history of nomadism; rather, they would refer to their community as being settled. However, while nomadism was at best lost in some immemorial past, their mobility was that of the present and of the near future. Not unlike many Romanians, many of the Roma from Ormeniș have been migrating over the past twenty years – since the fall of the communist regime – when the borders with Western Europe opened up (at least from the Romanian side). Of course, traditions of nomadism are different from contemporary migration paths (mainly the former are community based, and the latter are individual), but they also both relate to movement practices that people engage in.

While Roma nomadism is typically assumed (Fonseca, 1996), more recently scholars argue that the Roma mobility might not be the effect of their ethnical traditions, but in 'pursuit of employment, which was often mobile, flexible, and adaptable' (McGarry, 2017: 20), and that nomadism needs to be 'understood to be a fundamental component of Romani identity in the same way that speaking French is for the French' (Ibid.). Scholars, such as McGarry also steer our attention to the fact that those who write history were able to describe these mobile patterns as traditions rather than forms of evading 'state bondage, capture or manipulation' (McGarry, 2017: 20, citing Scott, 2009: 24).

As Romani people disobeyed these forms of control, their defiance was placed in the framework of criminality; this was facilitated by a legal system intimately connected with other literary discourses, and for centuries nomadism and criminality became both interlinked and associated with the term 'Gypsy'. This connection has been perpetuated over centuries, in Europe and beyond, leaving behind a strong social, legal and political legacy that often labelled those considered 'Gypsy' as criminals and nomads in need of punishment and rehabilitation (Dragomir, 2019).[7]

Of course, as mentioned earlier, nomadism comes at odds with the history of slavery that Roma people endured within the Romanian principates, where they were tied to land and to the people whom they worked for. However, some scholars (Crowe, 1996) argue that this was a partial process, as not all Roma were settled and enslaved: 'While robi' have been settled for extended period of times, many Gypsies continued their traditional lifestyle, particularly the Lajesi (Laieisi) and Ursari' (Crowe, 1996: 123). Moreover, Crowe continues, the habit of nomadism was re-enacted shortly after emancipation, leading to a return to traditional forms of mobility: 'Gypsy nomads lived in tents during the summer and in winter in underground cabins or shelters which they dug in the forest near villages, so that they might obtain fuel, also work for the peasants, and have opportunities for stealing' (Ibid.).

The light-hearted mentioning of 'stealing' in connection to Roma mobility is not exceptional or present only in racist works. It is rather a prevalent historical construction, still enforced today. Thus, the association with mobility and criminality, of those labelled as 'Gypsy' dates back centuries across Europe (Lucassen and Lucassen, 1997/2005; Mayall, 1988; Lucassen and Willems, 2003, 2012) and Asia (Radhakrishna 2000, 2001; Piliavsky, 2006, 2011, 2012; Dragomir, 2020). Over centuries, those in power imposed these categorizations, and as such they were able to tighten control over mobile groups and criminalize them.

While addressing the issue in terms of equality and emancipation, in the second part of the twentieth century the Romanian communist regime took a draconic approach towards the Roma, aiming to restrict both settlement and other forms of alternative economic gain (Necula, work in progress; Achim, 2005):

> Without ever being declared, public, systematic actions of repression (especially gold confiscation) and forced sedentarization were initiated in parallel, especially against traditional Roma (nomads and semi-nomads), camouflaged in the spirit of the time in propaganda formulas: 'Economic, professionally and socially, the Roma received in this regime the chance to integrate in the modern way of life, even if often in a forced way.' In essence, for the communist regime – like previous Romanian governments – the nomadic Roma were the ones who raised real problems (of the lumpen-proletariat type), imposing control measures on the part of the state authorities that were in permanent conflict of authority with the informal leaders of nomadic and semi-nomadic communities, the real aim of these measures being to eliminate the despotism of community leaders.[8]
>
> Necula, 'Studiu de Diversitate', work in progress

After the fall of the communist regime, in the early 1990s, came the democratic framework conditions for the political assertion of the Roma identity, which also meant that Roma are now recognized as a national minority, and thus receive a seat in the Romanian Parliament (Ibid.).

Different communities

One of the most well-known criticisms of the scholarly works produced 'about' the Roma is over-generalization. These works have been overlooking the crucial fact that the community is diverse (Necula, 'Studiu de Diversitate', work in progress). Most scholars who work with one Roma community tend to generalize their findings, assuming that all Roma communities are alike. Hence, the proud self-identification of the Roma participants, one made within the comfort of their homes in Ormeniş, might not be exemplary of other Roma with similar education, age and income bracket within Romania. Romani scholars (Dima interview, 2016 and Necula interview, 2017) argue that the Roma community is composed of many small communities.

Just as nomadism was hardly embraced by everyone, not all Roma communities are embracing the same identity. The degree of similarity among them is rather a matter of hot debate among activists and scholars, who have a hard time establishing both a common ground among tremendously diverse communities, and delineating among over-sweeping, over-generalized views. The diversity among the Roma communities around the world runs deeply: they speak different languages, they have different religions, live in various geographical areas, and have different traditional occupations, etc.

> I am not the same as all other Roma. Most 'Fierar' deny they are Roma as they do not want to be associated with 'Tzigani' with long dresses and moustaches. We do not even speak the language. They are all arguments that we are not like that! The model that 'Fierari' accepted as a successful one was the Romanian model.
>
> Ciprian Necula interview, 2017.

In an interview with Lucica from Ormeniş, I asked her: 'Are you a Roma woman?' She answered simply, 'Yes.' While knowing that identity is often an unreflective space, I continued: 'And what does this mean to you?' 'I am saying . . . well, "Romanizat",' she clarifies. I am confused, so I further ask: 'And what does that mean?' Lucica is patient with me, and continues: 'I mean, we speak also Romanian words, aside from Romany.' I nod and softly challenge: 'But what about from these categories: Căldărari, Ursari.' Lucica waits patiently for my question to end, and then reflects, 'I think we are Căldărari' (Lucica interview, 2017).

According to Grigore et al. (2007) the Roma are divided within several communities, separated mostly by trade or skill: 'Boldeni'/'Florari' (trading flowers), 'Caramidari'/'Caramizari' (referring to bricks), 'Fierari' (metal), 'Gabori' (Hungarian Roma trading mostly carpets), 'Xoraxane' (Turkish), 'Spoitori' (referring to working with copper), 'Căldărari' (making pots and pans), 'Lautari' (musicians), 'Lovari' (trading horses), 'Ursari' (entertainment, mostly with bears), 'Romungre' (Hungarian Roma skilled in trade), 'Rudari' (Romanian Roma working with wood), 'Argintari' (referring to silver), 'Vatraşi' (sedentarized and strongly assimilated Roma[9] into Romanian culture).[10] Necula ('Studiu de Diversitate', work in progress) also mentions the religious diversity of Roma in Romania:

In Romania, most Roma are Christians and a minority are Muslims (especially in southern Romania). In recent decades we have witnessed a process of re-Christianization of the Roma through a transition from Orthodoxy to neo-Protestant religions.

Necula, 'Studiu de Diversitate', work in progress

In my fieldwork in the south of Romania, in the village of Cetate, the Roma people immediately told me they are from the 'Spoitori' community. Similarly, in my conversation with Roma activists, who reflected and thought about their Roma identity a great deal, their particular identification with a specific Roma community was always made with ease. However, in Ormeniş the situation was different. When the Roma participants were asked about their Roma community, most looked confused, or simply told us that they do not know.

For example, during fieldwork we met Adriana, who was twenty years old, and when we asked about her Roma identity she responded: 'This is it, I really do not know', she said smiling. 'We are house of Gypsies', responded her grandmother, Doina (62 years old). Ştefania (28 years old) told us: 'No, no community.' Hearing this her child (11 years old) answered: 'Maybe Lăcătari', referring to a community unknown to me. His mother shrugged. Mariana (40 years old) detailed for us: 'I am a Gypsy of Roma ethnicity, but I don't wear a special dress, just my clothes; I wear mostly trousers. I speak exactly how I speak now', she said, referring to the fact that she does not speak Romani, the traditional Roma language. 'When I say I am a Gypsy, I am proud of this', she continues. 'Because, how could I say this . . . everywhere you go, maybe the Romanians laugh at Gypsy people, but when I go somewhere and they ask me, I say I am a Gypsy, not a Romanian.'

The much-appreciated scholarly distinctions are often blurred on the ground, with the Roma participants often comfortably inhabiting complex identities, navigating between labels, such as Roma, 'Gypsy', 'Romanian' and community-specific identifications, such as 'Căldărari'. Moreover, this diversity translated politically, with some Roma communities falling further behind in their access to rights.[11]

Justice and language: Roma versus 'Gypsy'

Identification with specific Roma communities is sometimes not a clear endeavour. As we have seen earlier in the introdction, in Doru's family, not all Roma agree about the name of their community, and while at the community level the people have different preferences between Roma and 'Gypsy',[12] at the scholarly and activist level in Romania the preferred term is Roma, and they argue for the annihilation of the term 'Gypsy'.

In my fieldwork, I noticed that while the Roma activists and scholars tend to predominantly identify as Roma, in communities the term 'Ţigan'/'Gypsy' is still a prevalent form of self-identification. Moreover, this divide often follows both generational and educational lines. In other words, typically, the more educated and younger a person is the more likely they are to identify and publicly claim their identity as Roma, and reject the term 'Ţigan'/'Gypsy'.

When I spoke with folks individually, the same difference of opinion persisted: 'I told my colleagues from university that I was Roma'. They kept saying, "Don't say you're a Gypsy anymore, because you're not a Gypsy." 'Doru related referring to the negative stereotypes that are often associated with the Roma.

> 'It's true, I repeated. I'm not a Gypsy, I'm Roma' (Doru, 40, 2016).

Differently, Mihai, also from Ormeniş, argued: 'I feel better if I am called a "Gypsy". When some say you are Roma ... What is this?' He gestures the term away and rolls his hand at his temple, signifying madness. 'I say Gypsy. Say: look, a beautiful Gypsy woman. A beautiful Roma woman? No. I say a beautiful little Gypsy, a perfect Gypsy. A Gypsy, a Gypsy, a Gypsy and that's it! Anyway, this is how everyone calls us: Gypsy. In Italian is Gitan, and in Spanish is Gitano. And I proudly say Yo soy Gitano!' (Mihai, 64).

'We are "Căldărari", says Lucica Adina (31 years old, 7th standard). But 'what does it mean for you to be a Roma woman?' we asked her. To this she responds, smiling: 'I like it, it's beautiful. This is it, we are Gypsy, that's how we say it, Gypsy, but in Romanian you say Roma. We also like to speak Hungarian, but we are Gypsy.' Trying to find out more, we ask: 'Do you prefer this term instead of Roma?' 'Yes', she says, and her neighbour added: 'This is how we are' (Cocoras Lucica Adina interview, 2017).

Because these terms are loaded and embedded in a history of racialization, this ethnical identification is not one that comes easily, but one that makes people pause, reflect, choose and assume one identity versus the other. Nevertheless, one's self-identity is not sufficient for recognition to be complete. For example, while in Ormeniş, Adriana who is twenty years old, recalled early memories of her education, while referring to herself as Roma:

> When I was at high-school – first semester – I was placed by chance in a class that was 'different'. My colleagues were of a higher society, they were speaking highly [i.e., eloquently] and different from me. So, immediately they knew I entered on special seats [i.e., reservations assigned for Roma pupils]. I do not

know how they knew. But I did not keep it a secret. They behave differently towards me; sometimes they would not talk to me at all. Mostly because of experiencing this, I left class – I kinda' felt excluded. The professors were OK, but if I needed help from other colleagues, they were indifferent, they did not want to talk to me. To deal with this, in the 2nd semester I switched to another class. There the colleagues were really nice – I keep in touch with them, even now we are connected on Facebook. These people also knew that I was Roma, but it did not matter. Maybe because in this group were also more Roma kids.

During interviews we asked Ștefania (28 years old), how she preferred to be called: 'Preference: Țigani. This is how it always was', she said, articulating her argument. Hearing this, her eleven-year-old son intervenes: '"Țigani" is humiliating, but "Roma" is not like that. I do not like being called "Țigani".' He continues pensively: '"Țigani", we do not think ourselves as "Țigani" we do not have the same habits – "Țigani" have long skirts with salba [necklaces], and their traditions', the child continued, marking the distinction between traditional Roma and his own community.

While young people mainly thought of themselves as Roma, there were some elderly people who appreciated being referred to as Roma as well. Jeni (50 years old, interview): 'Well, I don't know what community I am from because in our family we don't talk Romany. I know we are a Roma family, but we're not talking this language.' When I asked her how she would like to be called she said, smiling: 'Roma is better.' I probed further: 'Is there a difference between Roma and "Gypsy"?' Jeni laughs: 'There's no difference, but Roma sounds better.' Her laughter intensifies: 'It sounds better, more polite. We are talking like politicians now', she humours me sarcastically. I take her joke with a wink, and continue: 'What does it mean for you to be a Roma?' Jeni adopts a serious tone: 'Well, that's how we were born, it is from the family. There is no difference if you work and if you know how to treasure your money. And also, if you know how to respect others, you are respected also.' This touches on a sore point for the Roma of Ormeniș, and Jeni continues: 'But if you don't know how to be a human, you're not respected. We cannot say anything because we were respected no matter where we went, because we knew how to talk and how to behave. We are not drunken people; we are not trying to pick a fight or to start a scandal', Jeni says implicitly referring to the stereotypes that are often said about the Roma people in general, and from which she aims to differentiate: 'And here lies the difference: be a human. It means a lot. Because it is useless to be Magyar or Romanian if you pick up fights and you steal and you talk in a bad way, you are nothing . . . Right? At least that's how I understand the situation', she brings the point home: 'We never had any problems with anybody', she says referring to the animosities, which at times led to violence[13] that have been taking place in small rural communities between Roma and others (like Romanians and Hungarians). 'My man doesn't drink; we do not start scandals', concludes Jeni.

Similarly, Margareta (53 years old) tried to distinguish herself from the stereotype of Roma and 'Gypsy': 'No, we are not that kind of Roma; we are more like civilized Roma here', she says referring to the village of Ormeniş, 'we go to school. My children go to school in Braşov; here this normal just like Romanians. We are civilized Roma. For me Roma means to be civilized, like everybody'. While Margareta and Jeni admit their ethnic identity, they are also quick to distinguish themselves from the stereotypes associated with being Roma: creating problems in the village, not taking their children to school, drinking and being all together 'uncivilized'. Their thoughtful responses, trying to mark out differences, bring to light the in-depth knowledge that they both have of their communities, and of how they are perceived by others.

Overall, in Ormeniş, most of the folks who embrace the Roma identity – different from 'Ţigan' or 'Gypsy' – are either young and educated, or have been receiving informal education from relatives and neighbours about the racist implications of the word 'Ţigan'. While still not having an overall acceptance, the term 'Roma' is gaining currency within the community.

It might be argued that this use is one imposed from above, by elites and by non-Roma educators, and this is not an identity that sprung up entirely from the Roma people themselves. And this would be accurate. However, which identity springs from the people, and is not articulated and perpetuated (at least partially) by elites? Moreover, the term 'Ţigan'/ 'Gypsy' is a term that, while still in heavy use today both by Roma and non-Roma, has also been exogenous to the community, imposed on the people for centuries, until it became accepted as 'normal'. Thus, it is not surprising that now scholars argue in favour of the need to challenge the 'normal' use of 'Ţigan'/ 'Gypsy'.

Self-identification and multilayered taxonomy

Roma elites have been critically engaging with the 'Ţigan' term, stating that its use robs one from their human status, which has further implications:

> You can do anything with him, trick him, it's best to trick him, right? At the limit, you can even kill him, just as the Gadje can kill you because you are a Roma (in

a traditional sense) or a Gypsy in a social sense. That is, you are making fool of a man because it is defiled, it is not human … after a simplistic ontology: there are two completely exclusive realities, the Gadje and the Roma produced by social history especially the European one as 'traditional'.

Gheorghe, 2012: 321, cited by Necula, work in progress

Similarly, in her piece titled *Dear Gadje (non-Romani) Scholars*, Matache (2018)[14] argues for the decolonialization of Romani studies, specifically that the 'Gadje' scholars should stop using the term 'Țigan' ('T') or 'Gypsy' altogether, because of their negative connotations, which are similar to the 'N-word' within the American context, and insist on referring to the communities as Roma. This empowerment movement through self-naming is understood as one of crucial importance in defining the community and enabling it access to justice.

These efforts, while fierce, are rather new and not yet commonplace. There are authors who employ both Roma and 'Gypsy' (McGarry, 2017), or only the label 'Gypsy' (Stewart, 1997; Fonseca, 1996):

> Some Gadje scholars suggest that Țigan (T-word) identity and Gypsy as an umbrella term are more accurate and inclusive ethnonyms than Roma. They argue that the term Roma is a recently employed political term used by Roma NGOs and the European Commission (…) Romani identity has been constructed and strengthened by Roma on some agreed upon 'inside boundaries' or markers in relation to other groups on the basis of descent. Various political and historical contexts have built the ambiguity and the diversity of Romani identity, separating them in subgroups, names, dialects, or customs. Yet, if we were to follow a constructivist approach, instability, ambiguity, and fluidity constitute essential attributes of any identity. And in fact, such diversity also exists among other groups, including dominant majorities. Their ethnonational identities tend not to be questioned based on differences in "lifestyle", subgroups, dialects, etc. or clustered with other similar groups. Romanians in the north of Romania speak a different dialect from those in the south and have different customs, traditions, food, and clothes. They may display obvious similarities with some neighboring nations. The construction of the Romanian identity was recent, too. Yet, they are granted an undeniable right to their own identity.

Matache, 2017[15]

The answer to the question 'Who is a Roma?' is still very difficult to answer. This is because many Roma do not self-identify as Roma, but are typically identified as such by others, mainly by researchers, scholars and policy makers. This identification is one that intersects class, as many poor communities of Eastern Europe in general, and of Romania in particular, are identified as ethnically Roma even when they might not be such. In other words, people of a certain educational level, economic background and occupational status are categorized as Roma without sharing any ethnic or cultural similarities (Rughiniş, 2011; Surdu, 2016). Moreover, often – poverty coupled with lack of education and limited access to political power, as well as having certain professions such as horse trades, fortune-telling, etc. – is identified as Roma. Another issue that comes from the intersection of the Roma label with class (education, employment, housing, etc.) is that most researched Roma are those who 'fit this profile', and most researchers over-sample low income, poor communities, which in turn become 'the *favorite* place of research on Roma' (Surdu, 2016: 65).

The simple solution to this issue would be one of self-identification, and to count as Roma only those who self-identify as such. However, this process runs into a different issue: many Roma, knowing the negative stigma that often surrounds the Roma or 'Gypsy' label, prefer to identify 'as Roma when among the Roma, and Gadje when among the Gadje' (Lee, 2017 – Columbia University Roma People's Project).[16] Let us not forget that it is already proven that negative stereotyping of one's ethnicity leads to low self-esteem, and results in minimizing the ties with one's ethnic group (Grigore et al., 2007).

But, as powerful as the fear of discrimination is, this is not the only reason for keeping the Roma identity private. Romani scholars like Duminica (2017 interview) and Necula (2017 interview) declare that for many Roma the memory of the Holocaust is still haunting, and that – in an instinct of preservation – they identify as the majority population, and keep their identity a secret from the Gadje. Hence, even though the census of Romania acknowledges the Roma as 2 per cent of the entire population, Romani activists declare that the numbers are much higher, about 8 per cent, making the Roma minority in Romania the largest one, overtaking the politically powerful Hungarian minority.[17] As a result of reticence to self-identify as a Roma, the difference between those identified as Roma by others and self-proclaimed Roma is staggering. Studies have found that, of those identified by others as Roma, only '36.8% in Hungary and 30.7% in Romania considered themselves as Roma' (Ladanyi and Szelenyi, 2001, cited by Surdu, 2016: 62), leading to the conclusion that 'the definition of Roma varies a great deal cross-culturally and depending who are the classifiers' (Ibid.).[18]

Considering the sensitivity of identification and self-identification, while in Ormeniş we asked the people whom we initially identified as Roma – with the help of the Roma community leaders, and who after that were recommended by others as being Roma – if they were Roma, and how they self-identify further. All our participants self-identified as Roma, or 'Gypsy'. Out of over one hundred participants, approximately 40 per cent identified as 'Gypsy', even though the question that was addressed was 'Are you Roma?' To this, one half nodded, and the other half nodded and added: 'We are "Gypsy",' followed by 'and proud to be so!' Considering that the researchers were typically identified as 'Gadje', and thus representing the hierarchical status quo, the pride in their identity was remarkable.

It is also worth mentioning that the village of Ormeniş is a small place, where people feel safe. When researchers came into the Roma houses, they were often introduced by other members of the community, and therefore trusted. Given this familiarity, most of the Roma people of Ormeniş felt at ease in recognizing their identity. One could wonder if their answers would have been similar if they would have been asked to self-identify in other circumstances, or locations. Moreover, the proud self-identification of the Roma in Ormeniş might not be the norm in other geographical areas, with many Roma in other communities in various parts of Romania reacting differently.

Changes within the Roma community

The Roma community in Ormeniş, like many other Roma communities in other parts of the world, have been dramatically changing over the past decade. In Romania, during the communist regime, before 1989, the Roma identity was not officially recognized in census, and everyone was 'Romanicized'; after communism fell, the Roma still had a difficult time within the new 'equalitarian' regime, in which they have often been discriminated against and persecuted (Necula interview, 2018). While facing systematic discrimination, the Roma had access to education (which was still stratified, and often segregated), but often Roma children were placed in the last rows of the class, or told they are not as intellectually fit as the other students. Moreover, the precarious economic background of many Roma families led to the children being pulled out of school to help parents with their work, which in turn affected their access to higher education. In spite of these setbacks, over the past three decades, many of the Roma, especially in urban settings, benefited from access to education provided by the state, increasing the level of literacy, fighting through thick and thin (at times with the support of civil society institutions, such as the Open Society, Romani Criss, and Roma Education Fund), and some Roma made strides forward. Roma activists argue that as the number of literates grew, so did access to higher education for Roma, and this formed an exquisitely trained and educated Roma elite.

Thus, a new Roma elite emerged, an educated, well-spoken, articulated one that not only entered the middle class, while identifying as Roma, but also joined the new forces of the Romanian post-communist vibrant intellectual and artistic scene. As Roma actors, musicians, scholars, writers and poets have marked the scene of cultured life in Romania in the past fifteen years, and while bearing their Roma identity, they offered alternatives to the discourses that for too long have been essentializing their community. This does not mean that the Roma ascension to the public sphere is smooth or linear. The Roma elites I spoke with often shared with me the multiple burdens they have to carry, that the issues confronting the community are complex, and that they have to wear multiple hats: as activists, scholars, artists and at times political representatives. As we will see in the following chapters, Roma elites often confessed that they are tired. They have been working for decades now on multiple fronts, fighting powerful forms of structural racism, operating with limited resources and often accused that they do not fully serve their community.

While this process is mixed, these changes – maybe not as powerful as those taking place in the Romanian large urban areas – are felt in Ormeniş as well. While the older Roma people from the village barely know how to read and write, and many elderly women are illiterate, the new generations have a different outlook. Today, both girls and boys have gone to primary school, and many of them have completed at least two years of high-school. Referring to education, the entire Roma community in Ormeniş we interacted with, told us that they would like to have more schooling options for their community, and that education will empower them. This finding contravenes the stereotype that is usually attributed to the Roma, who are believed not to want to go to school, or to actively prevent their children from obtaining their education. Just like many Narikuravars, some Roma confessed that, maybe before they were reticent because they did not see what so much schooling could do for their children, but now they realized that it is important.

Specifically, the Roma of Ormeniş overwhelmingly said that they wish they had a high-school in their village, or at least a school where they could complete the two years towards their degree, and lamented amongst themselves how their children had to travel a long way to attend college. This issue was clearly outlined by Robert who is the Roma representative to the Ormeniş town hall. He has three girls, and the middle one goes to high-school in the nearby city. She was eighteen, bright eyes, long dark hair, oval face, tall and slim; she was dressed nicely, but modestly. Sitting at the small table in her living room, she was engaging everyone in a well-articulated conversation. In a well-spoken manner, she shared with me that she now goes to high-school, and that she hoped that she will continue and go to university as well. She was explaining to her mother how using the term 'Ţigan'/ 'Gypsy' was not acceptable to address their community, and that they need to use the term Roma – as it is more respectable. Her father entered the room as we were talking, with a cola bottle, which he placed on the table. As his wife poured the soda, he was pretending that he was not interested, and he made himself useful around the room. Finally, he pulled a chair a bit removed from us, and listened to our conversation. As his middle daughter was talking, I caught a glimpse of his proud smile. Later on that day he shared with me the everyday difficulties that they were encountering. His very modest salary from the town hall made it difficult to pay for the commute of his daughter (at least 15 lei, the equivalent of 5 dollars) five days a week to the high-school. This commute was exorbitantly expensive, and he explained: 'Most of my salary is being given to her commute, and that is even not taking into account that we need to make her a lunch box, and also give her some money, just to make sure that she is safe', he said quietly. We paused, and I thought of the other expenses that came with her high-school education: uniforms, books, computer, etc. It was clearly difficult for him. Because he worked at the town hall, he was aware of the support others were receiving to ensure the education of their children: 'It is not like the Hungarians', he said, referring to Hungarians who live in his village, whom – in spite of being a minority just like the Roma – are treated differently. 'The Hungarian government supports Hungarians in Romania for their children to go to school', he added. When he saw my puzzled look, he explained: 'The Hungarian government came and did a census in the Romanian areas with a large Hungarian population [like Ormeniş] and found out the needs of the Hungarian families in the villages. Now they regularly send funds to cover the costs of the Hungarian children going to a Hungarian high-school in the city. They have a bus that takes them every day. The Roma children do not have that', he said, sadly implying a reference to the funds, to the transport, to access to education, and to the support of a state that recognizes its people. The responses of Robert and his family highlight the challenges and transformations of the Roma community at large. They are Roma, proud to be so, willing to embrace their identity, to strive through education[19] and make demands of recognition to the state. Seeing the youth of Ormeniş so determined to make their mark, and strongly voice their views, assured me that while changes[20] are at times slow and assiduous, they are in the making. And that looking at the Roma communities, in Ormeniş and beyond, as a never changing community, caught in *illo-tempore*, is not only damaging, but also wrong.

Power: Internal and External Dynamics

What could I tell you? We're another type of Gypsies. There are many kinds. There are 'Gaboreştii' who are promising their children to marriage, and they are even sold for gold and fortunes, but not in this village!

Bodi Lavinia interview, 2017

Introduction

While hierarchies exist between communities, and those who share a tradition of mobility have often been marginalized and criminalized, there are internal hierarchies that people employ, reinforce and recreate. These orders are diverse, but here I will refer to two forms of internal hierarchization that I often encountered during my work with the Narikuravar and Roma communities: intra-community and gender.

As we have seen in the previous chapters, the diversity of people labelled as 'Gypsy' is often mentioned, but rarely fully analysed. Scholars typically refer to it in the beginning of their work, but rarely take into account in their study the policy recommendations and conclusions. For example, Zoltan Barany states that: 'In several Eastern European states, such as Bulgaria and Romania, tribal identity – primarily rooted in the traditional economic activity of a group – remains a significant bond. Suffice it to say that even in relatively small regions a dozen distinctive tribes might coexist' (Barany, 2002: 12). Similarly, Stewart (1997: 2) wrote: 'This is a culturally diverse community in modern industrial society.'

The diversity of the Narikuravar community is at times mentioned in passing. For example, in 2017 Anuradha explained that in the Narikuravar community there are three main groups, distinguished by their worshiping traditions. Thus, the groups worship one of the goddesses: Meenakshi, Kaali or Mariama. Depending on the goddess worshiped, they sacrifice bulls or goats. As we have seen earlier in the story of Sugan's marriage, when the Narikuravar marry they have to choose their partners from the community whose worshiping practices are different from theirs, and the woman takes the man's goddess for worshiping. However, there is a third group, but they are the 'lower' Narikuravar community and within whom intermarriage is rather frowned-upon.

To address the structural and contextual lack of information regarding Roma diversity, Ciprian Necula designed a complex project that studies this topic within Romania. This study – as seen in the previous chapters – offers a great in-depth look within the Romanian Roma communities. It is nevertheless important to understand that diversity is rarely horizontal, but often reproduces structures of power and hierarchies exist in the larger context. As we have seen in previous chapters, a vertical (while imprecise) hierarchization is enabled and enforced, with different Roma groups considering themselves superior to others. In a conversation in 2017, Ciprian Necula shared how his community of 'Fierari' is not only different, but also superior to other Roma communities from Romania:

> 'Fierari' is a different community – which is at times hated by other [Roma] communities – who call us 'caştali' – meaning a person without language, as we do not speak Romani. We understand it, but answer in Romanian. For example, my grandpa was suspicious of working with other Roma. He thought that they would trick him, because 'this is how they are', and this is something that was transmitted within the community. We were ok with 'Căldărari' and with the 'Lăutari' [Roma communities], but with the others we were always on alert. 'Lăutari' – on the other hand – we saw as our young brothers. Because they could not hold the hammer. Even though we thought of ourselves as superiors, we did not think of ourselves as aristocrat. All we wanted was to be 'in rand cu lumea' – same as others.
>
> Necula interview, 2017

Furthermore, in his work in progress study on Roma diversity, Necula writes:

> The leader of the 'Spoitori' [in Calafat, Southern Romania] explained that the Roma are grouped in neighborhoods, and the relatives generally live in the same area. Some of the wealthy 'Spoitori' built their homes among the Romanians, and they also 'pulled' their relatives after them. Basically, the borders between Roma communities are not only the fluid, invisible ones, given by belonging to the nation, the spoken dialect, but also geographical – the grouping by neighborhoods is done according to the nation they belong to.

This hierarchization is similar to the one that was reproduced among the Narikuravar communities. As we have seen above, Anuradha marked the internal hierarchization of Narikuravar families based on their worshiping traditions; but, just as in the Roma case, this hierarchization among different groups is not often addressed in scholarly analysis of community.

This intra-community hierarchization plays a significant role in accessing social justice, with certain people being less able than others to access recognition, redistribution and representation, while those from specific communities are situated in privileged positions that empower them to come to the fore and make demands on the state.

Class differences among those who move

This ethnic diversity and implicit hierarchization further replicates within the same community along class lines. Roma and Narikuravar communities are typically thought of in terms of poverty, and with limited access to economic/financial resources. While in total numbers this is an accurate description, it does not mean that all those who are identified as 'Gypsy' face the same poverty, but (as any other group) certain members challenge this presumption. Thus, a closer look reveals the Roma and Narikuravar's economic diversity. For example, in Romania, more than three decades after the fall of communism, not all Roma communities developed economically in a similar manner. When scholars focus on the most disadvantaged, often compact Roma communities, and bring to the fore their drastic marginalization and impoverishment, they often do not speak about communities that have managed rather successfully in bringing down at least some of the economic barriers in their struggle for justice (UNICEF/Preda, 2005).[1] But, as the scholarly oversight is in full swing, the media capitalizes on the exoticism of wealthy Roma communities, like Buzescu in Teleorman, south Romania.[2] These examples of Roma wealth are nevertheless outliners, used within racist arguments to delegitimize the need to change and support the Roma.[3]

Even if these outliers are (by definition) a rarity, the economic differences among the communities labelled as 'Gypsy' persist. For example, within the Roma community of Ormeniș the difference along economic lines mimics the geographical division of the community between the Main Street (Strada Principala) and the intersecting marginal street of Olt. During our work in the field, we found out that it is rather common for the Roma who live on Strada Principala to have ownership of land and of their house for decades; they are also visibly better off than those in Strada Olt, having larger houses, taller fences and higher ceilings. The folks from Strada Olt live on an unpaved road, with small, low houses, shaky fences and no direct connection to gas or water pipelines. This difference further reverberated into the way in which the people related to one another and socialized. In the main street, the older people would at times sit on a bench in front of their large house and interact with those who passed by. Their social practices are like that of the Romanians and Hungarians living on the same street, and like many other Romanians living in the countryside. However, the relations from the Strada Olt were more dynamic. The street was used as a common space for them to interact and do business, and to engage the children who were playing in the street, running from one door to the other. People were moving swiftly and engaging in the public space. The place was alive, dynamic and cheerful. The Roma of Strada Olt were aware of these differences. I was always asked: 'Will you come to see us on Olt Street?', referring to a common, larger 'us', separated from the people from the main street. They also always seek my approval about their community: 'You like it better here on Old Street, right? You will come back to us?', they probe ensuring that their part of the world does not get excluded from the conversation.

The Narikuravars were also divided along both class and geographical lines, but not so clearly. As they live in communal houses that are given by the government, on allotted land, and the space is used by many people who are at times occupying them only in a transient capacity, these class differences were blurred. However, in 2016, when I was at Sugan's place, he told me: 'You need to come see my house!' I was confused as I thought I was already in his home. So, I asked him. Sugan smiled and said that yes, they live in the place where we were seated, but this place was from the government. He did build his own house. With no other words, he stood up and showed me and the translator the way. We hurried up and followed him – some children from the neighbouring houses quickly joined us. We crossed the street of the settlement, and we found ourselves on the other side, which had seemingly newer and better houses. Sugan explained that the houses belong to another community, thus not to the Narikuravars. We quickly walked through the houses, on unpaved dusty land in which flowers and weeds were in abundance, to reach a construction site. Sugan stopped and said proudly that this was his house, or – better said – was becoming his house.

In 2018 when we returned, Sugan took us straight to the new house 'across the street. The home was ready!' The brand-new home was large, spacious and clean. It had a good-sized veranda, which led to a large double living room containing a large LD TV. The photos of Sugan, his family and of a famous Tamil superstar were adorning the walls. His wife showed us the well-equipped kitchen where she made tea. And then she took me to their private bathroom – a commodity that others in the community do not have. Their children were excited to have me around and they took me to their brand-new rooftop where the clean clothes were drying in the southern Indian blasting sun. Sugan also has a motorcycle that he uses for transport, and his older boy went to a private English medium school away from the community. Sugan not only had a different class position within the community, but also a certain clout. His deep voice and high stature were complementing his social demure of authority.

These class differences are important to highlight, because this study – while aiming to be inclusive and to ensure that it was reaching all members of the communities – at times tends to engage with those where access was more definable: with the ones who had cell phones and could communicate on social media (i.e., connected to the Internet), those who spoke multiple languages (including English), and those who were accredited by the community as people with power. And it is not surprising that the folks who met these criteria were most often men.

The blurred lines of gender hierarchization

The other differences in the community were drawn along gender lines. The way different gender identities are seen, understood and the dynamics they generate reflect the recognition of one's position and access to power within the society. The position of women in traditional communities tends to be subordinate and rather marginal – at least it is typically understood as such. However, a closer look into the gender dynamics of the Narikuravar and Roma reveals a more complex situation. On the one hand, the communities that still observe traditional customs have the roles clearly aligned along gender lines. On the other hand, being mobile challenges traditional gender roles, with both women and men being present in the public sphere. The tension between these forms of gendered dynamics become transparent within their daily lives, and at times bring the community at odds with the larger societies.

Knowing that racialization and discrimination do not affect all the same way, it is imperative to look at who in the community accesses justice, and thus to follow the intersection of gender and community/ethnicity. Roma and Narikuravar women often find themselves at the crux of discrimination (Crenshaw et al., 1996), both being severely discriminated against from members of other communities, and often being placed in subordinate positions within their own community. While these dynamics are not new, they have not been investigated in connection to intersectionality until recently (Kóczé and Popa, 2009;[4] Oprea, 2012; Schultz, 2012;[5] Ruz, 2019).[6] In India, specific intersectional analysis, research and implementation of policies with respect to the Narikuravar community has been, to date, scarce (Dragomir and Zafiu, 2019) in addressing gender specific issues.[7]

Recognition: the role of women

The role of women in historically marginalized and mobile communities is a topic of interest, but rarely are women from these communities – especially from the Narikuravar groups – asked about how they envision their role, or are invited to reflect about the daily gender dynamics. With this gap in mind, we asked women about how they understand their role today. As we will see next, there is a diversity among their views, which reflects both class and generational changes. Ravathi, who was 29 years old, said: 'Men and women are expected to follow certain etiquette. We are not supposed to cross the man when he is sleeping, or touch him with our feet. However, when the two are alone, this etiquette doesn't matter, but it has still caused misunderstandings and problems. As for the work, everybody has started to earn. The duties can be shared amongst the two according to their needs' (Ravathi interview, 2021).

Rajasekaran, a male in his thirties, offered to explain to us the role of the women:

> Generally, women have a big role in the community. I would say a bigger one than men. They could help their husband to sell products, even if it meant carrying their child with them. Otherwise, they are homemakers. In most situations, they don't waste time. When they aren't cooking, they make garlands, and go sell more products to other towns. In our community, it can also be seen that men are good at cooking in order to help their wives. As most of them are always traveling and roaming, men and women share the burden of everything.
>
> Rajasekaran interview, 2021

The Narikuravar women's role in the development of the economic life of the community was confirmed by Ravathi: 'Generally, we can't go near the gods we pray to. We worship the goddess greatly, and she is a big part of all important rituals in the community. We usually make garlands, we also go to local markets and bus stops to sell things like khol, soap boxes, and accessories. We take these, and try to go to crowded hubs. Some people go along with their husbands, and sell these things' (Ravathi interview, 2021).

Like many people around the world, the Narikuravar and Roma women take their position for granted and often sink into their daily dynamics and roles:

> Overall, before marriage, there aren't many restrictions for [Narikuravar] women. After that, they have many restrictions. First, when they speak to any other man, they must give respect and stand 10 feet away. Second, she isn't allowed to keep her innerwear at home. She has to keep it bundled up in the bathroom. Even their footwear shouldn't be kept near the house, it has to be left in some corner farther away. Even now they have to follow it. I have escaped all of this because of where I live, but my sisters still follow these things. Third, when cutting vegetables, or doing house work, nothing must touch their feet. Things are not supposed to touch the women's feet. Even if it's theirs, it has to be thrown away. If the girl does anything wrong, they won't include her in the community. They won't even give her water because that would mean she has to touch the tumbler. They usually leave, and live on their own.
>
> Jayachitra interview, 2021

During the ethnographic engagement, I was interacting predominantly with the women in the community engaging in gendered knowledge practices (Dragomir, 2019), which allowed me to understand the gendered hierarchies within the community. Through these interactions, I learnt how women and men socialized together, and also how women were able to retreat into their private space and have their forms of socializing. Also, to see how women embedded rituals of beauty, and how certain spaces and religious rituals were available only to men (Dragomir, 2020).

In Romania, the same gendered dynamics transpired. The Roma women in Ormeniş were always willing to allow the men to speak first, to express their views about the community at large, and to engage in a professional manner. At the same time, they were also eager to participate in public employment and seek jobs just like men, but, as they encountered both racist and a gendered hierarchized society, they were less successful. As a result, most Roma women of Ormeniş worked in their homes and were dependent both on the state for unemployment insurance and to their husbands for income.

Marriages: recognizing one another

The crux of (in)justice becomes obvious when important decisions are taken. And one's choice of a life partner is without doubt an important decision, one that includes more than the individuals directly engaged. It is thus clear that officializing romantic relationships is a process that is highly regulated – just as in every society. Looking at this process with care, we can also learn about the role one plays in the community, and how power is distributed. Ultimately, it also tells us how one's access to justice could take shape.

Working in the field in Romania, the most often heard stereotypes about the Roma community are related to their marriage rituals. While often referring to those living in the traditional societies, these rituals are nevertheless exaggerated, exoticized and used as denying access to the 'modern' society for the Roma people. Nevertheless, in my fieldwork it became obvious that only certain compact communities still hold in place marital traditions, while for others they are often a dusty memory of the past. Yet, the marriage within the community is still a prevalent practice. For example, Necula explains that in the compact Roma communities in southern Romania:

> Even though in recent years the community of 'Spoitori' in Calafat has adapted to some extent to modernity, there are cultural practices that have retained their traditional importance. These separate them from other groups of Roma and especially from Romanians. The tradition of arranged marriages, and the purchase of girls is a practice that is kept within the community of 'Spoitori' and, of course, the virginity[8] of girls is the most important thing: 'This will persist because in our community it is a rule. If I take a girl from you for my son, and I don't take her with money, it means that I, as a cousin, am no longer respected and the daughter will not be respected in my house either', [citing a 'Spoitor' Roma].
>
> Necula, 'Studiu de Diversitate,' work in progress

While marriages might not follow strict mating rituals, whom one marries is still strictly regulated, and transgressing the rules has dire consequences for the Narikuravar women:

> One of my aunts married another community man, and she lives outside now, and nobody gets involved with her. Even though she has had kids, grandkids, and her husband died a few years back, she is still not allowed to join in any community events or get involved in anything. If anything, her siblings would help her but even they aren't allowed to stay at her home. A man is supposed to take care of his wife and kids. He isn't supposed to have relations with any other women. If he does, he will be less respected in society, but there are not more severe consequences.
>
> Jayachitra interview, 2021

As I was in the Narikuravar community of Karamadai, next to Mettupalayam, waiting for the elders, I sat next to a teenage girl washing clothes. A few other teenagers shortly joined me on the pavement. 'We will sell necklaces and do home job when we grow up,' said one of the girls who stopped a minute from washing clothes. One cheeky boy came up and said: 'We will marry and have 3 to 4 children,' making everyone laugh. 'We only marry within our community,' explained another boy. 'If someone marries another community, we separate them from us.' Another one continued: 'We marry our relatives. We don't get girls from outside. But if someone marries another community person, they will be separated from us. Forever!'

The people of Narikuravar community often told me that they do not marry outside of their community. And within their small community, they maintain strict rules, based on their religious denomination, allowing people only to marry close relations:

> The people who follow God Chenamma is one group and people who follows Kaaliamma is another group. We change girls between us. While other communities use the horoscope to fix marriages, Narikuravars don't have anything like that. For example, I married my close relation (Aunt's daughter). My wife is from Thiruvannamalai. But I studied and grew up here. My wife is my grandfather's relation.
>
> Sugan interview, 2016

I followed: 'Could you marry outside the community?'

> Yes. That has happened before [he nods in agreement]. Now the Narikuravars go for higher studies for colleges, they fall in love with another people and they get married. But the thing is we will not accept them back into the community. We won't keep them with our community anymore. They have to live with their own. Our god won't accept it. So, we don't keep them with our families.
>
> Sugan interview, 2016

The idea of marrying someone outside of the Roma community is often taboo in Romania as well: 'I went to Spain (…) My middle boy finished high-school and had a classmate and wanted to marry her. She being Romanian, I did not accept her; and my son did not marry her' (PZ, in Necula, 'Studiu de Diversitate', work in progress). The rules about whom could marry were similar in Ormeniş, where both men and women told me that marriages outside of the community were not accepted, and the view that 'Rom should marry Rom' (Stewart, 1997: 61) was often voiced. However, different from the Narikuravars who preferred the family marriages, in Roma communities 'it was not Romanes to "marry close", especially not to marry first cousins' (Stewart, 1997: 61), a perspective I encountered in my fieldwork as well.

At times, I pushed my inquiries further and asked, 'How come one should only marry a Rom?' I was often told that even though the non-Roma would be accepted, maybe even welcomed into their families, because the family were Roma, they will never be accepted by the partner's family, and that sooner or later this will become an issue, which they saw as unsolvable, one that would push the couple to divorce, and everyone, especially children, would suffer as a result. Thus, the Roma were firm in pointing out that they did not want to form mixed families, but preferred staying within the Roma community. While mixed marriages are imagined to be the solution to ethnic discrimination, and a support to the community's social, economic and political mobility, this view brought to the fore the inevitable risks and costs of these alternative personal relations.

Education and gender

Marriages are correlated to education, and education is often thought to be the main solution to ending child marriages (World Bank, 2017).[9] As both communities are known for their traditional child marriage practices, the question of education and marriage are discussed in tandem.[10] For example, 'Drepturile Omului pentru Romi și Nomazi în Europa' argues that:

> In some Roma communities, girls' parents may anticipate that their daughters will leave school soon in order to get married and start their own family. There are cases when marriages between children have prevented girls from going to school, thus undermining their right to education and their subsequent employment opportunities. [However,] Positive awareness measures seem to indicate progress, an improvement in school attendance by Roma girls.[11]

Overall, in both Romania and India, the people I spoke with were concerned about school dropout, especially for the girls in the community. Moreover, they also mentioned that women in both Roma and Narikuravar[12] communities face specific and cruel discriminatory practices from other communities, and that these practices are visible and often intolerably painful while in school. They are faced with a double burden of both being women and suffering from the structures of patriarchy, and from inside community oppressive structures of power.

In 2020, Anuradha shared in an interview:

> The majority of the Narikuravar kids only study 'til the 8th grade. This community is big on child marriages and labour, but we are hoping that educating them will drastically reduce this. One of the main reasons to get their

daughters married is because when they go out on their own for long trips to sell their products, the girl will be alone at home – and because this is dangerous, it would be better to get her married.[13]

Anuradha's statement revealed how early marriages impact the community and especially the women, by limiting their development opportunities. However, it also brought to view that, different from women from other communities for whom being outside of their families/communities was considered a dangerous endeavour, the Narikuravars perceived that remaining in the 'settlements' was the real danger for the girls, while 'going for business' was seen as the normal.

Traditional internal structures of communities like the Roma and Narikuravar might not be supportive to modern, capitalist/neoliberal development, which makes scholars argue that: 'Legal and customary norms on the position of women are very archaic and they deprive Romani women of rights. Today, 96% of Romani women are unemployed, and 80% of them are illiterate' (Sabina Xhemajli, 2020).[14] However, it does not necessarily mean that these practices are necessarily 'depriving' or 'obstructing'. Rather, these practices need to be investigated within their own context and traditions, and their impact on the women and girls evaluated in accordance. For example, formal education, while embraced by many in the community, is not considered a goal in itself by all. Most Narikuravar women and girls of school-age I talked to were eager to study, but not all of them were able to. In 2015, when interviewing a group of women in the community in Karamadai, one of the girls proudly shared: 'Many of us are now educated. Some of us in the village are degree holders. Even recently one of us called Pandidurai came on TV.' While this statement was referring to a small number of people, it needs to be understood within the larger context of the Narikuravar community, where access to higher education for few people happened within a generation. Anand (in a 2018 interview) explained that: 'There is one Tamil actor Jeeva, who gives us money for education, mainly he is supporting the education of a bright Narikuravar who studies to be a doctor', he states proudly and hopeful for these endeavours. But one is left wondering how come the education of the brightest is left to the whims of private donors, and not systemically enabled through organized programming.

As the young girls from the community told me that they study as well, and that they 'take good grades also', I asked them about higher education plans. They stopped me briskly: 'No, no. If a girl is beautiful and if she talks with a guy then they will make them to marry to each other.' Then they share with me something that was all too familiar, something that I have heard spoken by parents of Roma youth in Romania: 'If girls go to higher education, far away from home, they might fall in love with people from other communities, and "go with them"' (Jeni interview, 2017):

'They are scared that the girl leaves her family. They think we will marry another person from another community', one of the Narikuravar girls says, drawing me back from my transnational reflections. Another girl intervenes explaining the marriage traditions: 'If we keep a girl when she becomes more than 13 that is a bad name for the family. So, we set up a marriage when the girl is becomes over 13' (Anuradha, interview 2017).

Thinking of how early marriages could drastically impede the continuation of a girl's studies, I asked what is the highest level of education for girls in their community. One young Narikuravar woman replied: '10th Standard. More than that we don't study.' Another one contradicted her: 'Some of them have studied 12th standard too.' 'Going to college is rare for girls, but it could happen', one of the girls shares about someone she knows from a Narikuravar community who lives in another village, and goes to college. And both confirmed that boys' education is typically higher.

I asked if the girls want to go, and they said they would, but this would make them 20–21 by the time they will marry and that is too old. I asked the question that baffles me: 'After they get married, they cannot go to college?' They seem surprised and respond: 'No. After marriage we will carry on our business only.'

One of women is 25 years old, and has 5 children: 4 boys and 1 girl. She says: 'One child is studying 6th standard and another child studying 3rd standard English medium. They are 10 and 8 years old.' She says she got married when she was the age of thirteen. Now she takes care of the business: 'Making necklaces, preparing food and wash clothing. Watching movies. We watch Vijay's movies. That's all what we do. We don't have much money to do other stuff.'

She also takes care of the spirituality of the community: 'I initiate for god. For that we go to Madras. Then my mother-in-law takes care of the house. I take my two children with me. The children who are going to school will stay here, and I will take the babies.'

'How about the husband?' I ask. 'He will take care of himself by himself', she answers, laughing. 'And my husband will take care of the children too.'

These diverse answers point to the current changes in the community, to the fact that young girls have access to basic education, but that higher education is rare, and that it is still a man's privilege. These structures and dynamics are embedded in tradition and supported by the current state of affairs. Lacking programmes to support and enable their education, and with family life and marriages often coming at odds with pursuing higher education, the girls in the Roma and Narikuravar community often face insurmountable obstacles. Limiting women's and girls' education of course furthermore translates in limited opportunities of entering formal employment, as in pursuance of careers.[15]

Economic underpinnings of gendered dynamics

Both men and women in the Narikuravar community I spoke with were proud to share that, different from other communities (in India and Tamil Nadu), the Narikuravars appreciate girls and they are happy when a girl is born. This is also related to the fact that in traditional families, the family of the girl receives (does not give) dowry (a long-standing tradition, which is currently illegal in India since 1961, but still prevalent).[16] Moreover, they showed me how, due to their nomadic tradition, they do not see private and public space as do many other settled communities. They were traditionally hunters, and therefore all Narikuravars participated in daily practices, in the wilderness and in the engagement with other towns. Because both men and women travelled, their roles have not been dogmatically assigned along gendered lines (men as bread-winners/ women home makers; men in public/women in private, etc.). Now that their hunting is illegal, they do business with neckless and other ornaments, but maintain similar gender dynamics with respect to economic participation: 'Now both women and men go for business. But before, some women went for hunting with men, or they stayed at home and cook food or to get rice, taking their children on their shoulders like we carry luggage', Sugan explained in an interview in 2016.

However, more recent sedentarization came with new practices, which follow more (ironically so) binary gendered lines.[17] While this change is not absolute, it still blurs the description, and still places women in a more domestic place:[18] '[Women] go everywhere by themselves', Sugan explains, implicitly referring to the fact that women from other communities in Tamil Nadu rarely travel by themselves, or without a man, in public places.

> They are not afraid to go anywhere. And they are doing business in foreign countries, like Singapore, Thailand, and Malaysia. For example, my 'small mother'/aunt is in Singapore for past two years for business. Selling necklaces and ornaments to foreigners and tourists. There is a big festival for us in Malaysia for Lord Muruga, who is believed to have married his second wife from the Narikuravar community and they do business there.
>
> Sugan interview, 2016[19]

The changes that everyone is going through in the economy are visible in everyday life in the community. Even though the changes are uneven, the Narikuravar women in Karamadai are an integrated party in the economy of their community, engaging in manufacturing the products, and also in selling them.

Redistribution: employment

As mentioned earlier, limited education further impacts access to employment and social mobility. The formal labour market is one of the most visible sites of gender inequality,[20] women's visibility in the high-end urban labour market in India is much greater today than it was a decade ago, but this is still unequal (World Bank, 2011).[21] The place of the Narikuravar women in the current rapidly developing global market is rather uncertain: 'Narikoravar women face many problems in entrepreneurship, and they follow traditional occupation and train their children in the same. So, many children are not able to acquire education due to their lack of interest and poor economic conditions within the family' (Naik, 1996: 153).

Because of limited education and limited exposure to the larger community, Narikuravar women, Naik says, are often unaware of the state programmes and schemes aimed to support them as they 'do not reach them properly due to their nomadic nature of living'[22] (Naik, 1996: 153).[23] Thus, even if state programmes are there to support them, they often cannot participate and further their social and economic status,[24] showcasing the poor policy design of programmes aimed to address the problems faced by the most vulnerable: 'STs appear to have done more poorly than other groups; they show the slowest pace of improvements in a range of areas. (...) Women are dying unnecessarily both in infancy and in motherhood; the outcomes are poorer among Dalits and Adivasis' (World Bank, 2011: 31).[25]

Representation: Gender Based Violence (GBV)

Limiting women, girls and transgender people's economic and social participation, constraining their educational pursuance, creates further obstacles in accessing social justice. As they live in remote areas where health care is limited (at best), they also experience health issues. Moreover, because official mechanisms to achieve justice are political, not having a seat at the decision table precludes their representation and political engagement. Thus, they fall out of democratic political representation.

GBV is always a sensitive topic, one that needs further investigation within traditionally nomadic communities, both in India and Romania. The statements below are based on limited data that came to the surface while I was in the field talking to women and girls. In the Karamadai community, the GBV issue came to the fore rather quickly. In 2012, when I arrived in the Narikuravar 'settlement', I was surrounded by the elder men in the community, and women were looking at me and smiling from afar. As I was working through a translator, I was mostly silent when one woman came to me, and started talking vehemently in Tamil. I looked at her and asked my (male) translator to explain what she was saying, but he quickly dismissed me (and her), and turned back continuing his conversation. As the woman seemed to be in distress, and really wanting me to know something, I called my translator by name, and asked him again. Only to be met by the same attitude. The woman insisted, and came close enough to be able to reach me. She pulled my hand to draw my attention to the bruises on her arm. Seeing this, I insisted that the translator help us. To this, he turned to me slightly annoyed, and told me that the woman was drunk. I encouraged him to tell me nevertheless what she was saying. The translator said that the woman was explaining that her husband was beating her, and that the bruises were the result of his actions. To this I felt powerless. The woman was asking for help and justice, but there was nothing I could have done as my position was limited and rather precarious. Similarly, a couple of years later, Joity, one of the Narikuravars in Tamil Nadu, explained to me: 'After we get married, we get beaten by our husbands. Life goes on like that.' My male translator smiles and translates this in obvious embarrassment. I snapped, and replied: 'Don't smile. Ask her about it.' He turns around, and asks her why is this happening. The woman answers: 'We have small fights between us in the beginning. 2–3 years after marriage we fight a lot.' The woman continues and shares: 'My parents drink a lot. So, when they are drunk, they come and ask money from me. If I give money to them to drink, my husband gets angry and we fight. He beats me.' I asked if this is common for other women, and the woman quickly replied: 'Yes, it is common.'

In 2017, Tamila Rasi shared: 'If the husband doesn't drink, we won't fight.' She quickly relates domestic violence to alcohol abuse, exposing in one phrase the two major issues confronting the communities. I asked about how she reacts to it: 'We do not react; we wait 2–3 days, and we adjust for it. We can't fight, and go out and stay alone', said Tamila in a matter-of-fact voice. I follow up by asking about outside intervention, like the police: 'No, we never go!' she says. 'If we go, they will give us divorce straight away.'

In Ormeniş, Romania, the issue of GBV came to the fore in a different manner (as mentioned earlier). Once we were on Strada Olt and having a fun afternoon in one of the courtyards, listening to music and dancing – all of us – Doru and myself were filming the encounter. One by one, the women in the group came to me, pulled me aside and asked me genuinely and in confidence not to place these videos on social media, because, if their husbands would see them, they would be beaten. Also, when we were interviewing the women in the village about their access to health care, sometimes they agreed to the interview after we assured them that their identity will not be disclosed. To this, they said that they did not mind their name to be associated with the research, but they do not want their husbands to find out that they gave the interviews, because they would get beaten. Women speaking unprompted and asking about these incidents of domestic violence, signals the commonality of these incidents in their lives.

While domestic violence, as a part of GBV, is seemingly prevalent in the Narikuravar and Roma communities, it is not endemic only to these groups. Globally, in 2013, 35 per cent of women have ever experienced physical and/or sexual intimate partner violence, or sexual violence by a non-partner (and this is not including sexual harassment cases). In some countries, the number can be as high as 70 per cent of women.[26] In both India and Romania, across communities, the rate of GBV is high. According to the UN Women database, in India 28.8 per cent of ever-married women, aged 15–49 years, experienced intimate partner physical and/or sexual violence at least once in their lifetime,[27] and the number who suffered in the last twelve months was 22 per cent.[28]

In Romania, 24 per cent of ever-partnered women aged 18–74 years experienced intimate partner physical and/or sexual violence at least once in their lifetime,[29] and the percentage over twelve months was 6 per cent.[30] Lifetime non-partner sexual violence of women aged 18–74 years experiencing sexual violence perpetrated by someone other than an intimate partner at least once in their lifetime was 2 per cent.[31]

Nevertheless, when minority women are both hit by discrimination from outside of their community, and also are placed in marginal places within their own peoples, we can expect the case of violence to at least mirror those of the larger society. They are, however most likely to be larger.

Representation: women's political voices

Direct engagement in politics of (certain) women from these traditionally mobility communities was also visible. In India, Anuradha participates together with her husband and nephew in all the political engagements. She fights equally and continuously in supporting the community's endeavour to receive ST status. She is a public persona and has a firm and well-known voice. This comes hand in hand with the traditions of the other political figures in Tamil Nadu who have strong female voices, such as Jayalalitha Jayaram, aka Ama. However, it is important to highlight that these forms of political representation are rather scarce, and the Narikuravar's and Roma's political representation is not widely spread.[32]

Necula's activist grass-roots work in Romania engages many Roma communities, but has proven (to this moment) unsuccessful in attracting Roma women as active members of Aresel, and in the civic initiatives he organized in 2018[33] (especially for work conducted outside of the large urban areas). He shared with me that they envisioned an ambitious recruitment goal, engaging over 200 Romanian communities with 20 per cent or more Roma inhabitants. In most communities, at the meetings (in person or on-line platforms) mostly the men participated; the majority of them were senior, in spite of the efforts of the Aresel members to engage the Roma youth. Necula also shared that the meetings were gender biased towards men. He identified this as a form of patriarchy, but added that this is not only in the Roma communities, but it is a generalized one. He said: 'In one community we organized a meeting and there were 120 men and not one woman. When we asked where were the women we were told, they "have to take care of the kids".' He continued by telling us that their work aims to cover a large part of the Roma communities of Romania; that they strive to be engaging, and thus it is best to simply unite the people, which means not to bring to the fore devisive topics, like gender empowerment (Necula interview, 2020). Thus, aiming to address one issue at a time, Aresel[34] and other Roma activist forums do not address gender inequalities Roma women encounter. Similarly, the issue of gender was not addressed full-on in India by the Narikuravars either. United (for now) in their goal of obtaining ST status, the role of women (and LGBTQ+) is not a part of their wide spread agenda.

During fieldwork in 2017, I also asked Necula about who are his activist partners, what are his network and strategies. To this he replied firmly: 'I have a problem with the coupling of the Roma and the LGBT movements.'[35] This he argues, is because many Roma do not want to be associated with other minority groups, especially gender minorities. 'I go out on the street, but not with gay men', he said, citing other Roma. His strategy is then as follows: 'We do not particularize our movement by booking at LGBTQI Roma.' Also, he brought to the fore that agendas are different: 'Let's not confuse agendas. The gender focus agenda might not serve the Roma agenda, at least in Romania', Necula comments in an articulated and passionate manner (Necula interview, 2017).

Necula's view is not necessarily shared by other activists or different groups and segments of the community. For example, in 2020 in 'Roundtable: Romani activists on women's rights', Sabina Xhemajli explained:

> The positions of Romani men and Romani women are clearly divided. Unfortunately, women have drawn the losing card. Their lifestyle is comparable to what it was five hundred years ago. The task of the Romani woman is to take care of the children, to maintain the household, and to hold together the extended family. As a mother, she knows precisely the details of her children's lives, including all of the stupid things they do. She often hides this knowledge from her husband, because she knows that she can expect harsh punishment for herself and her children from her husband, because as the mother of the family she is supposed to keep the children from doing stupid things. This lack of openness with respect to her husband weighs heavily upon Roman women – often extremely heavily.[36]

This competition between issues has of course been rather prevalent among activists across time, with gender issues always being pushed to the back of the empowerment agenda. And these techniques have been met by feminist criticisms, which always brought to the fore that within empowering those who are most vulnerable within communities, justice for the overall community could not take place.

Conclusion: Then and Now

Just like the other structured hierarchies and dynamics, the gendered dynamics are also changing. The Roma and Narikuravar women are navigating multiple terrains, in India, in Romania and beyond, which are in continuous, and at times rapid change. Their mobility – either community or individual – also exposes them to different gendered systems in which they have to define and redefine their roles. As nowadays, rapid transformations are happening within a generation, and women I spoke with often reflect on these transformations: 'Now everything has changed. Before, women couldn't come home after 6pm, now due to work, most women stay out; and sometimes even with the husband, if they do business together. As far as I can see, most people have changed' (Jayachitra interview, 2021).

Both the Roma and Narikuravar women I interviewed for this work live in transitional times. The world has drastically changed in their lifetime. The traditions of their ancestors might persist to a certain degree, and would create customs, but they have also greatly adapted to the new societal forms and dynamics. This transition is not smooth, linear or total. Certain aspects of their traditions emerge after a while, or as the people in the community mature. Others fade away, both from the life of the communities and the memory of the people, leading to complex – and at times contradictory – gender dynamics, which often challenge the simplistic gender divides, being simultaneously traditional and 'modern'.[37]

Thus, Narikuravar and Roma communities, like other communities, are both hierarchical and diverse. Work for social justice therefore needs to be understood along these lines of power and privilege, and to see that not all fights are similar, not all Roma and Narikuravar follow the same path, or employ the same tools. These power dynamics among communities and within communities mirror their access and their different manners.

This intra-community diversity based on tradition, have been challenged by the rapid changes in industrialization, technology and globalization, 'an ever-smaller number of Gypsies to adhere to the exact standards of ancient Romani culture and traditions' (Barany, 2002: 14).[38] But the transformation of gender hierarchies is harder to assess. The Roma and the Narikuravar have been adapting to and adopting the larger society's view of gender division. While this is typically celebrated as a sign of 'modernization' and 'progress' of their community, it is time to further investigate these values and examine if the larger national and international contexts are supportive of gender justice. This juxtaposition is clear when we compare the traditional Narikuravar and Roma practices of mobility, which placed both men and women in the public sphere, where women have been part of the business process, engaged in all aspects of financial decisions. It is important that we understand that communities as such have their internal hierarchies and that it is impossible to discuss access and practices of justice without acknowledging that there are different stratifications. And that justice needs to be achieved while taking into consideration those placed in marginal places within their own communities.

Stories: Women on the Move, the Other Side of Gender

Overall, in spite of the differences among traditions, most Roma and Narikuravar women, like many women across the world, are often caught within patriarchal structures of power, that are not necessarily specific to their communities. To speak about the Roma and Narikuravar women as victims of sexism within their community, reproduces implicitly the 'white savior complex' empowering researchers, readers, to re-enact a position of power vis-à-vis the communities. It is important to point out at every step the complex situation of these communities. On the one hand, women in Roma and Narikuravar communities are suffering from double, intersectional discrimination based on their gender and ethnicity/ community/'caste'. Moreover, they are also caught within often traditionally patriarch dynamics that place them in 'subaltern' positions.

On the other hand, and this is as important as the first, both women from Narikuravar and Roma communities define and redefine their position, in relation to their community, and to the larger society. In my experience, the women whom I met during fieldwork have been strong, resilient, vivacious, and able to take full-on, at times by themselves, racist and sexist society in structures.

Their strength and resilience were especially visible in the stories shared with me by women who, in spite of all, migrated and looked for a better place for themselves and their dear ones. This is not to say that women who stayed home while their male partners migrated were less powerful, as those who stayed home in the migration process often had to be fully in charge of their homes, while educating children, and striving to get at least partial employment. Because migration impacts all, the work of those who stayed behind in Ormeniş or in Karamadai was not by any means smaller. But I wanted to hear from those women who dared to move. Below are a few of their stories.

Kannammal (60 years old, Tamil Nadu, India)

I'm from the Narikuravar community. I was born under a tree in Arthur, Selam District of Tamil Nadu. I lived in the forest. I have travelled across north and south India and Malaysia. We sell our handmade jewellery on the street. There is a lot of torture from the police; they won't even allow us to sleep on the road. I delivered all of our kids on the road.

I studied up to 4th grade. My parents were Gypsies, they would leave us in one place and go for business. There was no proper care. We struggled a lot. We tried hard to go to school. It's really hard for us to travel from one place to another. People won't allow us to get into the bus and they discriminate. We beg them to get permission for our travel on the bus. Most of the time, we walk a lot. We used to live under the trees and in the forest. If there are no sales from our jewellery, we beg for food from the neighbourhood houses, even for the leftover rice water.

We do not have land ownership and we are living in the forest. We do not have any documents.

I order to promote my business, we saved some money and took a loan, and we went to Malaysia to sell our products and check the scope for our products. We travelled on a tourist visa, but there was not good business and there was high fear and pressure from the police. We paid the penalty of 400 Malaysian Ringgits ($100) and came home.

I always aspire to send our children to school. At least my children should study up to 10th grade and be like other kids. Because of education, other people build everything in their life. I would like to see our children also getting equal status and become better people in society.

Oana (31 years old, Braila, Romania)

I am from a Roma family. My dad is from a 'Firerari' Roma background, not speaking Romani language, and my mom from 'Ciobotari' Roma, Romani speakers. I had the opportunity to go to school, as my family was not facing economic limitations, and they constantly supported our educational growth.

When I was 14 years old, my parents decided to move to Bucharest, to facilitate going to college, for me and my older brother. I attended high-school in the capital, which was a school opened to teaching Human Rights, and volunteered in NGOs since my teenage years. In high-school, I learned English, Spanish and German. Then I attended Law School and I started working for Romani Criss, an NGO for Roma, ever since my first year as a law student. In 2013, I was granted a fellowship for conducting my LLM studies in Human Rights at the Central European University in Budapest, for one year, and then collaborating with an NGO for another year. The LLM programme was in English and had six modules, which included diverse themes such as: International, Public Law and Human Rights. Since 2016 I have been working at the European Court of Human Rights (ECHR), Strasbourg, France, where I currently am.

When I first moved from Romania in 2013, I was twenty-six years old. I left together with my husband, who was my fiancé back then. I received the fellowship I mentioned above, and he received a grant to study in the same university, in the Political Science MA programme. We left Bucharest in August 2013. I remember how my father drove us to Budapest, and I started crying from the moment I walked across the door, to the moment we were out of Bucharest. I suffered leaving my parents behind, as I had been living with them until then. It was tough leaving my house, my friends and my country.

I was also optimistic and excited to see how my new life will turn out. Everything was new and for some time, rather overwhelming. Coming to a new country meant embracing several 'new' moments. It was the first time when I did not live with parents, when I cohabited with my fiancé. Was the first time since finishing high-school when all I had to do was to study, because I was not employed.

The biggest obstacle I encountered in Hungary was the language barrier. If in other countries you can manage in English, there it was difficult to find English speakers; and Hungarian, I could not understand one word. It was hard to get used to always hear around me a language from which I could not understand absolutely anything. I did not struggle to learn the language because I lived in an international bubble, my LLM colleagues were from all over the world and English was the main language. And also, we had no long-term plans in Hungary. We wanted to finish the MA programmes and come back to our country. I did not find myself in difficult situations because of not knowing Hungarian; but the toughest part was to get used to being away from my parents and friends.

In November 2015, I found out that I received the job at ECHR. With one eye I cried, and with the other one I smiled. We had just come back for six months to Romania, I was already adapted to life back home, and settled in my nest in my parents' home. It was tough to pull away one more time. My husband was working back then at the Ministry for European Funds (i.e., in Bucharest, Romania) and he had to resign and come with me to Strasbourg. Both Budapest and Strasbourg were our common choices, which we made aiming to better our lives and to enrich ourselves, not financially, but as human beings.

In Budapest, I went because I was longing for a period in which I could focus only on study, not work and study, as I have done during my undergraduate studies. And those passionate about Human Rights look at ECHR like to some form of God: an abstract concept, yet so present in our lives. This is why I came to Strasbourg. As I could not miss the opportunity to come to the place about which I read in the textbooks.

All these have been professional and spiritual accomplishments for me. But these come with a high price. I get to see my parents only once in few months, and I away from my country. I do not know how much others saw me as a Roma migrant woman in Hungary or France. Rather, I was seen as a Romanian migrant woman. However, I was always careful that people knew my ethnicity, and I always said that I wanted that those looking at me to see a Roma woman. And as it seems natural and unexceptional that I am a woman, my ethnicity should also be regarded as natural, ordinary, nothing special to talk about, but something to be respected.

My experiences are common to any woman who leaves her country, in spite of her class, country of origin or ethnicity. Crossing borders gives birth to similar feelings: you start a journey, you embrace the unknown, but you are hopeful. No one thinks they are leaving for the worst. But you have to start from zero. It takes time to adapt, and not always are you received with open arms, and you have to make yourself be welcomed. You finally get used to it, and the new country becomes 'home', but deep down in your heart you long for the other 'home'.

Ananthi (48 years old, Tamil Nadu, India)

I was born in Arthur Village in Selam District of Tamil Nadu. I was not born in the hospital; I was born in the open space. My parents were not able to educate me, I studied up to 2nd grade only. We are Gypsies, we used to live under the trees and open spaces. There itself we cook and eat what my husband brings from his hunt.

It was very difficult to go for a toilet or take a bath. Even it's hard for us to get into the bus because we take all our household stuff with us. When we go to big cities like Delhi and Mumbai, the people there didn't accept our business and the police tortured us. We went to Malaysia for our business on a tourist visa, and they sent us back to India due to visa issues. On my return, we occupied some land and started doing agriculture for forty years. The government took land from us due to lack of legal papers.

Again, we went back to our traditional occupation in Tamil Nadu and started sending children to school. While we are doing business, we take girl children with us. We always feel proud to be women. However, women from other communities will not treat us in the same way. They won't even allow us to sit on the stoop of their house. We always live as a group. If the government provide us land ownership to live in one place and residential schools for our children, it will support us greatly to grow equally with others. Thank you.

Maria (61 years old, Timisoara, Romania)

May I speak Romani? I am Roma. Here [i.e., Germany], there are more money. At home we had nothing; children did not receive financial aid. What can you do with 160 lei? [i.e., the amount given by the Romanian state for children; approx. 35 euros/month]. Here you receive one, maybe two hundred euros, and it is much better than home. Home [Romania] is 'vai și amar' [untranslatable; approx.: 'Oh, and the bitterness of life', or 'horrible, horrendous'], you starve to death; you can't live on 160 lei, and pay for electricity, water and gas. Here, you do not pay for anything, because they [i.e., the state] offer you everything and you live life well. Here, you have all you need: food to eat, you have money. But at home is poverty.

Thus, I tell you, here is better; home is 'vaişi amar'. In Romania, they do not want to do anything for our kids, to give them monthly allowance; or my pension for which I worked for in Romania. I wanted to retire due to my health, and when I went to the Romanian doctors they asked: 'What is your ailment? It is nothing.' But I suffer from heart and lung issues. I walk around with a bag full of medicine, but they did not want to approve my retirement. I worked for twenty years, but they do not want to give me pension. They [i.e., Romanian state] said: 'You do not have the age for pension.' 'But I am sick sir, how can you leave me like this?!' 'We do not care. Go to you doctors; if they agree to help you, is ok, if not – no.'

And so, I was left without pension. I was hoping to stay home like a lady and wait for my pension, not to leave abroad and struggle. Unfortunately, it can't be done. In Romania you starve to death, and you have nothing. When you have any money in your pocket, people attack and rob you thinking you are rich. And in reality, many times you have nothing to eat. But people do not know this. Romania is poisonous [poverty]. Here, for better and worse we have all we need. Health is the only thing missing.

They betrayed us in Romania. They cut the funds that they owed us, ended all programmes that helped us. Here is much better. And our children come here also because they have nothing to eat at home and can't support their own children. They have no choice. Here, if they work, they have a good salary. My son-in-law worked in Romania and they were giving him 100 lei per week [i.e., approx. twenty euros/week]. What can you do with this? Starve to death. How can you pay your utilities, food and all the other needed things? There is no talk about being healthy, either, forget about it. I would like to ask for help for my children and my grandchildren.

Gayathri (29 years old, Tamil Nadu, India)

I was born in Sakara village in Perambalur district of Tamil Nadu, India. I lost my dad at a very early age and my mother couldn't take care of me, so I stayed with my grandma until the age of five, and after that, I started going with my grandma for business. At the age of six, they put me in a residential school. I studied in a girl's school. After high-school, I did my teacher training course and I'm at home now. At an early age itself, I used to travel with my grandparents for business. I was afraid, being a girl, and there were no bath and toilet facilities. I used to take a bath in the mud pools and lake water.

Now, I'm at home and travel with my husband for the tattoo business. I have two girl children, and we have our home now. We have some land, but there is no document. Me and my husband have to take care of us, we don't have our parents and in-laws. I haven't been abroad, but we travel across Tamil Nadu to places such as Kolli Hills, Ooty, Thiruvannamalai, Arthur, Selam and so on. While we are travelling we always face the challenge of accommodation, we can't get a room.

We mostly travel as a group of five or more with few bags, but hotels and guest houses won't allow us to stay and the fare is also not affordable for us. Every night is trouble for us. We mostly stay at the bus stand. Some people look at us in a weird way. There is no freedom for women. Being born into a low caste, there is discrimination, and we feel inferior.

Other community members always look down at us. Our women feel more freedom at all places, but society is not looking at us in the same way. We have taken some efforts for women's freedom, but it's not continued. Thank you.

Monnica (24 years old, Constanta, Romania)

I grew up in the Roma community in Toflea, Romania, where both my parents are originally from. I speak Romani, Romanian, English, French and Spanish. When I was seven years old my parents decided to move in the capital, in Bucharest, where my sister and I could have access to better education and to better life conditions. After a short while, I had the opportunity to cross borders by myself. When I was eight years old, I wanted to go to a summer school in Great Britain, where I had to study English. There, I had my first contact with nations from all over the world, but especially I came in contact with a language, which I did not know, and I had to learn without anyone translating it into my own language.

Even if at first it seemed impossible, and I literally hid in my room, where I was eating only crackers and ham because I could not ask for anything else, things started to slowly change and started making sense. And after a week, I already forgot what it means impossible!

Gymnasium and high-school I finished in Bucharest, where I also learnt Spanish. After high-school I decided to go to France, in spite of the many clichés about the Roma that were circulating, in spite of rumours that Romanians were not welcomed by the French because of prejudices. These did not stop me from moving to France, continuing my studies. For it was important to have an education and a first-hand perception of the world, and I was convinced that people would perceive me as I was going to present myself, regardless of clichés. This is why every time time I introduced myself, I mentioned I was Roma. I wanted people to see that there are different types of Roma, just as there are different types of French or Swedish people, etc. As there are different social classes in each country, it is the same in the Roma communities, and I wanted people to know this. I feel that it was, up to a certain point, my duty.

When I moved to France, I did not know how to speak French. All I knew was 'Bonjour' and 'omelette au fromage'. Which meant that I was polite, and I would never starve. The issue was that I did not like cheese, but I had to eat it, as it was the only thing I knew how to ask for. When I started speaking French, I slowly realized that people considered me a bit rude, even though if you would have asked me, I was very polite! But in France, for example, when we buy a baguette in a boulangerie, as a sign of respect for the people working in the boulangerie, we should bite the tip of the baguette. As I did not know this, the boulanger was rather annoyed with me. Later, I figured this (custom) out, and then I made him smile.

Here – in France – I was never confronted with any acts of racism, so I do not know what this means. Usually, if people were a bit impolite, or if they were unhelpful in certain circumstances, I never took it personally, or as a sign that I was different. Because I am not different! We are all human beings. We all face rejection, but it is important to never give up, to go forward and not make a drama out of a rejection by taking it personally. Probably, if I had been disillusioned after my first rejection, today I would not be studying at the Sorbonne, one of the best schools in the world. Here, I study Economics, and I am in the final university year.

All of these were possible because I never regarded my position in the society as one of a Roma woman, as others do. I saw myself strictly as a woman. Or better said, as a human.

These stories show how the processes of migration/mobility of Narikuravar and Roma women takes place today. This is a process that is more individual than it was in the past, when women were moving together with their families. Seeing the strength of women from Narikuravar and Roma communities, I conducted interviews with the women who were in their mobile process. In these encounters, the women's resilience, force and courage to work through the different environments and strive, at times against all odds, was evident.[39] Moving, or being mobile, has been for many of the Narikuravar and Roma women a way to access justice. As we will see next, the struggle for justice of members of these communities takes long, complex and diverse avenues, which are both formal and informal.

'Our Justice'

In an interview in 2017, Nelu Pavel, who is a judge in the traditional Roma system, shared with us details about 'the Kris'. He was a 48-year-old Roma, with a Masters' degree in Public Administration, and held a political seat in the southern part of Romania. He comes from a family of Roma judges, and has been adjudicating hundreds of cases. He highlighted that when judging, his main interest is to 'bring peace' among the parties. Pavel specified that Kris works within the traditional Romani communities, where members respect the traditions and customs, which are paramount components in obtaining justice and maintaining the peace. This, he explained, is due to the fact that the truth of the allegations is established based on the cooperation of the members of the community. When one of the parties is asked to give a deposition, the person swears that they are telling the truth. Swearing has no legal implications, as upon finding out the falsity of one's allegations, there is no legal punishment. However, within tightly-knit communities the implications are stronger, deeper and dire. If one is not being truthful, they lose 'their honour and the respect of the other community members; they become impure', Pavel explains. The retribution for lying is also envisioned as a curse, it can bring distortions of life onto one's family: Children could be born with birth defects ('boala copilului') or become sick, even die as a punishment for their parents' deeds, Pavel detailed. Hence, when speaking during Kris, the Roma have to decide between lying, which might lead to loss of health and wellbeing for their family, or telling the truth and risk paying the fine as requested by the judge in case of being found guilty. Pavel explained that the Roma often opt for the second, i.e. telling the truth, thinking 'if I am healthy and my children are well, I can always make money back; money come and go, but family and children's wellbeing is important'. So, they do not lie under oath. While describing these customs, Pavel also mentioned that these are particularly true for communities where the Roma tradition and customs are important, which – as we will see in communities like the one in Ormeniş – is not always the case.

Pavel also highlighted that 'Judgment of Peace' is not about final judgments, but is about reaching peace and a good order in which both parties feel that justice was achieved. This often implies a fine to be paid to the grieving party. This fine is established taking into consideration the fault of the party and the overall economic situation of their family. 'If someone is not wealthy, putting too much of a fine on the person could break them, as they might not be able to pay, and further resort to violence', Pavel said, highlighting that it is important to ask for an equitable payment that would in turn be seen as an honourable gesture in restoring the peace of the community.

Introduction

According to Mills et al. (2017) legal systems 'are grounded in a particular constitutional order. Constitutional orders, in turn are grounded in people's fundamental beliefs about the nature of reality, including their ontology, cosmology and epistemology' (Mills et al., 2017: 260). It is thus important to understand the social justice systems within specific contexts and interpret them accordingly. Like many other indigenous legal structures, the Roma and Narikuravar justice systems operate in everyday life,[1] along the national and supernational ones. Thus, similar to other communities that have nomadic traditions, they often have to navigate a double-folded justice system: The one of their community, and that of the larger society. While for most part the two systems come in accord, at times due to different traditional cultural norms, the two could be at odds, placing the community members in the delicate position of interpreting and accommodating both.

Justice through someone else's eyes

It is rather well-known that within the larger/national legal system, the Narikuravar and Roma have been historically and systematically discriminated against, treated differently and negatively. For example, across Europe the 'Drepturile Omului pentru Romi şi Nomazi în Europa' Report of 2011 found out that:

> Roma are treated violently by the police both in places of detention and in public places – for example, in Roma neighborhoods, during police raids. In a number of cases, when the criminal investigation into such acts was initiated, it appears that it was clearly discriminatory and biased. (…) Isolated Roma settlements have received special attention from the police, often in the form of intrusive raids.

Roma, who were in cars or other vehicles, were discriminated against in 'stop and search' police operations. The registration of the ethnic profile was also reported, in the context of the displacement of the Roma outside the national space.[2]

Under the national/EU and Indian justice systems, those labelled as 'Gypsy' have often been marginalized, discriminated against and disproportionally met with violence (Dragomir, 2020). In India, the study of the contemporary treatment of the nomads under the law has not received the same attention as in Europe, and as result we have less data that explains their position. Nevertheless, scholars have been referring to nomads in India along similar lines: 'Violence against nomadic tribes constitutes a social context unique to the community's existence as marginal people outside the purview of the hierarchical caste system and sedentary people' (Kolekar, 2008: 569). Moreover, according to Berland and Rao (2004), nomadic communities are the most neglected and discriminated social group in India. While situated worlds apart, due to their (assumed) common history, the connection between the two traditional systems of justice has been previously explored:

> Whenever there is any sin or crime committed by Roma, they go to Kris, which is like the Panchayat system of traditional India, and refers both to the abstract concept of 'justice' and to the institution responsible for settling disputes among different extended families. (. . .) To solve the problems and for a fair justice, a judge is selected from the tribe not belonging to the party involved. He should be known as an impartial person and should have a national reputation. The Kris offers an opportunity for young men to practice their won skills. (. . .) The jurisdiction of the Roma tribunal (Romani Kris) is limited mainly to actions for damages and cases concerning women (abduction, wilful desertion and the like). Its chief power lays in the ascendency of the community over the individual, and the moral pressure exercised by the tribunal, for this Court has no right to inflict corporal punishment.
>
> Shashi, 1990: 107

The comparative analysis of the Roma and Adivasis is welcome, but often faulty of exaggeration, lacking in detail, and without looking at the differences among communities and their inherent dissimilarities of justice. For example, Shashi talks about these two systems in a universal manner: 'The members of the court are always appealed to by the plaintiff. He notifies an elderly Gypsy who convokes the others. When summoned, the defendant has to submit to the procedure of the Kris. But no trial can be held in the absence of one of the contestants' (Shashi, 1990: 108). To a certain extend the process described by

Shashi (1990) reflects some of the traditional justice practices however, as they are rooted in local histories, this is painted in too-large brush strokes. Thus, to overcome this shortfall, in what follows, I will detail the connections between the two systems based on the qualitative research I have been conducting in Romania and India.[3]

Traditional 'Kriss' and 'Panchayat'

Given their 'Orientalizing' and discriminatory historical treatment, also due to their nomadic traditions, it is not surprising that both Roma and Adivasis have been looking for justice within their own community,[4] creating rules and practices to address injustice. These forms of justice are typically referred to as Kriss[5] for the Roma communities, and Panchayat for the Adivasi/ Narikuravar.

Romano Kriss

The Roma traditional justice system, or 'Kriss',[6] is described as 'a gathering of Gypsies, almost always men, though sometimes including an old woman, [who come] to adjudicate disputes between Rom over matters as diverse as compensation for divorce, accusations of theft, cheating at horse deals, and betrayal to gazo authorities' (Stewart, 1997: 57). According to Crowe (1996), these forums of community justice were typically led by 'the "Buljubasas", who wielded immense political and judicial power and received two percent of the Gypsy tribute'. Moreover, 'the Buljubasas were intermediaries between the Rom and local officials' (Crowe, 1996: 23).

It is important to point out that the traditional Kriss system is understood as entirely based 'on the willingness of each Gypsy to acknowledge his moral ties with other Gypsies and so to consider their needs emphatically. The judgment given in kris were no more than the advice of one or more men no one was compelled to heed, since the men who gave their opinions did so as individuals not as representatives of some abstract system of idea of justice' (Stewart, 1997: 57). Thus, as we have seen above, it presupposes ethnic community ties that are perceived as valuable and worth preserving. Without the willingness of the members to participate and to accept the verdict of the community leaders, the judgment is a mere 'advice' – as Stewart suggested. However, one can imagine some communities with a high level of interdependence where these decisions have an impact, and cannot be disregarded or treated as 'advice', especially by those members who are lacking resources for surviving independently (such as women).[7] Nevertheless, as per Nelu Pavel's description above shows, the overall conceptualization and legitimization of the traditional Romani Kriss highlights the importance of the intra-community ties, and of the acceptance of the common traditions and leadership. As there is no formal, enforceable punishment for one's deeds, once the community ties loosen, the role of the Kriss is severely diminished.[8]

Narikuravar Panchayats

Panchayats are forms of traditional community justice that are neither specific to the Narikuravar community, nor to the Adivasi. They are rather found at different community levels across South Asia. For example, community or regional Panchayats co-exist with other Panchayats that operate for a fragment or a specific community, and are typically referred to as a 'village council', 'a former group of five influential older men acknowledged by the community as its governing body; [or] an elective council of about five members organized in the republic of India as an organ of village self-government'.[9]

The Narikuravars explained that they have their Panchayats within their communities, and also participate in the large, regional councils. As Rajasekaran said:

> About the general [i.e., regional] Panchayat, there is one person representing our community. Because this is done through the general election through the government. So, amongst our people, one person was elected to be a part of the [regional] Panchayat, where there are nine members in total. His name is Vijayakumar, and he is one of the ward members. His job is mainly to get resources for the Narikuravars: Drinking water, addressing supply demands, and to allocate government schemes to all areas. He tells them how much our people need, and they distribute the funds. For example, you know the housing scheme? He got two houses out of ten for our locals. This is the kind of work they do.
>
> Rajasekaran interview, 2021

The selection of Narikuravars within their own Panchayat is typically based on the power they have within the community, i.e. their economic and political clout: 'In a Panchayat, they get four–five leaders, each from every district. People decide the leaders based on the money they have, and on the number of sacrifices they have made to either Goddess Kali or Meenaksh over the years. If somebody has killed ten goats, one per year, they will be the leader if that is the highest number. So, in every village there will be someone' (Jayachitra interview, 2021).

At the community level, establishing a Panchayat is seen as a straightforward process: 'If somebody wants to start a Panchayat, they have to spend about 500 rupees arranging for the meeting. So, about 50 to 100 people come to the Panchayat discussions. There are no [formal] systems or rules. It is more spontaneous. And the solution is also implemented among the members informally' (Rajasekaran interview, 2021).

During fieldwork in 2018, the Narikuravars in Mettupalayam described the Panchayat system along similar lines. Sugan said: 'When we have a problem that we need to solve in the community, we can take an instrument (similar to drums), and go around the settlement and ask for a Panchayat.' He explained that this is one way to get immediate attention on a wrongdoing that took place, and to find a remedy. A Panchayat will be formed ad-hoc among the leaders of the community, who would hear the case, and pass a judgment.

The traditional selection of the members of the Kriss and Panchayats are both gender-biased, as women are not a part of the judging committees. In Romania, one Bulibaşa in Olteniţa cited by Necula (work in progress), representing the community of 'Spoitori', said that they select their justice leaders mainly based on one's overall reputation: 'The authority of the local leader comes from his ability to mediate relations with the authorities. (. . .) Bulibaşa deals only in the [Roma] community – that is, they discuss issues only about the [Roma] community. If anyone has a problem, they call me, I intervene, we'll see what it's about' (Necula, 'Studiu de Diversitate', work in progress).

Referring to the Roma community in Calaft, Necula presents the interview with one of the community leaders who explains the selection process slightly differently:

> Generally, the leader is one of the richest people. The acquired wealth attracts the respect of the other members of the family. I am part of a group of judges that is all over Oltenia. I participated into trials all over Oltenia . . . I'm going everywhere Roma people ask . . . All the families that recognize the [Kriss] judgment in the community turn to the well-known judges, regardless of their [specific] community. (. . .) We are a big family; 50–60% of Roma from Calafat are my family. I am recognized as a moral authority . . . We see how a man thinks, how he dresses, how he speaks, what level he has in society, if he is otherwise respected and listened to.
>
> PZ, Spoitor, community leader

In other Roma communities, which tend to be more integrated/'assimilated', like the one in Ormeniş, there is no longer a Roma court, and this role is at times assigned instead to the church and its leaders: 'We had a community leader here:

Old Vaida', Doru told me in 2017. 'He was a pastor, but also acted as a ruler. He imposed the Roma rule, the people listened and respected him. But he passed away. Now, we have a [new] pastor, but he is not a real leader', Doru says and then stops pensively, reflecting on the situation of who takes on leadership roles: 'It's hard to say. In general, the elderly people are respected in the community. Some are great, but others less.' As the Roma community of Ormeniş is further divided in the Main Street and Olt Street, Doru says that in the latter – where poorer Roma live – the church plays an important role, dictating the rules and shaming people. Then, if this is not yielding success, and 'if conflicts are not resolved, they go next to the police'.

It became obvious that in the Roma communities (as in many other close groups) one's image, in terms of their moral character, wealth and social clout, plays an important role in assigning and maintaining one's leadership role. Compared to the Narikuravar Panchayat, the Romani Kriss is more formalized, and more procedural. However, as we will see next, Romani Kriss tends to be more symbolic, with less power over implementing their decision on the community level.

How the traditional practices of justice work

While conducting work about social justice, I knew very little about the indigenous justice systems. Most of the literature covers Western-centric views of justice, and uses them as universal instruments in assessing justice, equality and fairness around the world, and throughout history. My fieldwork brought to the fore both the limitations of the theories of justice, and the understanding that due to their traditional nomadic lifestyle, the justice processes of the traditional Roma and Narikuravar have been kept within the community, and little is known outside. When we asked about their process, Rajasekaran explained the basic functionality of their Panchayat: 'People usually gather in a place and the person who appealed usually organizes the meeting. Then, they request four main elders to discuss the matter with everybody openly. Usually, these are small disputes that could be solved internally, and in the case that they are not resolved, people may choose to appeal to more bureaucratic methods' (Rajasekaran interview, 2021). Ravathi gave us an example: 'If a woman touches something with her feet, she will have to pay back with a new item or the money in order to properly settle the matter. Mostly these kinds of issues are talked through verbally' (Ravathi interview, 2021).

Romeo Tiberiade is one of the mayor's counsel for Roma issues in Craiova, Romania, and one of the Roma Kriss judges. In an interview in 2017, he explained the process:

> I can tell you, from my point of view, in the Roma communities Kriss is not judgment, but an advice. You are not allowed to judge anyone outside of official institutions. But within a family you can analyse, advice, and get an advice from the leaders. So, when in a community there is an issue, the two parts involved come in front of the elders asking to see who is right, and who is to blame. The elders being wise and tempered, find each time a solution to stop a future violence, and any unwelcomed acts. The elders can judge this even for three long days.
>
> Romeo Tiberiade interview, 2017

The role of the elders in the community is a topic that was brought about often during the interviews both in Romania and in India. 'The elders' are seen as the (default) judges: 'Elders can judge any case, except murder. We can ask for the support of the elders to stop the revenge and the violence' (Tiberiade interview, 2017). They are also seen as pillars of the society, and disrespecting is a concern even in communities who do not practice Kriss:

> Well, that is not allowed. You will not let them, if you can. If you can't, it is better to leave than to get into a fight with them. Because the ones that would do such a thing are very aggressive, so you cannot say a word to them. Especially us, the older ones, do we have a word in front of the young ones? Not at all! Because they would leave the elder alone and they will start to insult you.
>
> Micu Eugenia interview, 2018

'That is a shameful thing', agreed Ms. Bodi. 'So, if he [i.e., the elder] is beaten or insulted, I would tell the police. If my relative would disrespect an elder, I would scold him, but if he would be a stranger, I would be afraid because he could beat me also', said Elena Bodi (2018 interview in Ormeniş), reflecting on justice and the age divisions within Roma communities.

Gender roles and dynamics

While the role of the elders is a topic of importance, most of the time the Panchayats and Kriss today address issues of gender relations, dynamics and roles in the society. In the past, the traditional justice systems addressed most of the community issues, especially those related to monetary exchanges, and sometimes to violence, but now these are typically handled by the outsiders' system, through the police. Traditional justice systems' power nowadays has been severely reduced, and their work is mainly in the field of personal relations, a field not regulated (at least not in detail) by the state. 'Marrying inside one's clan is the biggest sin. For example, if two people that worship Kali were to get married, they would be looked down upon by society, not allowed to walk the streets, come to other people's houses, and drink their water. Overall, these people will be treated awfully, as it is as forbiden to marrying a brother or sister' (Ravathi interview, 2021).

Marriages and gender relations have been one of the important topics that kept recurring in the conversations about traditional forms of justice, both in the Narikuravars and Roma communities, and seem to make up the main group of cases that come under the scrutiny (and possible jurisdiction) of the Panchayat and Kriss:

> As far as I can see, the problems are usually related to marriages. In my community, it is acceptable for a widow to remarry. There are also no oppositions to mutual divorces. However, it has to be presented in front of a few people. They neither need any legal means, nor go to court. If there are fights between community people, it isn't seen as a big issue, and can be solved easily through this method. As everybody resides in the same locality, the proximity makes it easy to solve the problems faster.
>
> Rajasekaran interview, 2021

Rajasekaran detailed about the typical cases that need the intervention of the Panchayat ruling, which typically revolve around regulating marriages:

> For example, my aunt's father married another community girl. Her family was opposed to the idea, and both of them were still kids, and did not have proper guidance. This was almost 60 years ago. But because he was a government employee, and had a stable income, he didn't feel the need to stay dependent on the community. However, they couldn't participate in either communities' festivals.
>
> Rajasekaran interview, 2021

Who one marries is a sensitive subject, and tensions can escalate quickly:

> If they marry for love, both families should agree, and approve of the other family. If this is done, there will be no problem. If they marry without families' consent, they will have to face the Panchayat. In these cases, the Panchayat has the power to separate them. For example, 35 years ago, my aunt married a 'Modaliyar cast' (from another community), and ran away together. After this,

there were intense discussions and Panchayat meetings. They even got him to the police station. But then my grandpa had a gun, and he started shooting inside the station. So, problems used to be bigger before.

Ravathi interview, 2021

In Romania, the woman's virginity on the wedding night is a topic typically discussed in connection with the Kriss:

Romano Criss was not something concrete [i.e., formally enforced] – people taught these traditions which were striving for a long time. In the past the biggest issue was the girl's virginity. They had to show the blood-spotted sheets after the first night of marriage. If the girl was not a virgin, the boy had to cut his finger and bleed on the sheet. This was a big issue. If this proof did not exist, they would split up.[10]

Relationships outside of marriage tend to be highly regulated and are also the purview of the community council:

If a man touches [i.e., has sexual relations] a woman, they will conduct a Panchayat for him. If the man is married and touches a woman of age, or another married woman, they will conduct a Panchayat, and settle the matter with 'swami sothu', meaning hereditary money in our families. Then, they have to make the sacrifice of an animal and there is a full ritual. The person has to hold an offering, and do certain things. A woman can't tell anybody, because she will be beaten up. Before marriage, when the girl is still young, anything is accepted. But after a certain age, these rules get extremely strict. These kinds of words are considered highly offensive when said by a woman. Like this, before marriage I can go to anybody's house, and behave the way I want to. After marriage, nothing is supposed to touch our feet. If I touch my own stuff in my own house with my own feet, we still have to throw it away, and it can no longer be used.

Ravathi interview, 2021

The Roma community in Ormeniș has been assimilating into the large (modern) Romanian society, and tends to regulate less their personal relations. Corcoaraș Mihaiu, amusingly making references to the larger Roma community, but (proudly) referring to how the Roma in Ormeniș have become more Romanian-ized told us:

In our ethnicity is either breaking up, with normal divorce cases in the Courthouse, or if there are children involved, they forgive each other. But, there was never violence. But this sort of problems in Proverbs in Chapter 6 shows that if jealousy confronts the man, there is no mercy on the Day of Judgment. So, it is very true, because of jealousy, the man is capable of transforming into a beast. And there were cases, indeed, some men became beasts. But anyway, this community from Ormeniș is more civilized compared to other villages or communities. And we see things in different ways.

Corcoaraș Mihaiu interview, 2018

Balint Firu's view also confirmed this development. 'Some are forgiving each other; others are breaking up. The police intervenes in these cases, [so] if they reach to the court, then yes. But you know how it is, if both parts are reaching a common ground ...', said Balint Firu (interview, 2018), leaving his thought unfinished, but understood. This change in the justice system took place in Ormeniș over the past four decades.

Janos Vaida, explaining the difference that still persists among different Roma communities – and in doing so assigning value to the process of modernization, which brought change into his community – said:

Some years ago, there was an incident. A man was in a group of Bulibașa, and was with a woman – but they were both married [to other people]. They ran away, when they were over 40 years old. After that they weren't allowed to live in that community. They had to come here, to Ormeniș, in secret, and they stayed a lot of time here. They lived here. They were Gypsies, but more traditional, the kind that wears hats and makes rings. They have these rules, but us – we don't have them. We started to be more civilized.

Janos Vaida interview, 2018

Considering that both Kriss and Panchayat depend on the willingness of the community members to accept the ruling, punishment and enforcement are difficult to effect:

When someone does something wrong, they are fined. It depends on the kind of problem and the circumstances. Not many problems occur with physical violence. It is mostly fighting about marriages and money. If two people wanted to get divorced, they would present their sides to the elders, and try to make them live together. However, if the majority thinks the reasons are valid, they let them get divorced without having to appeal in court. If there is disagreement, money may be used to make the settlements. In most cases, as the dowry is given by the husband to the wife, the settlement is given back to the initial owner.

Jayachitra interview, 2021

As a result, the members of the Panchayat try to find acceptable ways for the grieving parties, and would also not come into conflict with the laws of the land. Rajasekaran said, pointing out the tensions between traditional forms of justice and the supra-national one:

These days, the general constitutional rights are being respected, so the severity of the consequences have reduced, and nobody is even willing to punish so harshly these days. Some of the traditional punishments include carrying a rock around a tree, kneeling on the ground, and thoppukaranam. Now even these are not there anymore, and can be seen as a violation of human rights in these modern times. To solve any issue, only verbal methods and compensations are being used.

Rajasekaran interview, 2021

Role of women in Kriss and Panchayat

While women's position in the community and their personal lives fall under the Panchayat and Kriss jurisdiction, often women have no judicial power: 'Women are not judges; they are not a part of the Kriss. If they are the grieved party, a male family member (typically their father or uncles) would seek justice and act as her guarantor within the Kriss. This is due to the fact that women do not have the same right as men within the traditional Roma communities', Pavel explained. 'It has been like this since our forefathers', he continues by pointing out the Roma traditions. He then details that 'in the older days women were not even allowed to walk in line with men in the street, even less to be a part of Kriss, which is the honour and duty of the male' (Pavel interview, 2017).

While in Ormeniş, the Kriss is not enacted, people know that 'women cannot get involved; they are not allowed from the Bulibaşa' (Vaida Cerasela interview, 2018). In turn 'the men are judges here. Everything is after how the man says it' (Corcoraş Noe interview, 2018).

The exclusion of women from the Kriss is also acknowledged by Matras, who argues that: 'The precise rules differ, but usually women cannot take on a role as a member of the court ("judges" or "arbiters"), and more often than not they are not allowed to testify in the courts, either, though only some communities impose restrictions on their presence and hearings' (Matras, 2014: 50–51).

Similarly, Doru explained that within the Roma traditions gender dynamics are more hierarchical. These hierarchies are often taken for granted, and 'they seem normal, because they are not acknowledged by women as such. Women have to respect the men, and this is visible in the Romano Kriss' (Doru interview, 2017).

Within the Narikuravar communities, the situation is rather similar, while quite complicated. 'Only men have the right to be in Panchayat', said Jayachitra.

She also argued contrary to some common beliefs that: 'There are no women elder-leaders.' Elderly women have a minimal role as 'they could give suggestions, but nobody will follow what they say' (Jayachitra interview, 2021). Ravathi also explains that while women's role is not in the Panchayat, they participate indirectly by praying and getting their will through gods: 'We worship the goddess greatly, and she is a big part of all important rituals in the community' (Ravathi interview, 2021).

Nevertheless, the view of the two women, Jayachitra and Ravathi, was not shared by Rajasekaran, who argued that in the Narikuravar community 'there are no [gender] restrictions. A woman can be a candidate in the [Panchayat] elections if she wants. Even my mother contested as a board member 15 years ago' (Rajasekaran interview, 2021). Thus, while it is rather unclear if women could officially act as judges on community matters, it is obvious that their role is limited, and often marginal both in the Panchayat and Kriss.

Times they are changing, and so does justice

These traditional justice practices have been in place and functioning for centuries within the Narikuravar and Roma communities. However, over the past four decades research on rural local administration shows that the traditional Panchayats have 'almost disappeared or [have] gradually decayed from the rural scene. Even among the traditional societies, this much cherished traditional institution seems to have lost its importance. This is believed to be true of the tribal communities as well, where the panchayat is stated to have hardly any significant role in the local affairs owing to modernization' (Murti, 1981: 48).

While some Narikuravars and Roma still practice traditional forms of justice, for those who do not live within compact communities, their role has been greatly diminished. For example, Jayachitra shared:

As my family lives apart from the community, we don't face any problems that need any counselling from the community elders. If we had a few people around us, something might come up. Living in a city is completely different, so the routines and problems and conflicts vary as well. So, I have not experienced the need for confronting the Panchayat. If the kids fight in school, we just go talk to their parents and the principal, like other communities. If there was a problem with the family back home, I go back to the village, and talk things out within the family.

Jayachitra interview, 2021

Similarly, as the Roma community from Ormeniş shares the village with Romanians and Hungarians the practice of the Kriss is a mere reminiscence for many, while for others it is a time-honaured story they heard as children. These changes in the Kriss and Panchayat do not take place in a vacuum; they rather come together with other changes that have been taking place within the overall communities:

> Now everything has changed. (...) Only about 10 per cent still don't know how to live and survive in these fast-evolving times. Our people have to work every day to make a living. But most people don't have the practice of saving up. Which creates a problem. Only about 20 per cent save money. Most people earn, eat to their heart's content and start over the next day. People like me get monthly salaries, so we need to manage our finances more. Their priority is eating properly, and taking care of their body. But some people aren't clean, and aren't aware of what it means to groom themselves.
>
> Jayachitra interview, 2021

These changes reflect on the ways in which justice is understood and conducted. Transformation of the justice system (within a generation, even faster) is almost tangible, so community members often reflect upon them:

> We are on the verge of change.... Traditions are changing. In the past, the girl was promised to the boy. It did not matter if she hated him. Now they have been migrating, flying to the foreign countries, and they seen some other things. They changed what they want, and how they behave; when you start to see something else ... you transform. It can be good, or maybe bad. I rely on this principle: if you are not educated, you are at a loss; even if you fall in love with someone, even if he finds a job in England, and makes more money, it is still not better [on the long run].
>
> Doru interview, 2017

Policing and justice

The changes that have been taking place in the Narikuravar and Roma traditional justice systems are not at random. One of the biggest changes developing across recent decades is the increasing role of the police in Roma and Narikuravar lives. This is not a new occurrence, as the police have been intervening rather brutally in the lives of those who are identified as 'nomads' and 'Gypsies' (Dragomir, 2020) for centuries. It is rather an increase in the state's attempt to control and curtail the movement and the activities of those labelled as 'Gypsy'. More recently, an increase in policing has been remarked internationally: 'Discrimination between the police and the nomads is a standard model. Roma were treated violently by the police both in places of detention and in public places (...). In a number of cases, when the criminal investigation into such acts was initiated, it was clearly discriminatory and biased' (Drepturile Omului pentru Romi și Nomazi în Europa Report, 2011).

Like the Roma and nomads in Europe, the Narikuravars also face terrible discrimination at the hands of the police:

> The question of whether the police help or not is a touchy subject here. Why I'm saying this is because, for example, the forest officers are always thinking about taking something from the Narikuravars – mostly money. They look for their benefit in any situation, and aren't fair or just. They don't operate under a legal licence or a registration. So, they just go to places – like bus stands and railway stations and temples. They just take documents with them – like property documents – and conduct their problems privately. And obviously, this causes problems for the Narikuravars who are present there during this time. Even if it is things like maintaining security when an important person is visiting, there is still trouble caused. They mistreat the people. That is what the community faces with the police.
>
> Rajasekaran interview, 2021

Descriptions of the police intervention in an intrusive and corrupt manner in their daily lives has been something that Narikuravars often shared. They told me that the police regularly came into their 'settlements', and looking for bribes, they pick up some people, and place them in jail. They would do this charging them with illegal hunting, which is a part of the Narikuravar tradition, for which they are well-known. Thus, the police use the Narikuravars' traditions as a legitimization for harassment.

Police practices do not aim to bring peace in the community, like the Panchayats and Kriss. They are rather used to control and punish those who are deemed as a problem for society. These are often forms of harassment of those identified as 'Gypsy', and are regular/daily practices. When I asked Vali, a Roma woman from Ormeniș, to share what it means to be a Roma, she said that: 'Whenever she goes into town, she dresses particularly nice, so she won't be discriminated against. She felt confident when she was at home, but whenever she entered stores, shopkeepers followed her around, or even threw her out on suspicion of theft. This was done because, in spite of her behaviour and nice clothes, they focused primarily on her race and identified her as a "Gypsy"' (Dragomir, 2020).

These forms of control over one's ethnical identity, gender normativity and their bodies are also enforced through the over-presence of the police. As we will see in the following chapters, at the end of the school year celebration of the local school in Ormeniş, next to the teachers and the priest, the local policeman gave a lengthy speech in front of a predominately Roma audience, in which he threatened the children and their parents, scolding them about the future/possible scandals they might cause over the summer break.

Instances as such show how, while police presence and enforcement are not new endeavours, they have been 'normalized' and internalized by the Roma people of Ormeniş. When we asked the Roma to tell us about the police in the village, the Roma whom we interviewed were quick to deny their personal involvement. Their response was somewhat surprising, since we did not ask this, but asked them to reflect on the police role in the community. But their prompt replies point out the distance that they wanted to mark between themselves and the possible police intervention, as Micu Eugenia exclaimed in a 2018 interview:

> Eugenia: The Mayor is helping us. But we didn't need his help because there were no problems.
> Interviewer: Can you give us an example?
> Eugenia: No, because we never had problems; so we did not go to him or to the police.
> Interviewer: For example, if someone was violent or if there were any scandals in the village that happened to be connected with you ...
> Eugenia: No, no, it never happened. We didn't have problems like these. Because if you mind your own business, you do not need this help.

Moreover, when directly asked whom do they turn to in case of need, the Roma in Ormeniş say that they would call the police, 'To the police! Automatically!' firmly replied Zoltan in an interview in 2018. But the Roma admit that they get differential treatment from the police. This treatment is rarely fair, especially when they are asked to intervene in issues that involve members of other communities. In a 2018 interview with Matilda Elves, she said:

> Matilda: [I turn]To my mother.
> Interviewer: But if someone is violent, or there is a scandal?
> A lady from the room screams out: To the Police!
> Interviewer, asked to confirm: So, you're going to the Police?
> Matilda: Then I am going directly to the Police!

'Well, we go to the police, because we don't have any other place', also said Vaida Cerasela (2018 interview), pointing out the limited support that the Roma get.

Well, first I would call the police. There were times when we needed to call the police because of scandals. There was a big scandal, because of lands and ownership. Some neighbours jumped my brother. I immediately announced to the police. We are 5 brothers and only boys. We intervened so it would not turn out to be so bad.

Corcoraş Nae interview, 2018

Veronica shared about the aggressiveness of the policeman in Ormeniş:

Police came here [i.e., in Ormeniş], so I think we need to respect them. There is a new policeman, I don't know his name, but he is very respectful, and he talks so nice with the children and people. Of course, God forbid, if you're not violent, because otherwise he can be violent as well; if he likes. But with us, they are very respectful. And with the women and men … And I saw him also with other people, not just with us, with everybody. He's not bad, what can I say? He's not bad.

Corcoras Veronica interview, 2018

In India, some of the Narikuravars also internalize the need for the police and justify their treatment of the community:

I don't think they treat the Narikuravars unfairly. They encourage people to seek their help, and say that they will solve the issue. They make the people sign a document to make sure the fighting has been resolved. If anything, they speak a little harshly, but that is all. I don't think this is any different from other communities. [For example] There was a problem with the children at my neighbour's house; they fought a lot. The police raised their voices to discipline all of them, and then they tried to solve the issue verbally. As they couldn't reach a mutually agreeable solution, the police made them sign a document stating that neither family would interfere in the others' business. They warned them that if they got another complaint about this, they would be arrested.

Ravathi interview, 2021

Their views of the police, while often ambivalent – as reflections most of the times are – are seemingly positive. Highlighting the violent police practices towards the Roma, Balint Firu said:

To be honest, I have a good opinion. I feel protected with them. I cannot say anything bad about them. I admire them because they protect us. But I don't agree with this idea that there are some hooligans who pick on the police, and are shot on spot. Wait a minute, there are other methods also. I just saw something now on TV about this. That time when a Roma man used the sword, but he should not have been shot for this. Why didn't they arrest him? This morning,

I heard at PRO TV that one Roma insulted a policeman, the police shot him, and he died. And there were two policemen there! They could have bound him, and beat him well. But you don't shoot the man to death. Maybe he was drunk, or sick. They should have sent him to jail, or to re-educate him, or to send him to an asylum for disabled people.

Balint Firu interview, 2018

Firu's reflections on police brutality, on the unnecessary brutal response that they display when dealing with the Roma people, has chilling similarities to police brutality towards Black people in the U.S.A. (Schwartz, 2020), and reminds of racialized state practices of aggression around the world. Furthermore, these words point out to the similar practices of aggression that the contemporary states employ towards their racialized 'Others'. When we asked the Narikuravars if the police act in a fair way towards their community, the same ambivalent view came to the fore:

Some officers scare away the people by saying that even if you spend all of this hard-earned money, the person is already dead. This fear makes most people withdraw their complaints. There is corruption. They tell the people that they will have to pay this much in court as well, and instead take the money and come to some improper conclusion. That is what happened in this case as well. They could have taken this case further, but the person guiding them drained them of money. What could my sister do? She has three children. All of them are still in school. And all her husband left her were loans to pay back. Her income from selling garlands and other items can't cover all these costs. This kind of life is very hard.

Jayachitra interview, 2021

Their stories point out the corruption and police violence towards racialized and historically marginalized communities that are global issues that erode the trust of the communities in the state and the police, while disrupting the life and fibre of these communities. Moreover, as these practices are rarely officially reported or taken into account, there is no urgency of change in the political and social arena. The goodwill of the Roma community is often extended to the police, but that does not mean that the Roma of Ormeniş are unaware of the injustices in the system.

'Of course, the Hungarian and Romanians receive better treatment in the hands of the police. The Roma people are left aside', as Laioş Alexandru (2018, interview) clearly stated his view, which was mirrored by the other Roma in Ormeniş. 'Well, just so you know that they're not making a fair justice. If you're right – they don't admit it. Especially if you're Gypsy. If we fight between us, the police will sanction us. But if there will be a fight between a Gypsy and a Hungarian, the Hungarian has already an advantage. Because we're Gypsies. That's life', said Vaida Ecaterina (interview, 2018), pointing out the different police treatment of the Roma.

As Ecaterina mentioned, often there is an internalization and acceptance of the injustices that confront the Roma communities:

What can I say? There is a little discrimination. But generally, Roma people are making problems. It is their lack of culture and education; their poverty, and they tend to shoplift small things. Because if we talk about stealing, the ones from the top of the country are stealing in style. The Hungarians are not shoplifting, to be honest. The Roma are forced to steal firewood, because of their poverty. Or they need to steal corn or potatoes, and they are caught right away. That's it. And then what are they saying? 'Look, the Gypsy shoplifted!' The Romanians and Hungarians are more educated, and they are stealing with intelligence. They rob a bank, or they are taking a loan that they do not intend to give back, you know how it is. The Roma people cannot do this. They can't even reach a bank. If a Roma man is not educated, he doesn't even know how to speak well, or to dress appropriately. He smells, he stinks, he is not well received. He steals from where he can. And he is caught very fast. But the man that is well dressed and steals from an ATM is harder to get caught because he is smart, and he knows how to do it. And you talk with him with 'Mister'. I met a lot of people like this aboard, this is their only job. In Budapest, there were Romanians who were stealing. And you were calling them 'Mister'. But if it's a Gypsy you will call him 'Gypsy'.

Balint Firu interview, 2018

Firu's complex and poignant analysis of the justice system, and the position of the Roma, reveals the accuracy of perception of those labelled as 'Gypsy' in the face of discrimination and racism. While they hold ambivalent views of the police force, they sharply analyse the hierarchies of power existent and enforced regularly in the larger society, pointing out the perils of criminalization, showing how 'white collar' crime often goes unpunished.

Rajasekaran also reflected on the same unjust practices of control and punishment at the hands of the police and those in power:

In urban areas, in bus stands, our people are mistreated. Recently, on the train from Chennai to Thiruvallur, our people were doing business selling handmade items. The police took all the products, and destroyed them. Even though we tried to protest things like this, when it's election time, they do not see the need to address this issue. Some verbal promises have been made. The police said they wouldn't interfere with their livelihood. However, no written confirmation has been made, or asked for. This is because the Narikuravars will have to stop their business to pursue a lawsuit, and this affects their daily pay, and they can't afford this.

Rajasekaran interview, 2021

The structural differences, which are both social and economic, are often reflected in how justice in the hands of the police can be done. When one cannot find the time and the means to address issues of justice, when making things fair means taking away resources injustice becomes a daily occurance, and often goes unreported. Thus, the persecution of those identified as 'nomads' or 'Gypsy' continues. The Narikuravars, like the Roma of Ormeniş, know that justice is rarely given if one is identified as 'Gypsy'. 'One of my sisters' husband went hunting because of Corona', Jayachitra said, referring to the COVID-19 pandemic that induced severe poverty among the Narikuravars, 'and he died because of a wrongly, and illegally placed windmill. The owners wanted to cover it up, and so they threw him in a well one kilometer away. This was even in the newspaper. His name was Ravi. I have all the evidence, but nobody is doing anything, even if we talk to them', shared Jayachitra (interview, 2021), highlighting the different treatment those labelled as 'Gypsy' receive in front of the law.

Our justice

Faced with these profound and systematic injustices, it is foreseeable that whenever possible the Roma and the Narikuravars are looking for alternative justice practices:

> Most of the time, we seek the advice of the elders in the community. There is nobody specific to take care of particular issues. Within the community, there are around four people, and they sit together with all parties involved to solve the problem. If it's just me, I will take it up with the elders of my clan. If it involves marriages, elders from both clans will talk. The act is an arbitrary body. The members are not fixed, whoever is available will come.

Rajasekaran interview, 2021

Thus, for the issues that could be resolved internally, the Narikuravars prefer reaching out to their own leaders:

> There are leaders within our people. My uncle is the leader of the street. There are divisions like this. If we need anything or there is a problem, we take it to

them and they get us what we need. If it is a family problem, we talk it out ourselves. If that doesn't help, we appeal to the Panchayat, which has all the leaders. So, we gather under a tree, and they let both parties present their perspectives, and then conclude on what is just.

Ravathi interview, 2021

When I asked the Narikuravars about their justice, and what do they think is just, their response was that being a Scheduled Tribe[11] was just. It became quickly obvious that for the Narikuravars to access justice in their own terms, they needed to be seen as Adivasi and ST. This was a step necessary (but not sufficient) towards their access to justice in their own terms. For the Narikuravar the fight is focused towards achieving this goal:

Everybody is working toward that. Rajasekar sir, Sankar Sir, and Anuradha ma'am are also trying to get this ST status. We are working with them as well. We are trying to reach out to MLAs, MPs, and ST ministers with letters and arranging meetings with them. Although the bill has been passed, they have not acknowledged it or put it into action.

Radha interview, 2020

While for the Narikuravars it is crucial to make claims in the name of their ST status to achieve justice, in Ormeniş, the idea of Roma justice was more diverse, and rarely followed traditional lines. For example, Firu's perspective resonates with that of many other struggling and disenchanted Romanians: 'Only this: I am bothered that the people that are ruling our country, being so educated, they are stealing without shame. And they are proud of it. This is what I don't like. Since 30 years, they are stealing without stopping' (Balint Firu interview, 2017). His, and others' views of justice were rather aligned with the tripartite views on justice – i.e. redistribution, recognition and representations – presented by Fraser (which will be analysed in detail in the next chapters).

Conclusion: tensions between systems of justice

While understanding of justice is particular to specific communities (and of course individuals), overall, access to justice for those who have been traditionally on the move has been scarce within the larger, state centralized systems: 'Tamil Justice has not helped. The Narikuravar has had no help. We have had nothing so far. Because we are MBCs, we do not get any special help. I have studied this much, and I still don't get any help or advantages. We have all protested too. The most basic thing is spreading awareness. To tell people what rights I have as an Indian living in Tamil Nadu', articulated Rajasekaran (interview, 2018) on the techniques of achieving justice, while identifying with the larger national ethos.

The consoldation of historically unjust systems of justice, where their visibility was scarce, and their presence often criminalized, leads to the creation of alternative forms of community justice. However, these systems of justice are not frozen in time, they are also changing in tandem with the larger societal and political contexts. Thus, if justice systems are based on the ontological understanding of the community, as practices are changing from nomadic to sedentary, and becoming more 'modern', integrating more into the mainstream, we are due to see the Roma and the Narikuravars seeking justice within the larger (national and international) institutions. As such, the current alternative that is now taking shape is integrating communities within the justice of the state that has monopoly over violence, often represented by the police practices of control and punishment. Policing has thus become the main way to adjudicate and administer justice within Roma and Narikuravar communities. However, their interjections rarely take into account differences in traditions, histories and positions of those who have been occupying for centuries marginalized positions in the larger hierarchical systems. Acknowledging the dignity of traditions, and of the community's legal systems, is paramount in articulating long-lasting, sustainable and fair systems of justice that accommodate all its members. Until then, facing these oppressive systems of power, Narikuravars and Roma are left to engage in alternative formal and informal practices of justice, as we will see in the next chapters.

Discrimination and the Politics of Denial

Discrimination and schooling

Following Doru's advice, one afternoon in June 2016, I went to Ormeniş. It was a Friday, the last day of their academic year. Anca, Doru's wife, has been working in the local school, teaching Romani, and counselling both formally and informally the Roma children. The ceremony was set to start at 9:30 am, and it was difficult for me to reach it in time, as public transportation from the main city to Ormeniş was unreliable, and scarce. Thus, I had to come by car. As I made my way to the village, I kept thinking how difficult it must be for the Roma children to get daily reliable transportation when returning from their city high-school back home. The day was sublime, with the sun shining powerfully over the luscious green of the area situated outside of the busy city of Braşov. I was familiar with the road to Ormeniş, but I never ceased to be impressed by the beauty of nature, which at times looked pristine, with small villages appearing round each corner making a surprising sight. As I entered the village, a bit after 9 am, I saw the buzz in the streets. Young girls and boys in dark bottoms and white shirts, carrying large bouquets of flowers. They were wearing festive dresses, had their hair done, walking quickly, calling each other's names, and smiling.

I reached the main building of the village: 'Caminul cultural', a building on the right side on the main street. The building resembled many others in the Romanian villages, constructed during communist times as a centralized space for people to meet, to 'become cultured', to hold meetings, but ultimately and mainly to hold the weekend 'disco' party. Built in the 1970s or 1980s, under the national guidance of the communist party, Ormeniş' cultural place had seen better days: The orange paint was washed out and peeling, the structure seemed shabby. The doors were heavy and rusty, the toilet had low pressure water at the sink, and no toilet paper in the stalls. Trying to grasp my bearings, I stood in the yard, surrounded by the people who were excitedly coming in. If other times my presence – as the stranger – would garner a lot of inquiring looks, now adults and children were passing me by without a second glance. Doru came into the courtyard, and together we stepped inside. Almost everyone was seated, or preparing to do so. The room was simple, and probably had witnessed many events along the years. In the back, it had a wooden stage with red curtains, in front of which the organizers had placed a table with four chairs on which were seated the local Orthodox priest, the policeman, the Catholic priest and the school principal. The teachers were already honorarily seated in the first row. Anca was also there, among the other teachers, and Doru was in the back.

There were about 200 people and the room was buzzing with children's voices; while the teachers tried to quiet them down, the noise persisted. In the small seats were the Roma women whom I knew from the village; they held young children on their laps, laughing and talking. The children were talking to each other, and the Roma men I met earlier were in the back wearing tight shirts, quietly looking and sizing up the room. I took a chair, and sat on the side in front of the room, close to the stage, and looked around.

Separated from the main seats, there was a row of about 20 chairs, perpendicular to the other rows of the room. It looked odd, but I just assumed it was for practical reasons, so they can sit more people. However, when I looked closer, I saw that the children seated on the odd row were dressed alike, in some sort of uniform, different from the other kids. (Later, Doru told me that they were students from the Hungarian section of the school.) Rather confused and excited myself, I just sat and waited for the show to start.

The principal of the school, a middle age, undescriptive Hungarian man, took the stage and asked all to be quiet, but he was not successful. Speaking over people's voices, he started the ceremony by saying platitudes, such 'as we look at the future', which did not seem to impact anyone. He then gave the statics of the school: From a total of 180 students, 20 dropped out of school, most of them in the 1st and 2nd grade. With this highlight, the principle set the tone for the rest of the ceremony and invited the Orthodox priest to talk. Wearing a black monastic robe, with a gentle voice that could hardly be heard over the humming of the room, the priest did not manage to get the audience's attention.

The priest was immediately followed on stage by the village policeman; a tall young man in uniform, he started speaking in a booming voice, scowling the participants in the room for not being silent and disappointing the principal and the priest. The room rapidly quietened down. Even though he was introduced as a figure that was going to talk about the general wellbeing of the community and traffic rules, his speech rapidly spiralled into talking about criminality. He said that everyone in the audience needs to make sure that during the summer vacation they do not get into fights with their neighbours or with their friends; and, if conflicts do *arise, they should come to him and not 'make their own justice'. His speech came at odds with what I was told (too often, and usually unasked) during the interviews in the village – namely, that criminality does not exist in the community, and that everyone gets along well. His advice seemed to be referring to some concrete experiences, but it was tempered by his ego, which empowered his (seemingly) misconstrued scowling at the same time. The room was now silent; everyone was listening to the policeman. In an act of bravado, and to further mark his authority, he put his left hand onto his belt in a cowboy-like move, while holding the microphone with his right hand. He finished and sat down, full of himself, and the Catholic priest continued with his brief and uneventful speech.*

The programme continued with children's performances. When the Hungarian children were performing all teachers were applauding; the school principal had his hands fully extended in the air, enthusiastically clapping. But when the Roma kids were dancing the clapping was scarce and most of the professors did not participate, rather chatting with one another. Only Anca was clapping to all the children's performances.

Now and then, the teachers turned their heads to where I was sitting, measuring me and whispering. A Roma boy pulled up a chair and sat next to me. Dressed in a red shirt and black pants, he was a small, slim boy, with short hair and a bright outlook. His brown-green attentive eyes were paired with a quick mind and big smile. I smiled back as I recognized him from my past visits to Ormeniş. Assuming an accomplice's tone, he started explaining what was going on in the room, and who was who. A group of young Roma girls and boys took the stage, performing a Roma dance to traditional music. The girls were wearing a lot of makeup, looking like small adults in colourful dresses and traditional Roma skirts. The boys were wearing black pants, sunglasses and traditional black hats. Then the group danced to the music of Michael Jackson.

After the ceremony, when I asked Anca, she told me that a Hungarian teacher placed her pupils in that special row, so they can be away from the Roma people in the room. I paused to think about it, and I realized that their uniforms also proved that the Hungarian parents could afford a special dress for extra-curricular activities. The Roma children were all dressed differently; some with dresses and skirts too big for them, making me think that they probably borrowed from older siblings. Seeing children in the same village, of the same age, going to the same school inhabiting such massive structural differences was a disturbing sight of grim reality. In addition, the Roma children's performances – while engaging and good – were not as well orchestrated as the Magyar ones, suggesting that they did not have a lot of teacher support in preparing for the event. It was painstakingly obvious how many more obstacles the children from the Roma community have to overcome (compared to those of the Hungarian community) to access the same success within their village.

When the performances ended, I went to the back of the room. Doru was waiting for me there, and showed me the garbage on the floor as some people in the audience, mainly Roma with their children, were strolling off – even though the ceremony was not over yet. Looking at the garbage, Doru sighed. 'I understand them', he said, referring to the non-Roma in the village. 'I am ashamed and upset too, but you know, there was no garbage bin anywhere in sight. What were the Roma supposed to do? They [i.e., Hungarians] often comment negatively on Roma behaviour – but what were they to do if there were no garbage bins in the room?' he said in a sad, quiet voice.

We left and went to Doru's home. The village was still buzzing with young spirits, jumping around under the blasting late June sun. Back at Anca and Doru's apartment, I asked them about the strange arrangement of chairs. Anca was preparing coffee, and without looking at us, she confirmed that it was the Hungarian teacher who organized the pupils as such. She then added with disgust that even if the teacher had not orchestrated this setting, the Hungarian pupils would still have sat in separated seats from the Roma. Their discriminatory behaviour was already formalized.

Anca continued by explaining that in school children learnt in segregated classes: Magyar (Hungarian) and Roma/Romanian classes. This, Anca said, establishes the feeling of superiority of the children from the Hungarian community. While they go to the same school, they are taught how to not interact with Roma children. She described how, before the school lunch, all children need to wash their hands, and form orderly lines. According to the rules, not all children eat at the same time; the Roma kids eat first, followed by the Hungarian kids. However, a small break between the two groups was instituted by the Hungarian teachers. During this break, the cleaning ladies come into the lunch room and wash the tables, washing-basins, etc., with chlorine: 'After the "Gypsy" kids, you need to wash with chlorine', Anca said in anger and sadness, citing the attitude of the Hungarian staff.

I encountered that this idea of the need of chlorine in the 'Gypsy part of town' (as Hungarians often referred to it) was widespread. As I wanted to stay in Ormeniş, I asked Doru and Anca where I could rent a room. They recommended one of their neighbours, Lucica, who agreed to host me. I went one afternoon to her flat and she received me with open arms, while being quite nervous about my presence. I took my shoes off as we entered the modest three-room apartment, which was the home of four generations: An elderly man, his daughter Lucica, her *husband, her son and his wife, together with their two-year-old daughter. Lucica's boy and husband were away for work, so she could host me. The rooms were clean and crowded with things, with old carpets, blankets and appliances orderly aligned and folded. Lucica humbly showed me around saying that they live modestly. I assured her that the apartment was really good and not to worry about me. Nevertheless, she took me to the bathroom. Confused, I followed her thinking that she needs to explain something that I already knew about the building: There was no gas in their home, so water needed to be heated in small appliances to have a warm bath; otherwise, we could only have cold showers. But that was not it. Lucica opened an old door and showed me a simple and spotless bathroom, and she proudly said: 'We cleaned everything with bleach for you!' This damn bleach business again. I looked at the bottle of Clorox on the sink, and I felt the smell of this harsh chemical instill in my nostrils. I turned my head to her encountering her proud smile, but I did not have it in me to probe. I just said: 'Please, you really shouldn't have. I am really OK, and your home is lovely and clean.' But her remarks about the need of chlorine in Roma homes revealed the internalization process of the discriminatory practices Roma in Ormeniş (and probably beyond) are faced with. Lucica's home was clean, there was no need to use chlorine for me, but the informal education of the Hungarians in the village created expectations that she was trying to comply with.*

The re-occurring bleach reference indicates the belief that because Roma live in unsanitary conditions and have poor hygiene, are therefore a threat to public health. The solution is not thought to be (as common sense would have it), addressing the conditions that are assumed to put all in peril. Differently, the solution is imagined to be a prevention of disease transmission from the Roma to the non-Roma. Limiting Roma mobility and their interactions in the name of public health is not a new (racialized and discriminatory) practice, but one that has been used for hundreds of years in Europe (and in the colonies). Those on the move, and often labelled as 'Gypsy', were considered to be a health menace.[1]

This incident reminded me about the time when I first visited Anca and Doru's home and how I was impressed and a bit uncomfortable with how spotless their home was. I was scared to sit anywhere not to disturb the perfect order of their dwelling. Later Doru confessed: 'My wife cleaned the whole house knowing that you are coming.' I told him that she should not have done it, as I was convinced that the house was kept immaculately. He nodded smiling, and added: 'She was so nervous that a "gadje" would come to her home, and for sure that you would be concerned about cleanness, so she wanted to make sure that her house was spotless.' Trying to dismantle stereotypes about the community's hygene made the Roma much more *aware of their homes. Struggling to achieve a presumed standard of cleanliness, to fight a preconception about one's life based on their community, is one of the pillars of systematic racism and discrimination. It is a race that cannot be won, as the standards are not precise, not visible, not unmoveable, and a race where any detail, any gesture or word can 'disqualify' one in spite of their best efforts.*

Ormeniș, 24 June 2016

The dynamics I observed in Ormeniș were not exceptional. Throughout the years, I have been exposed to how a myriad of informal discriminatory acts against the Roma imbued everyday life and the structures of their society. The experiences outlined above highlighted how segregated the Roma community was; how criminalization was still a part of everyday discourses, with the police treating the community as a possible arsenal ready to explode; and how the situation is different from how the Roma described it during the interviews. Moreover, these encounters showed how, overall, the Roma community of Ormeniș was in transition, just like other traditional communities in the world, just like the Adivasi in India.

Recognition: structures of racism

What kind of Rom are you?

I don't know. Mostly being discriminated. When you are trying to get a job you are discriminated. They are simply ignoring you, mostly because you are Roma.

Dadu Aurica Marcela interview, 2017

We are Orthodox. Well – we know more languages. It is good and beautiful. We are proud that we aren't other kind of Roma. We are normal Roma.

Cocoraș Veronica interview, 2017

The (mis)recognition as 'Gypsy'

The (mis)recognition of Roma among Romanians, and Narikuravars among Tamilians, is typically related to the 'Gypsy' label. This is the result of a long racialization process that categorizes people, which both formally and informally places them in the social hierarchy. Both in Romania and India, being labelled as 'Gypsy' is often a social sentence to be endured. If one is (mis)recognized as a 'Gypsy', their equality and access to rights needs to be continuously affirmed and exercised, rather than assumed or taken for granted. While there might be notable exceptions in admitting one's ethnic identity as Roma and accepting them as equal members, this inclusion is often limited to specific groups, and has a fast-approaching deadline.

Ciprian Necula is now a well accomplished Roma activist, politician, researcher in international institutions and an academic. He is often invited to speak on mass-media channels, and is considered one of 'the good ones' from his community; he is now highly respected and appreciated, especially in selected elite Romanian (and beyond) circles, but his earlier life was marked by racism and discrimination: 'I grew up in Dristor [a neighbourhood in Bucharest]', he recalls during an interview in 2017. 'In my "hood" there was no one with higher education. When I was in Dristor, others identified me as Roma. First of all, because of the colour of my skin. No matter what we say today, people identify you as such.' As he speaks, I look at his skin colour which, while not really different from that of many Romanians, is nevertheless identified as 'dark' by racist-trained eyes. He continues:

Also, because in my building my grandparents lived at the 3rd floor, my mom and I at 7th floor, another aunt was at 6th floor. There was no one else like us in the neighbourhood. My grandpa worked downstairs in front of the building. He had an old car which he used as drawers to store his tools. He worked from there as a blacksmith and made a lot of noise, but he was tolerated because he was offering valuable services to the building. So, he was a 'gospodar', a good worker, so the Romanian neighbours did not mind him.

But, Necula says that not always was his Roma identity easily accepted, as he was often racialized:

In school I was identified as Roma because of the colour of the skin. Teachers played an important role. I was a good pupil; I was among the best in my class – at least until I decided to become a vagabond [he adds laughing]. When I was in third grade, I was given a 7 [equivalent of a C grade], and the teacher marked in red ink my paper, but I did not make any mistakes. I went home and I was sad, and my mom came to school with me to see what was the issue. The teacher told her: 'If to a "Gypsy" I give a ten [i.e., A], to a Romanian what should I give, a 15?' My mom was very upset, and got into a fight with the teacher, so I had to change schools. It was traumatic. Of course, my colleagues often call me 'Țigan' and so on [he says as in passing].

Necula's story is neither unique, nor unexpected. Roma children encounter these racist attitudes on a daily basis, and this solicits family members to prepare and protect them from racist encounters:

I was prepared by my grandma and others, so I would not be bothered if other kids are mean and say: 'You Gypsy', not to be upset. I was prepared to enter in the grown-up world. I had to face it. Especially when the teacher would say to the other children 'You drown like a "Țigan" at the shore' [synonym with not able to finish something] – I felt really bad, so I bow my head. When I was in high-school, in 1996, I saw Madalin Voicu on TV, who openly acknowledged that he was Roma, and he was supporting the rights of Roma. So, when I finished school, I called the Roma Party I started my activist path. And I entered the Roma movement. However, I had negative stereotypes about the Roma from my family, from mass media, from the entourage I had. So, I had internalized this [racism].

Necula interview, 2018

Also, in 2012, Cristiana Grigore wrote in the opinion section of the *New York Times* her story about growing up as a 'Gypsy' in Romania:

My parents and grandparents were well aware of the negative stereotypes of the Gypsies as rootless thieves and beggars, and they took pains to protect me. As a little girl, my mother dressed me in pale colors and cut my hair short so I would not look like a Gypsy. My father warned me never to steal, and to always associate with smart people. I can understand why my grandfather, a blacksmith, was so proud of buying a "corner of the village" and building houses for his children. My grandmother was a healer—not through magical powers but by volunteering to take people to the best doctors in the capital. (...) I grew up believing it was better not to be a Gypsy, yet I couldn't fully belong to "normal" society, either. I learned that I must not be the best in school.[2]

Grigore's experiences are not unique, as the Roma presence is often criminalized and exoticized even in their own country by people in their proximity. F 19 said in an interview with Roxana Marin in 2020,[3] recalling how in high-school she was:

The only Roma in the class, all my classmates knew. Although I was never directly discriminated against by a colleague, there were always racist stings or comments. In these situations, I always said something to sting them back. Somehow, they said that I was not like 'those bad gypsies who steal', for them I was still a babe. For others, we were aliens with exotic and unheard-of traditions.[4]

While in everyday life the identity of Roma comes under question and is equated with the 'Gypsy' label, legally the Roma's status[5] in Romania is less ambiguous.[6] The Roma have been declared to be a national minority and as a result they are beneficiaries of certain rights including the right to have education in their preferred language, and in localities where the minority numbers are 20(+) per cent of the local population, that signs, street names, etc. would be bilingual.[7] While this has been in effect since 1993, almost three decades later its implementation is still to be desired.

According to the European Parliament rapport of 2020: 'The current framework lacks coherence between priorities. Thematic areas of activity such as political participation, Roma art and culture, Roma language and Roma history should be explicitly mentioned in the post-2020 policy, as additional measures for the four main priority areas: Education, employment, housing and medical care.'[8]

In India, discrimination of the Narikuravars follows the logic of 'untouchability'. Even though it was legislated by the Untouchability Offences Act, 1955 and the Protection of Civil Rights Act, 1976 that declaring untouchability is a crime, modern forms of practicing 'untouchability' have been persisting.[9] India's discriminatory practices have a different historical background, which (while unpredictably similar) are based on 'caste' and 'untouchability'.[10] One of the places where the discrimination based on one's origin is painfully visible is temples,[11] which become sites of exclusion:

> I never used to go – I hated going to a temple in Salem District. There is a small place called Attur. This happened only in this particular temple. I am not generalizing all temples. Just this one. Usually, all community and caste people pray in that temple, but when the other communities go to the temple, we don't go. We will go when there is no crowd, on our own, [we] pray, and come back home.
>
> Prathiban, 20, interview, 2016

Fearing these discriminatory practices, at times the Narikuravars try not to disclose their identity: 'Some people are insecure, and scared that if they disclose to others that they are Narikuravar, they will not be accepted, and such people usually hide this detail from others. But I don't want to hide so. I openly told that I am a Narikuravar' (Prathiban, 20, interview, 2016).

Painstakingly similar to Grigore's experiences, even when the Narikuravars make strides forward and succeed in accessing equal rights, they are still worried about how they are seen by others:

> You know, in my mind I was saying to myself, you have to adjust to them. Are they asking me questions about who I am, but because I'm just coming from the minority community, and they feel that I got my achievements and my degree

because of that? Because, really, I'm good in my studies. Do, they feel they are too good for me? Or, maybe I am a concern to them? I feel discriminated in my mind.

Rajasekar an interview, March 2021

The fear of discrimination runs deep, and impacts the very self-understanding of the community. It is not surprising therefore that many Narikuravars, especially in the presence of other communities, do not inform them about their ethnic background. This is also to avoid the label of criminality they have been associated with for centuries:

> In both Europe and India between 17th and 19th century those who are not settled and frequently labeled as 'Gypsy' are often presented as 'criminals'. This intersection of nomadism and criminality is visible in both legal framework and literature of the time.

Dragomir, 2019: 62

Even today (i.e., 2021), the Narikuravars are often described in the media in connection to criminal acts: 'In a horrific incident, a gang of 12 Narikuravars were arrested by the forest department for killing a jackal using explosives near Jeeyapuram in Tiruchy on Monday. The group of miscreants went for honey harvesting to a village. While returning, they spotted the presence of a jackal roaming around. So in an attempt to hunt it down, the accused used country-made bombs and blew its jaw off', said a senior forest official. Reportedly, the incident came to light after a police constable spotted the group of Narikuravar drinking tea at a stall with the carcass in a shady bag. Seeing their suspective behaviour, he enquired with them. During the initial inquiry, it was found that they had hunted the jackal', added the forest officer.[12]

Thus, they are often assumed to be criminal, treated by officials as such, and imagined to be 'guilty' until they are proven innocent. This treatment is furthering the communities' access to recognition as equal members of the society, with equal rights and freedoms. These axes of racialization, misrecognition and criminalization intersect, forming a crux of discrimination (Crenshaw et al., 1996), which impacts the Roma's and Narikuravars' access to basic rights, such as education, housing, health care and employment.

The Roma often face 'suspicion and mistrust', and are seen as 'scape-goats and outcasts' (Crowe, 1996: 149). This is 'rooted in centuries of prejudice, [as] the negative public image of the Roma is an historical constant' (Ibid., 238). This misrecognition of the Roma identity at times has extreme and terrible repercussions that escalate into hatred and violent outbursts against those labelled as 'Gypsy' (Fonseca, 1996; Matache, Facebook, 2020).

Lack of redistribution: being denied access to resources

Being labelled as 'Gypsy' often impacts access to all areas of life,[13] including but not limited to access to basic human rights, such as education, housing, health care and employment. To ensure access to these rights, governmental programmes come into play. However, communities labelled as 'Gypsy' both in India and Romania often face dire conditions and extreme limitations when accessing them.

Education and schooling

Anca and Doru work in education within Roma communities, striving to bring equitable access to school and quality education for Roma children of Ormeniş. It is not surprising that these topics were always important points in our conversation, and issues that have been engaged with and cared about deeply. As we have seen in the example at the beginning of this chapter, the village of Ormeniş, while it has only one school, provides in effect segregated education. Of course, officially the separation between Roma children and others was made based on language used for their education, and the Roma kids are assigned to the Romanian speaking section. In effect, the Romanian section is composed of Roma children, which allows educators and staff to segregate the groups, and to enforce discriminatory practices (such as cleaning with bleach only after the Roma children).

The local school in Ormeniş provides education until the 8th standard. To further their education, the pupils need to go to the nearby city of Braşov and learn in urban high-schools. However, as we have seen previously, the transportation to those schools is sporadic, inefficient and expensive. These factors create insurmountable obstacles for even the most dedicated students, and while many of the Roma would like to further their education, they often find it really difficult. In the past, to accommodate their special social and economic circumstances, programmes – such as adult education – have been in place in Ormeniş with the support of the state. They were remembered by the Roma I interviewed as positive endeavours that supported the community. However, as funds were no longer available the programmes stopped, and with them the possibilities of their schooling died out. As many scholars (Sigona and Trehan, 2009) point out, this lack of programming is often based on how the community is seen: Many officials still hold essentialist views that imagine Roma culture as antithetic to formal education, and blame this on the Roma's nomadism. While the dropout rate of Roma children from schools is alarming (Andrei et al., 2011), the assumption that this is an inherent ethnic trait needs to be severely interrogated by turning the tables around and asking uncomfortable questions such as: What type of education is provided that many Roma (and Narikuravar) reject? Moreover, when in school, how is work with communities done to accommodate those who have different traditions, including those who are mobile? How are formal education systems able (or not) to accommodate different manners of schooling? And, importantly: How realistic is access to schooling – considering aspects such as: Transport, cost, meals, safety etc. Until these questions are addressed, policy making risks reproducing vague, incomplete and essentializing views, which further racialize and discriminate communities.

Of course, the situation of the Roma in Ormeniş is not exceptional. According to the World Bank report of 2014:

> Roma students' participation to compulsory education is considerably lower compared to their non-Roma neighbors, with a significant gender gap in favor of boys. Enrolment rates in compulsory education are significantly lower for Roma compared to non-Roma children living nearby. In the age group 7–15, the enrolment rate of Roma is 78% and that of non-Roma living nearby is nearly 95%. Significant gender gap can be noticed in case of Roma students: 76% of girls are enrolled, vs. 81% of boys in this age group. This gender gap seems to be specific to Roma: Among non-Roma students, girls have higher enrolment rates (97%) than boys (93%).[14]

As in India, Kalpana Kannabiran's study of 2017 revealed that 'although there is a proliferation of private schools across the country, (…) children from the most marginalised communities continue to attend government schools' (Kannabiran, 2017: 1). The Narikuravar community of Karamadurai faces similar issues. They have a local school where children can study until 4th standard within the community. Their 'settlement' school is rather remote, and during community visits I found that it was difficult to get and keep committed teachers willing to commute to remote areas, and of course who are willing to work with communities that are often perceived as 'polluted'. To this the people in the village saw one solution: The Narikuravars from the community get educated, and then become teachers back home. This solution is nevertheless far from perfect, for it takes a long time – this is a generational solution; it does not take into account that after being educated individuals might want to move to other communities; and of course, that this approach might encourage isolation of the Narikuravar children.

These issues also bring to the fore one fundamental point that is as sensitive as it is overlooked: How should the Adivasi/Narikuravar children be educated? What type of education is most conducive? In my conversations with the community activists and leaders, like Rajasekaran and Anuradha, their view was firm: Residential schools for Narikuravars, run by the Narikuravars (with the help of the government and of other civil society bodies) is seen as the best form of education. They both shared with me that this is the way to ensure social mobility for their community, that children would be supported logistically and economically, while also being protected from discriminatory practices of other communities, who 'do not understand us' (Anuradha interview, 2017). While residential schools are highly regarded by the Narikuravars, they are also seen as 'a partial alienation' (Gupta and Padel, 2019). In these schools, the Adivasi tribes have low literacy and high dropout rates, combined with losing their traditional knowledge and reducing their value system. Moreover, according to Gupta and Padel (2019) these schools have tribal children being taught a version of modernity that alienates them from their tribal culture and forms of life.

The issue of separated schools for those labelled as 'Gypsy' is not endemic to India, but to Europe as well:

> In the Czech Republic, segregation persists, despite the 2007 decision of the Strasbourg Court in the case of D.H. and others vs. Czech Republic, and the adoption of a new school law in 2004, which restructured the special needs education measure. (…) It is estimated that 30% of Roma children are still educated in schools for children with mild mental disabilities, compared to only 2% of non-Roma children. These practices are also present in other countries. The Commissioner took a stand against all forms of segregation in education and called for clear obligations and measurable progress in the field of desegregation and inclusive education. Desegregation must be combined with the support measures needed for children to adapt to integrated classrooms and succeed and excel in education.[15]

(Mis)recognition under the 'Gypsy' label is intertwined on the ground with practices of (mal)distribution and (mis)representation. As such, those who are labelled as 'Gypsy' are often excluded or marginalized from state support in education, housing and health care. Thus, the Commissioner Report of the Council of Europe (2011) outlined the systemic discrimination faced by Roma children and their families, whose right to education is trampled on, as 'in some countries, the fact that Roma and nomads do not have personal documents has a negative impact on school enrollment.' Lack of public transport or funding for it, as well as lack of school supplies are additional obstacles for Roma students trying to attend a school.'[16] Contrary to the belief held by many about the Narikuravars' and Roma's reticence to formal education, in the communities in which I did my research, education was seen as one of the most basic needs for their community to succeed, and to address the other (interrelated) issues.

Limited access to education is also the result of lack of adequate housing. While supported by special governmental programmes,[17] Roma and Narikuravars are often allocated to unhabitable and/or undesired housing areas, which further reinforces structural racism. For example, in Europe:[18]

> Discrimination against access to housing is reported in a number of Member States; it often takes the form of refusing access to public and private rental space, which is accessible to others, or even refusing to sell housing to Roma. Some local authorities have pursued a policy of segregation in terms of housing. This has sometimes been accentuated by the insulating walls erected near Roma neighborhoods. Such destructive measures must cease. Many Roma continue to live in sub-standard conditions in most European countries, without heating, running water or sewer systems.[19]

Structural racism of (un)housed communities furthers discrimination, and has repercussions on their access to health care and health care insurance. In the research conducted in 2017 with Mara Zafiu, we had fifty-one open-ended, qualitative interviews with Narikuravar women, who revealed how not only did the Narikuravar women (in our study) actively seek health care access, but that they were eager to use government provided health insurance schemes. However, due to their limited education, poverty and poor housing/mobile life style, they received health care only in emergency situations, and often needed to pay for those services from their small earnings, which increased their financial burden (Dragomir and Zafiu, 2019).

Similarly, in their 2012 work, Das and Mehta showed that while Adivasis have been making significant gains in health indicators, they have poor access to health facilities, as 'in most states in India, Scheduled Tribes live in physically isolated hamlets, in remote regions and districts and in hilly and forested areas with poorly staffed health centers' (Das and Mehta, 2012: 3) and they are still confroned by a higher than average child mortality (Das et al., 2010).[20]

When working in Ormeniş, similar issues relating to access to health care became obvious. The Roma women recalled stories of giving birth on the road because of not receiving medical assistance in time, as the ambulances took too long to reach the village. They shared with me the reticence that the local doctor exhibits each time they come into her office. How they are always pushed to the back of the line, and that sometimes they need to wait for days to be seen by the doctor.

As I was conducting fieldwork, I was hosted by one of the Roma women in Olt Street. Her home was a modest house at the end of the unpaved road, with no current water, and with the toilet in the backyard. Jeni was 53, but looked considerably older. As we were talking in the kitchen, a young boy, about seven years of age, was also with us. Jeni was telling me how hard it was for the Roma women to receive health care. She said that some years back she went to the doctor because her stomach was growing, and she had a lot of problems with digestion. When, finally, the doctor received her in the office, she asked her a few questions, but never consulted her, as in: She never touched her, or sent her for any tests. However, after a brief visit she was diagnosed with cirrhosis (i.e., liver cancer) and given medicine. Jeni started the medication and took it for weeks, but her health was worsening. When it became unbearable, she called for an ambulance, and she was taken to the hospital in Brașov. There, she was informed that she was seven months pregnant. Hearing this she was surprised, as she thought she had reached menopause, and asked the emergency doctor if she should keep taking the cirrhosis medicine. But as the tests proved, she was only pregnant. The boy was born shortly after, and Jeni was grateful that the boy was born healthy. As she said this, Jeni lovingly looked at her son, gently stroking his short hair.

The lack of proper medical attention and engagement with the women from the Roma community is notorious. In India, the Narikuravar women shared similar experiences:

> In hospitals, as soon as others see us, they hold their nose – as if we stink. They think we smell badly; we do not take bath – like that. Even during work, people do not come nearby us. They stay away and buy things. They always humiliate us. Public used to threaten their children by saying they will hand over the children to us, as if we are dangerous or horrible people. Sometimes, I shouted back at them, and asked them to treat us as normal human being.
>
> Velakani, 20, in Dragomir and Zafiu, 2019: 75

As the discrimination against those labeled as 'Gypsy,' persists in all instances, it revealed the systemic prevalence of discrimination in health care. Doru shared during one of our encounters: 'We face many instances when doctors did not pay attention to us. Especially, during the night in the emergency room. When they see us, they say: "What?! you are here to disturb us in the middle of the night". "Hei! slow down" [he continues as if answering the imaginary medical staff] "we are not here socially, but because we have a problem." This is the treatment we typically get, especially from the nurses' (Doru interview, 2016).

The lack of medical attention for the Roma is (again) not only specific to the sites I researched. Referring to Roma across Europe, Földes and Covaci also highlighted that:

> Health inequalities experienced by Roma people living in Europe presents a persisting challenge for health research and practice. Available literature on Roma and health agrees that: (1) Roma people suffer from poorer health and unhealthier living conditions compared to majority populations, (2) better data are needed to explain the Roma health gap and design better interventions to reduce this gap and (3) the poor health of Roma is closely linked to the social determinants of health.
>
> Földes and Covaci, 2012: 37[21]

Also, in India, women from Adivasi communities are more likely to bear 'the high burden of preventable diseases [as] there are large disparities between different classes' access to health care, with the poor, women, and Scheduled Tribes and Castes having the lowest access' (Dragomir and Zafiu, 2019: 65–6).

Redistribution: poverty and employment

The Roma and Narikuravars' systemic marginalization has been for a long time entangled with their structural exclusion from formal employment. To overcome this, in India, there have been special reservations for Adivasi employment. However, these special rights are not rights that are accessible to all. According to the World Bank, only:

> A few elites among the STs had access to and benefited from reserved jobs, while a significant proportion [of Adivasis] served as manual labor in construction projects. (. . .) Only a little over 8 percent of Adivasi men are in nonfarm jobs to start with and that these are clearly people who may have acquired upward mobility over several generations of education and movement out of rural areas. In public employment, too, it is often not possible to find qualified ST candidates even to fill the reserved quotas.
>
> World Bank, 2011: 45[22]

Overall, the economic situation of the Adivasis is dire:

> While India is widely considered a success story in terms of growth and poverty reduction, Adivasis in 2004–05 were 20 years behind the average. The poverty headcount index for Scheduled Tribes fell by 31 percent between 1983 and 2004–05. In comparison, poverty fell by about 35 percent among the Scheduled Castes and by 40 percent at an all-India level. The relatively slower decline in poverty among Adivasis means that they are increasingly concentrated in the poorest deciles. Comprising about 8 percent of India's population, Adivasis accounted for a fourth of the population living in the poorest wealth decile in 2005. More worryingly, in states with high tribal populations (more than 10 percent of the state's total population), Adivasi households exhibited poverty rates that were higher than the rates across the nation as a whole in 2004–05.
>
> Das and Mehta, 2012: 1

This situation is even more calamitous for the Narikuravars, who – while facing extreme poverty as other Adivasi communities – are not recognized as ST (but are MBC) and therefore they compete with many more communities for government reservations. The Narikuravars often brought up these issues during our conversation. There was nowhere to work in their small 'settlement', and outside jobs were really difficult to procure. Obtaining formal employment was a difficult endeavour, even for the educated folks. Praveen is a young (24 years old) Narikuravar man from Karamadai. He is married, and both his wife and him have BA degrees; Praveen also has an MA in Computer Science. However, none of them could find work in the nearby towns, so now they are living at his parents' home, hoping to find employment.

Limited employment opportunities, and therefore ways to empower themselves economically are often a sobering reality for those labelled as 'Gypsy'. During the interviews, both the Roma and the Narikuravars often told me that being from Ormeniş, or from the Karamadai 'settlment', and sometimes because of their name, their ethnic identity is identifiable to possible employers, and this limits their chances of getting a job. In addition, even if they get a job in the city, transportation to work is both expensive and limited. In Romania, a round trip bus ticket to Braşov is almost 5 $/day, which is a considerable amount of money that is often unavailable to folks looking for a job. For the people in Karamadai, transportation is even more scarce, and unreliable. Furthermore, obtaining employment is also linked to having a permanent address, and an ID that many Narikuravars do not have.[23]

This situation forces them to look for alternative employment options closer to home (or far away). In Ormeniş, the Roma often have to work as daily-labourers for the Hungarian and Romanian farmers, helping them in the fields. However, these menial jobs are unsteady, and do not pay enough to ensure their survival. The Roma women I spoke with told me that they would like to be hired as cleaning ladies at the school or clinic in the village, but that it is hard to get these jobs, which usually are allocated to the Hungarian and Romanian women. As a result, for the Roma in Ormeniş, the main source of income is their unemployment insurance that they receive monthly, but it is never enough to make ends meet.

Exclusion from employment opportunities furthers long lasting discrimination. In a multi-country (Bulgaria, Czech Republic, Hungary, Romania and Slovakia) research of structured narrative interviews conducted by the European Roma Rights Center (ERRC) in 2006, with 402 working-age Roma, it was documented that there is massive systemic discrimination in the area of employment (Hyde, 2006).[24] Finding employment is often obstructed by structural discrimination, which is 'intensified by prejudiced and stereotypical views'. This is typically blamed by the non-Roma on 'the Romani culture and their lifestyle; they do not fit with the discipline of work. Roma do not have the motivation to work; they are unreliable, lazy and prefer to live on social assistance than earn a living.'[25]

These deeply rooted stereotypes were refuted again and again during my fieldwork within Roma communities. Roma men and women were often telling me how difficult it was to make ends meet, *because* they could not find employment in their area. They did not refer to the state or to unemployment insurance, but they referred to the lack of employment opportunities because of being identified as Roma. Those who 'pass' as non-Roma have to hide their identity to keep their jobs. Mihaiu Corcoraş (interview, 2016) shared with me his experience of working in the city:

> I was working, and doing a good job. Then, we needed more people to work for us, and I called on more people from Ormeniş, whom I knew were looking for jobs. Soon after they started working, I was called by my boss: 'Why did you employ "Gypsies"? Listen if you do not fire them, we will change our collaboration.' I wanted to take a stand, but the others, my partners, said we need to be silent and we did. And like this it was all good.

The issue of discrimination in employment persists further after hiring. Doru, who is highly educated, reflected upon his experiences at work in schools: 'When they want something, they call us Roma. When you make a mistake, you are no longer a Roma. You are a "Gypsy". "Hey 'Gypsy' why did you do that?" they often reproach. But the term "Gypsy" is ugly, and it is a tool used to hurt us, to make us feel bad and to get us to react', he explained in 2017.

Endemic discrimination of the Roma and Narikuravars hinders their inclusion in the labour market,[26] and often pushes them to migrate and to the informal market. Besides creating dynamics of exclusions and reinforcing hierarchies of power, these techniques are long-lasting, leading to circles of poverty, criminalization and racialization. Moreover, as Gheorghe and Mirga (1997), and Necula (personal communication) argue, this structural issue is problematic as the Roma risk being perceived as an ethno-class:

> Historically, the Roma have been treated as an inferior and undesirable group, which has generated, through social exclusion and marginalization, a precarious general economic situation for most members of the Roma community, especially for those living in compact communities. (...) 'It seems that the political dimension of the Romani issue is nearing a solution as a growing number of states recognize the Roma as a legitimate national/ethnic minority and as the appreciation of the human rights problems faced by the Roma increases. Other issues will move to the fore, those concerning social problems of the Roma: Education, housing, employment, and health care. Because of the underdevelopment and marginality of the Romani community, the growing unemployment, especially among the Roma, and the demographic growth of the Romani community, there is a danger of its evolving into an ethno-class or underclass, and thus further perpetuating its marginality in society' (Gheorghe and Mirga, 1997).
>
> Necula, unpublished work

The danger of this association between class and ethnicity is something that might affect Indian communities as well. Thus, addressing this would be an important step in addressing redistribution for Roma and Narikuravar communities, and thus it is paramount that a common front is created to combat what 'sociologists, labor economists, and most Gypsy leaders agree [on:] that the vast majority of Roma became unemployed because they cannot compete on the labor market' (Barany, 2002: 174).

Politics and representation

To date, both Roma and Narikuravars have modest political representation. The Narikuravars do not have any one representing them in local, state or national politics. If they would be identified as Adivasi, or as ST, then their political representation might be different. Scheduled Tribes have several reserved seats in the Parliament of India, State Assemblies, urban and rural-level institutions. As STs still face political marginalization, reservations of political seats have become the primary means of empowerment, meant to ensure the 'redistribution of political resources in favor of the marginalised communities' (Ambagudia, 2019: 44). Nevertheless, to date 'the political reservation system has brought both hope and despair among the STs' (Ibid.).

In Romania, the Roma Party was founded by Nicolae Păun and Gheorghe Răducanu in 1990. It currently has one reserved seat in the Romanian Chamber of Deputies. However, in 2012 the party has signed with the PSD (the Social Democratic Party of Romania, which is a left-wing party, whose corruption issues have been making waves over the past three decades) a political agreement of mutual support in parliamentary elections, hoping to further the implementation of objectives aimed at the Roma community.

Roma politicians ('asumaţi' – i.e., self-identified as Roma) like Petre-Florin Manole,[27] who is a deputy in the Romanian Parliament, or Dana Varga who was the State Adviser in the Cioloş government,[28] joined the PSD ranks in national politics. Others, like Damian Drăghici[29] have joined the Group of the Progressive Alliance of Socialists and Democrats, and have been representing Romania in the European Parliament since 2014.

These politicians are sometimes seen as separated from the community, not in touch with the 'grass roots politics', following their individual goals and not those of their community, or even being pawns in the national political schemes that further the interest of the majoritarian (corrupted) leaders. Thus, while they have visibility and a certain political clout, their work is in effect limited, with NGOs and other members of the civil society playing a more relevant role in the life of the Romanian Roma.

The Narikuravars in Tamil Nadu do not (yet) have political aspirations. Narikuravars are faced with similar obstacles, like many other Adivasi communities:

> Physical remoteness and smaller numbers have gone together with political isolation and low voice in decision making for the Scheduled Tribes. There have been measures to assure defacto autonomy and self-rule to Adivasis, but implementation has been patchy. The Indian government's response to vulnerability among Scheduled Tribes has been proactive and has included a mix of constitutional and budgetary instruments.
>
> Das and Mehta, 2012: 3

In turn, the Narikuravars hope to garner the attention of the current people in power to ensure that their views are represented, and their immediate needs are addressed. These multiple structural forms of discrimination and marginalization reproduce and reinforce hierarchies of power that place the Roma and the Narikuravars in 'subaltern' positions, which – as we will see in the following two chapters – they fight on many fronts.

Discrimination: denial and acknowledgement

Racism, discrimination and xenophobia are structural. They work through rules, legal measures, institutional processes and everyday practices. They are taught from a very young age. We are all taught, formally and informally, how to distinguish who looks and is like us, and who does not. We train eyes and other sensory organs to inform us of the minute differences. This information ends up creating structures of power and hierarchies that we all inhabit and reinforce. As such, these structures of oppression are intertwined, and at times difficult to untangle and point out.

Concepts like race and ethnicity/community gain currency in social science, and are in full use in classifying people. However, in the case of Roma and Narikuravar, in general with communities labelled as 'Gypsies', these differential markers, these classifications are not so precise. While on the level of everyday interactions, people can tell 'who is' Roma or Narikuravar, when asked to explain how can one tell, the task is complicated, and answers are imprecise, at best referring to their skin colour, clothing, social status, geographical presence, language and speaking/social manners. One day, as I was preparing to go into Coimbatore with my new translator to meet urban Narikuravars, I asked: 'How will we meet them?' To this he replied: 'They are in the roads, in some well-known areas.' I insisted, and asked how will we know they are Narikuravars? He shrugged his shoulders, and answered slightly annoyed by my assumed disbelief: 'I know them. By looking at them.' I received the same answer in Romania when I asked how some knew some folk were Roma. Often my interlocutors would roll their eyes and tell me that of course they 'know', and if I insisted, they will say 'by their dark(er) colour, clothing or behaviours'. This esoteric knowledge of the community is based on the informal means in which people are classified, and reiterated by the ways in which we interact with folk coming from different groups.

The outsider knowledge is at best imprecise, but often generalizes, placing diverse people under racist labels: 'In Romanian eyes, it does not matter how many years would pass, we would still be "Gypsies". They will continue to discriminate us. Wherever you go and knock at a door, when they hear our name or where we are from, you are no longer received as you should be', shared Doru (interview, 2016). He continued:

> In Romania, racism is as strong as it gets, and no one does anything about it. I myself think: 'I am Roma and I am small. I can't do anything else.' I can see this attitude happening at the level of our small locality, but also at the country level. All are talking about the state help that Roma receive. I am tired of this. Maybe I'm a little pissed off about it as well. When I think about development, I can see that the Roma have no chance.
>
> I don't encourage my community to ask for state programmes to help either, because our community is used to receiving ... the system got them used to it. Social assistance has become the main source of income, and that has a lot to do with it. The system and the politicians want to create dependency because they want to destabilize the community, and ensure that the Roma do not form [political] alliances. So, they blame it on the Roma's work ethic, [and] then give them social aid, which doesn't even buy them the daily bread. The poor Roma indulge in poverty.
>
> Doru, 42, interview, 2017

Raul (interview, 2017), a young Roma from Ormeniş, also shared with me the palpable dynamics of racism he faces: 'I tell you honestly only Romanians and Hungarians call us: '"Gypsies" borâţi" [i.e., vomited]. I don't want to offend you', he says apologetically, acknowledging that I am not from his community, 'but if you work with someone in a company, and he knows you're a "Gypsy", after a few minutes you're a '"Gypsy" borât" for him', Raul continued, signalling the widespread discrimination he often encounters.

Raul comes from a long-lasting Roma family, and as his mother says 'we are Romanian-ized "Gypsy"', meaning that they had been living together with Romanians for generations. Physically, in spite of the dire training that Romanians have to 'detect' the Roma, Raul could be seen as a Romanian. But Raul knows that this identification is precarious, and – when ethnically identified – he is likely to be the victim of discriminatory practices.

While the persisting, prevalent, systematic and historically rooted forms of racism are visible in both Romania and India, when asked directly – not all Roma and Narikuravars I engaged with – would admit that they are confronted by racism in their life. This attitude puzzled me, and I started my inquiry into how they perceived forms of racism.

People like Doru and Anca were confidently articulating the racist and discriminatory behaviour they encountered: 'The people in the village say: Put all of Roma in one boat, and send them into the sea, so they will all drown. And they claim that if this would happen, then there will been no need for police in our village', Doru told me during an interview in the summer of 2017, referring to the Ormeniş non-Roma's view, which implied that the Roma are the cause of local crime, and not having Roma in the community would lead to the end of criminality.

Similarly, Eva told me as we sat down and had coffee in her friend's home:

'Gypsies' are not well-seen; especially those who are not educated. And even if you are, you are still a 'Gypsy' to them. But we are human beings, man! Like everyone else. If you do not go to this school, or had certain possibilities it does not mean you are inferior. Especially if you do not hurt anyone. The 'Gypsies' here, who are day labourers, work for the Hungarians, and are still called 'Gypsies', with no first names. They got used to behaving like this towards us; because they are allowed to. If we work for them, we are humiliated. I can't take that. I could not be humiliated as such. I have a name. And you know it. Just call me by name.

Eva, 47, interview in Ormenis, 2017

The denigratory behaviour of Hungarians towards the Roma of Ormeniş was also articulated by Mihai (64 years old, interview, 2016): 'The Hungarians were used to have "Gypsies" as their servants, working the land. Because of this they think we are inferior – but what kind of inferiority are we talking about?!', Mihai said, referring to how class differences are being reorganized into systems of oppressions, and hierarchies of power that often place the Roma in 'subaltern' places.

This hierarchy is often perpetuated in the media, as Rodica (53, interview in Ormenis) told us: 'Mass-media presents us like this. There are some Roma who make stupid things and spoil our image', she says, referring to the way in which the media often use the Roma image as a scapegoat, and also exaggerates the dynamics within the communities.

However, while Rodica admitted that the media is biased in its portraying of the community, when I asked her about experiencing discrimination in her daily life in the village, she negated it. She said that her children did not experience racism in schools, and that her daughter is 'well liked' at her job. Similarly, even though she recognized the systemic discrimination of the Roma, when I asked him about his individual experience at work, even Doru said: 'I do not face discrimination on the part of the school staff. If I were ever faced with it, I would know how to answer them. Honestly, at school I consider myself superior to them', he says, referring to his graduate degree and his pursuance of his doctorate. 'I have the attitude of superiority. Also, keep in mind that these are also well-trained colleagues. (...) Generally, when people are professional, and well-prepared, discrimination disappears. For example, when I was in college, students didn't perceive me as a Roma' (interview, 2017).

While talking to the Narikuravars in Tamil Nadu, the same direct denial of discrimination was often exhibited: 'No, nothing like that has ever happened' (Vijaya interview, 2016).[30] But the experience of discrimination often transpired. When I first went to the Narikuravar 'settlement,' I met one of the elder men in the community, the one who described himself as the 'president of Gypsy'. I asked him what is their relationship with other communities. He promptly responded: 'They are good. They do not think we are thieves.' As I was unfamiliar with the community and its relationships with others, I was surprised by this answer. However, after the visit, the translator pointed out that the Narikuravars are referred to as the 'vagabonds', and assumed to be petty-thieves. This brought to the fore the prevalence of negative stereotypes, which reinforced dynamics and hierarchies, and also revealed their inclination to deny these discriminatory practices.

Denial of experiencing racism and discrimination has been observed and studied by behaviourists and physiologists (Crosby et al., 1980; Guidmond and Dubé-Simard, 1983). While this scholarship is helpful in understanding the phenomena's psychological behaviour consequences, as well as the sociological education implications, the political implications – specifically its ties to accessing social justice – are not yet thoroughly explored.

In her work, Fage Crosby (1984) looked at women and gender discrimination and argued that while women are disadvantaged by their gender, they are not likely to acknowledge that fact, and often deny their own 'victimization'. Even more puzzling for her was that 'at the very moment that a woman denies her own disadvantage, she recognizes that women are generally disadvantaged' (Crosby, 1984: 372). In Crosby's view, women faced with gender discrimination formulated an incomplete syllogism that otherwise would follow: 'If all women are disadvantaged, I am a woman, therefore I am disadvantaged.' This logic leads to asking 'how to make sense of women containment in spite of obvious dissemination' (Ibid.). Researchers, Crosby tells us, have found many examples of groups who were unwilling to pay the psychological price of affirmation, as it is too hard to go against the status quo, and chose to deny being subjected to disadvantages. Crosby reflects that 'this could be understood as a symptom of people's need to believe in a just world. ... We want to be sure that people get their just desserts, and that we will engage in cognitive distortions to convince ourselves that people are actually the recipients of their deserved outcomes' (Ibid., 374–5). An alternative explanation that Crosby presents is a cognitive bias as 'the difficulty of inferring discrimination from individual cases, but easier when speaking about a larger group, if data is provided' (Ibid., 379).

Roma scholar Margareta Matache (2016, personal correspondence) describes this refusal to acknowledge discrimination as the result of internalization of racism: 'Roma have internalized and reconciled themselves with the inferiority status imposed by *Gadje*, to the point in which anti-Roma racism experiences become normalized behaviors or Roma would try really hard to fit into the white cultural norms.' Furthermore, internalizing racism is typically related with a feeling of disempowerment and fatalism.

Similarly, in his now classic book on prejudice, Allport (2012) explained that members of minority groups tend to accommodate to majority opinions, and in turn internalize the negative image of themselves that dominant groups exhibit. Thus, according to this argument, many Roma and Narikuravars deny the experience of discrimination, not because they do not perceive it, but because they feel it is futile to bring it up, as the system has been designed to continue its hierarchical structure. For example, many times during the interviews, participants would add that there are some in the community who do not behave in an honourable way, and therefore are the cause of the discriminatory behaviour, which is a fair response to anti-social elements.

Ambivalence and dignity

Another reason for the refusal to acknowledge discrimination was suggested that it is done because the Roma and the Narikuravars recognize discrimination, but admitting they suffer from it – is admitting that they are victims. The victim status is one that sits uncomfortably with people who see themselves as victors and survivors against all odds. Margareta Matache (2016, personal correspondence) argues that another plausible reason for these denials of personal experience of discrimination based on perceived 'Gypsy' identity is not because they do not experience or fail to see it, but it is due to the fact that once they admit it, they lose their dignity. She said:

In a global context in which Roma have no access to discourse powers, non-Roma continue to portray Roma as inferior others. This type of symbolic power prevents Roma who experience anti-Roma racism to be able to feel safe or to be willing to talk about it. For instance, some of the young people we worked with in Serbia emphasized a sense of shame and discomfort to talk about the humiliating experience of anti-Roma racism. We also experienced that in Romania, when we used 'testers' at Romani CRISS to prove the discrimination of Roma youth in public places. Many agreed it was still a humiliating experience to talk about, even though they put themselves in that situation.

People from the Roma and Narikuravar communities acknowledge the difficulties that their community are struggling with, but at the personal level they refuse to engage with them, and in this way preserve their human dignity. This is an important factor that needs to be understood in the context of conducting qualitative research, where the participants and the interviewer (and interpreter) spend a great deal of time together, participating in different activities. As relationships tend to be (more) horizontal, participants present themselves in a more equalitarian way, and admitting personal victimhood could possibly jeopardize their position vis-à-vis the person in front of them.

Fear, economic dependency and equality

The third explanation was suggested by Doru, who bluntly suggested 'it is fear', suggesting that Roma are afraid that their proclamation of discrimination might reach the ears of local authorities, who might use this as leverage in refusing to give them social assistance. Just like the Roma in Ormeniş, the Narikuravars in the Karamadai settlement are highly dependent on rations, and live on land with no proprietory rights. Therefore, this dependence on state resources might influence their responses to the question of discrimination.

Matache also agreed that: 'As many could anticipate instances of discrimination, they also create defense mechanisms to protect themselves (e.g. some wear nicer clothes when meeting with the *Gadje*; others don't stay long in the sun so that they can maintain light skin complexion)' (2016, personal correspondence).

Another factor is implicit in the dynamic of the research. As I am not from the community and I am perceived as a part of the larger majority, the participants did not want to create any frictions, and wanted to please. Not to create a negative image of themselves and potentially insult the interviewer, the participants deny being discriminated against, and thus preserve their dignity. Moreover, for many of the participants who fear loss of social and economic support, and who would like to preserve their individual dignity, it might not be clear what discrimination is or how it works.

Rather than asking for one cause for these denials, I suggested looking into a more complex framework, which presents the intersection of fear, dignity and lack of awareness and understanding of discrimination practices. This intersectionality could explain further how some of the respondents deny experiencing discrimination.

Conclusion: beyond discrimination

The European Commission for Human Rights recommended that 'Member States must ensure that their national legislation and practice are in line with the case law of the European Court of Human Rights and the European Committee of Social Rights in all these four areas. Of particular importance is the immediate relocation of Roma children to integrated educational settings – where they receive the necessary support – in the classroom, but also in other relevant forms – so that they succeed – and excel in the educational process.'[31] Furthermore, they advised that 'the human rights situation for Roma and Nomads must be addressed as a whole, and the various areas addressed simultaneously'.[32] The Commission further declared that 'wherever possible, targets should be set that go beyond the four EU goals of Roma integration', related to access to education, employment, health services and housing.

Similarly in India, a World Bank report urged that 'addressing the development needs of tribal groups will be central to attaining India's goal of shared growth'. Furthermore, they argued that 'more discussion of tribal aspirations and problems from their point of view is needed, rather than an examination of such issues through the lens of policy makers, the bureaucracy, or the civil society' (Das and Metha, World Bank Report).[33]

The enduring phenomenon of racial discrimination requires immediate attention. The adoption and implementation of anti-discrimination legislation is a necessary step, as shared by Roland, a Roma activist from Budapest, Hungary:

> Roma are victims all the time. It is time to change this political narrative, which makes us seem to be a victim by ourselves. Over the past decades we went to various international conferences; we discuss what are the problems within hours of speeches. We do not talk about the huge power, the economic power that over one million people have. But, there are not positive narratives created [about the Roma] by the mainstream. You hear the negative one, and you start believing in them and this creates a cage for you. It is extremely difficult to get

out of the cage. So, Roma do not understand how much they are really discriminated against. Racism is not extraordinary. It is a political way to thinking and a form of victimization creating certain obstacles, so when we try to get our voice out it is more difficult.

Roland Ferkovics interview, 2016

Following this vision, the next chapters aim to empower these voices and challenge the narratives of victimization, by showing how Roma and Narikuravar fight these entrenched forms of racialization and discrimination in numerous ways.

Formal Practices of Aiming for Justice

Attention: Romanian political parties that have registered for the European Parliament elections
To: All candidates for a seat in the European Parliament (regardless of party, ideology, region, ethnicity, religion or gender).[1]
Ref: #Aresel! #That's enough! #Enough! #Enough! #Eleg!

Dear [political] candidates,

During the electoral campaigns, our vote, of the Roma, is equal to that of any Romanian citizen, and you know this best, because suddenly in the Roma communities electoral representatives appear. But, the rest of the time, we are no longer treated with the same interest and that's why we say #Aresel! #That's enough! We know that many times you avoid going through 'Gypsy', to see the problems we face every day and the reality in which we live. As long as local politicians vote for 'Gypsies', the mechanism works, politics goes on, and we continue to struggle in poverty and segregation, generation after generation.

We, after 28 years of democracy, say #Aresel! #That's enough!

We believe in the common good and humanity, not in manipulation and corruption!

We do not generalize. We know they are different politicians. There are those who choose to ignore 'Gypsy', or those who talk about inappropriate public policies for most Roma, theoretical luxuries, such as organic food or the transition to electric cars. There are those politicians who forget or choose to ignore that more than half of the Roma families barely survive from one day to the next due to the systematic marginalization, poverty and discrimination they are subjected to in Romania.

For this reason, because you ignore us, we tell you #Enough! #Aresel!

We are citizens of this country, and you represent us. We also want you to talk about our needs and problems!

Ladies and gentlemen politicians, #Aresel with the old techniques of obtaining Roma votes!

We, the signatories of this petition, regardless of your 'attention' and the remaining promises at this stage, do not vote for you without publicly presenting solutions for the socio-economic inclusion of Roma, combating hatred and discrimination against Roma and promoting Roma culture from / to Romania.

We, dear candidates, want you to respect the following principles for the Roma community in our country:

1. *Always use the word Rom when referring to us. We are Romanian citizens of Roma ethnicity, and you represent us by the vote with which you were invested.*
2. *Publicly condemn discrimination and geographical, school or hospital discrimination against Roma and initiate resolutions in the European Parliament to financially penalize (minus points on European funding, for example) local authorities promoting ethnic and gender segregation and discrimination.*
3. *Come and discuss with us, in our communities, where your policies need to make a significant difference. This will make it easier for you to understand our problems.*
4. *Organize meetings with local government representatives to stimulate interventions and investments in Roma communities.*
5. *Hire Roma young people in the office of MEP and prepare them for a political career.*
6. *Encourage the civic and political participation of Roma women and take into account the gender dimension when formulating public policies for the Roma ethnic group.*
7. *To propose European strategies based on local solutions, based on public consultations with members of the Roma communities, integrated (i.e. to reflect all dimensions of local issues) in the social cohesion programs of the European Commission, the Romanian Government and local authorities.*

If you assume the above principles, dear candidates, we are waiting for you on May 18, 2019 at the EU2019ROMA political forum to publicly present your perspective and vision regarding the Roma community in Romania.

Introduction

The document above is a manifesto created by Aresel, which is a Roma civic initiative created in 2018. I learnt about it during one of our extensive conversations in 2020 from Ciprian Necula, who is its founder. He explained how the Roma movement in Romania needs a platform where they could support the fight against systematic racism, one that would empower Romani citizens to complain to authorities, and hold responsible those in power when they commit discriminatory acts. Aresel's platform and actions are the result of decades of work on the part of Roma activists, who have been engaging in formal acts to achieve justice. While not identical, their formal processes are not different from those of the Narikuravars in India. In both communities, their struggle for justice has been active on three planes: Combating discrimination and racism based on their ethnicity, obtaining a better economic situation, and having a saying in politics (i.e., decision making). Thus, their social justice practices are aligned with Nancy Fraser's (2000) tripartite theory of justice: Recognition, redistribution and representation.

Tripartite access to justice, Nancy Fraser

As mentioned in Chapter 1, to reveal the practices and process of accessing justice, I use Nancy Fraser's tripartite theory of social justice. Fraser (2000) showed that justice is typically understood as having access to recognition and distribution. Therefore, 'injustice is misrecognition, a form of subordination rooted in institutionalized patters of cultural values. And, injustice is maldistribution, meaning economic subordination, rooted in structural features of economic system' (Fraser, 2000: 117).[2] In 2009, Fraser also added political representation as the third pillar of justice.

In what follows, I will use these theoretical tools and analyse the Roma and Narikuravar practices by looking at the ways in which they address discriminatory practices of recognition, representation and redistribution. While analytically distinct, they are in practice interlinked and interdependent, facilitating or impeding equal treatment of members of the Roma and Narikuravar communities.

Different from the widespread stereotypes that are bandied about Roma and Narikuravars, according to which these communities self-isolate and do not participate in a community-based formal process to request equal rights, during my work in the field in both Romania and India, I observed how both communities engage in complex strategies to draw the attention of the state to their struggle and to achieve rights and justice. Their work stands as a testimony of contemporary social movements that 'move beyond both anti-statism and state-centrism in order to develop a politically enabling engagement' (Gunvald Nilsen, 2013: 615).

Their processes of accessing justice are neither equal in length or strength, nor do they share an identical time-line. While far from being the same, as they operate within different political, economic and social systems, with different long-lasting histories, within (and at times against) which the communities are working, they nevertheless have similar goals, using similar elements, tools and methods. As we have seen in the previous chapters, the two communities have been facing marginalization and racism for centuries under the 'Gypsy' label, and have been striving to make a place for themselves. Thus, it is not a surprise that their efforts are focused on recognizing their identity, understanding that officially and legally re-aligning their recognition has implications over their economic and political stands as well.

(I) The Struggle for Recognition

Both communities have struggled throughout the years with their misrecognition as 'Gypsy'. This means that their identity was not rightfully recognized, that it was misrecognized or wrongfully recognized by other communities and given the 'Gypsy' name, 'an identity, [which] has implications for integration and belonging' (McGarry, 2017: 99).

In Romania, for hundreds of years, the Roma's misrecognition often fell under the label 'Țigan' (in Romanian). The term was used to address different and complex identities, which only converge at times. Also, under the name 'Țigan'/'Gypsy' many indigenous tribes in India were referred with the same colonial term[3] (Dragomir, 2020). In both countries (and more) the word 'Gypsy'/'Țigan' is equated with that of 'nomad'/'vagabond', and criminal (Ibid.). These over-generalizations generated misrecognition patterns of communities, while also creating unity among them. Thus, engaging critically with these labels, and demanding that the state recognize them as Roma and Adivasi, provokes the process of recognition, creating a 'sense of us' (Cohen, cited by McGarry, 2017: 102). In both communities people battle racist labels, and try to change them either by re-articulating their meaning, or by replacing them with labels that offer the needed recognition.

Narikuravars as Adivasi

The Narikuravars are unofficially addressed as 'Gypsy'. As the name is in English, and many members of the community do not speak the language, the meaning is rather foreign to them. Moreover, as the English language still occupies a place of prestige in India, with its identifications connected with colonial rule, the 'Gypsy' name is identified as positive. Thus, the term 'Gypsy', in different spellings, is often appropriated. In trying to create the connection with possible international networks and funders to support their causes, at times the Narikuravars use the name 'Gypsy' in their social media. For example, on 27 January 2021, Rajasekaran posted on his social media the following announcement:

> Hello my dear friends,
> Its my kind request that if you need to donate your used mobiles/laptops/data cards/computers in working condition, please give it to our children. It will be great helpful for our students to attend their online classes. The donated material will be shared among 3 different schools that are running for *gypsy children education in Perambalur*, Trichirappalli and Mayiladudurai. The students are suffering a lot.
>
> Rajasekaran, 2021, Facebook post, author emphasis

Since 2017, the Narikuravar activists, like Anuradha, have continuously shared with me the situation of their community: 'We [the Narikuravars] are in the MBC [i.e. Most Backward Class] category, we are missing out on a lot, and we should have ST [i.e. Scheduled Tribe] status instead. Tamil Nadu is the only other major state where Narikuravars are still not in the ST category.[4] So, we use our registered contacts to get this tribal status' (Anuradha interview, November 2020).

Anuradha's claim refers to being officially recognized by the state within one category as a path that allows them access to opportunities and support. To date, Anuradha argues, they are categorized as a vulnerable community, but not as vulnerable as the Narikuravar community is in reality. As a result, they are placed within the wrong category, and they have to compete for funding, seats, etc. with less vulnerable communities, which are often better prepared, more educated, with a stronger network, etc. Due to this unfair competition for reservations,[5] they end up falling short, and being denied state support.

The ST status is a categorization (or recognition), part of a nationally designed and locally enforced hierarchical system. This stratification has the forward classes (rarely mentioned), followed by Backward Classes (BC), and Scheduled Castes

(SC) and Scheduled Tribes (ST). These categories are further diversified, and in the state of Tamil Nadu[6] they are: Backward Classes (BC) and Most Backward Classes (MBC). In the state of Tamil Nadu, officially the Narikuravars have been classified as a 'Most Backward Class' (or MBC) for decades:

> Currently we are an MBC community, and this is not something we want. If you compare us mark-wise in colleges, we score less. Other students – from other communities – study in better schools that even teach English, whereas the government school we go to is lacking. In colleges, our quotas aren't good because we are an MBC, so we have to go around meeting people and collectors and IAS officers to get seats in the college.
>
> Rampa interview, November 2020

The Narikuravars have been fighting for the past thirty years for their official recognition as a group at the very bottom of the hierarchy, as the most vulnerable, and therefore entitled to most reservations. Other Adivasi communities, officially defined as 'Scheduled Tribes' and 'Primitive Tribal Groups', typically live within forests, which is/was their main form of socio-economic access (Rangarajan, 1996).[7] Those communities whose traditions conform to these categorizations are more likely to be legally recognized as ST within the Indian legislation, and as a result they have access to special minority rights.[8]

The Narikuravars argue in favour of their ST identification based on similarities with other Adivasi groups, which – according to the Minority Rights Report (also in Chapter 6) – have the lowest socio-economic indicator in India, are regarded as primitive and tribal, typically speak their own distinctive language and maintain their distinctive way of life. The Narikuravars' battle for this status has been ongoing for decades: 'The Narrikurovars have viewed themselves as "Adivasi" and have been attempting to gain ST status. When asked why they should be recognized as such, they answer, "because our community needs it," and point to their poor living, economic, and social conditions' (Dragomir, 2017).

The current Indian reservation system is justified as a measure to address historical injustices by providing sustainable reservations (similar to the U.S. Affirmative Action measures) in education, employment and political representation aimed at increasing the opportunities for these communities. Thus, according to the Government of India, Ministry of Heavy Industry and Public Enterprises (2016): 'Objective of providing reservations to the Scheduled Castes (SCs), Scheduled Tribes (STs) and Other Backward Classes (OBCs) in services is not only to give jobs to some persons belonging to these communities.

It basically aims at empowering them and ensuring their participation in the decision making process of the State.[9]

Being seen amongst the most disadvantaged socio-economic groups in India would offer the Narikuravars their needed recognition. This, in turn, transforms into tangible benefits, making being an Adivasi/ST a desirable official identification,[10] which provides 'positive discrimination measures' dating back to the 1950s Indian Constitution. More recently, to ensure the progress of its most vulnerable, in 2012 India released the 12th Five-Year Plan, which included programmes to support historically disadvantaged populations, aiming for inclusive health, education, drinking water and sanitation, and provision of critical infrastructure in rural and urban areas.[11] As such the 12th Five-Year Plan[12] 'places special emphasis on expanding access to these services and views it as a critical role of government in the development process' (12th Five-Year Plan: xiii).[13]

Considering the possible advantages that one would receive for being recognized as ST, it is perhaps not surprising that this status is often a point of contention:

> Getting ST status means that members of the group have access to highly desired tangible benefits such as political representation, reserved seats in schools, and government jobs. Over the years, social and political mobilization has led to the number of STs growing from 225 in 1960 to 700 today (with overlapping communities in more than one state). As the number of communities clamoring to be recognized as ST expands, so do the number of people who question the legitimacy of awarding ST status, bringing the criteria of this recognition under increasing scrutiny.
>
> Dragomir, 2017[14]

Thus, while quite counter-intuitive at first glance, the struggle for the Narikuravars is to not be recognized 'up' on the social hierarchy, but 'down', as an ST, so they could compete for the reserved seats with similar communities. This, they argue, would be a fair competition, one that would ensure that Narikuravars have access to more state support, which over time would lead to their progress as a community.

Their current MBC categorization 'is a misjudgment by others, not by us', Rajasekaran told me (November, 2020). His voice is echoed by many in the community, who vehemently argue that MBC status is wrongly attributed to them, and fervently ask that they should be recognized as ST.

Strategies of recognition

In the 1980s, M. G. Ramachandran, the then Chief Minister of Tamil Nadu, proposed to the Union Government to include Narikuravars in the ST list. On 18th December 2013, the UPA government was forced to issue a bill (160/2013) to include the community in the ST list. Prior to the issuance of this bill, Narikuravars convinced DMK president Karunanidhi and Tamil Nadu Chief Minister J. Jayalalitha to write to the Central government. However, on 21st February 2014 when the bill was floored in the Lok Sabha none of the members supported the Bill. This led to its lapse.

Round Table India, 2016[15]

The process of qualifying for ST (or SC) status is a political process, one which has been ongoing for the Narikuravars for over thirty years:

The main thing is getting an ST status. In states like Karnataka, Kerala, and Andhra Pradesh, they have been successful in getting these rights. Here, however, there is still a denotified community. This is a social injustice. So many politicians come and go. Nobody speaks for these people. During the Manmohan Singh government (13th Prime Minister of India), we got a little recognition and managed to get the bill to the parliament. However, because of the Telangana partition issue, this bill lapsed, and that was the end of it. In Modi's government, we got it to the parliament again, but it never passed. To try this again, we have to take it to the cabinet, and then the parliament.

R. Vijayasundaram interview, November 2020

The Narikuravars often talk about the long process they undertook to date, which while making strides,[16] has been unsuccessful. Arun Kumar shared his story:

My dad's name is Mahendran. He died in 2017. When he was alive, he led a lot of protests continuously. We took it to major cities like Chennai and Delhi to get more recognition of ST. After my father, although lots of people are trying to keep it up, it isn't on the same scale anymore. But most of these protests go unheard because they always seem to have bigger problems. Politically, there is nobody to support us at a big level [i.e., national politics].

Arun Kumar interview, November 2020

Speaking to Rajasekaran, he repeated for maybe the thirtieth time: 'This is a long-term engagement; our work is never done.' Taking a deep breath, he explains the politics of Tamil Nadu: 'There is a triangle: BJP, AIADMK and DMK – triad of parties', he says, referring to the parties that are the most powerful and typically dominate the state's politics.

National politics come at odds with local politics in the case of the Narikuravars. Since 2014, the Indian central government has been led by Prime Minister Narendra Modi, and the Bharatiya Janata Party (BJP).[17] Emphasizing the greatness of the Indian past and its traditions, BJP and the central government find themselves in an awkward position when trying to accord more rights to historically marginalized communities, especially to those suffering from castism, an issue at times thought to be taken up by the opposition party: Congress. However, according rights to historically marginalized communities is sometimes applauded by the Indian right:

> Hindu nationalists have also taken the major step in delivering historic justice to Indic nomadic forest dwelling communities which were branded as criminal tribes by the Protestant colonial administration. Narikuravas were categorized as 'criminal tribes' in 1871 by the British rule. Both eugenics and protestant worldview were behind this legislation. It took five years for independent India to denotify them. Still, these nomadic communities were placed only in the categories of Backward Classes (BC) thus effectively excluding them from empowering themselves. Though the then Tamil Nadu Chief Minister Dr. M. G. Ramachandran had recommended placing them in the ST category, the central governments have largely not cared for this demand. The Modi government though, on May 25 [2016], approved bills placing Narikuravar and Kurivikaran communities in the Scheduled Tribes (ST) category.[18]

In spite of these strides at the central office, the Narikuravars did not succeed in changing their status. This is, as Anuradha and Rajasekaran often told me, also due to the fact that the Narikuravars do not have the backing of any political party. No party pays them court because their community is too small, meaning the number of votes they can provide is not crucial in determining elections. So, Rajasekaran often tells me: 'We need to work concomitantly at all of them.' But as their political expertise is minimal, and their connections to the larger political sphere non-existent, the Narikuravars are often lost in their struggle: 'We do not know where to go, and whom to meet', they say.

They strategize by reaching out to all political leaders whom they think might help. Once they identify them, they engage in a long-term laborious process, which starts with the Narikuravars putting in writing their request. I asked how do they ensure that their message and letters reach the political leaders. 'We have to give it in person. They do not respond to emails or to mailed letters, so we need to go in person. We have to appraise them and to make them happy,'

Rajasekaran says, laughing nervously, and adds, 'it is very different here in India.' He continued by explaining their strategy of diversifying: 'We work with more parties to gain their support, because only through them we can go and demand. So, we need to lobby to more parties, hoping to get them interested in our issues' (Rajasekaran interview, 2020).

The same strategy was outlined by Rampa: 'We are trying to reach out to MLAs, MPs, and state ministers with letters and arranging meetings with them' (Rampa interview, 2020). Similarly, Vijayasundaram said:

> We tried to get the attention of certain politicians. Other than this, we have tried to give our representation in many forms: [To the] central minister, central executives, and IAS officers that wish us well, and department secretaries to governments, and officers that used to work here and who were promoted to Delhi; these are the kinds of people we try to get connected and well acquainted with. We need to create a lobby in Delhi, and I think we can establish that by January 2021.
>
> Vijayasundaram interview, November 2020

This process cannot be on pause even during a global pandemic. In spite of the recent COVID-19 national lockdown, the Narikuravars still tried to pursue their ST status agenda, and reached out to politicians. 'Recently we tried to meet AIADMK representatives in Chennai', Rajasekaran explained in December 2020. While they were not successful, their work was not deterred. Seeing the difficulties they face when trying to reach out to politicians at the state level, I asked if they tried to appeal to powerful parties at the national level. To this, Rajasekaran responded: 'We tried to work with BJP in Tamil Nadu, but now they changed their representatives. We knew Radha Krishna. But now, he has no role,' he said in sadness, and emphasized further: 'He has no power – it has collapsed.'

Faced with swift changes in political power, the Narikuravars expeditiously adapted their strategies: 'We do now lobby with local and central ministries to get them the [necessary] data', i.e., to support their work in making a decision in favour of changing the status of the Narikuravar community from MBC to ST. In addition, activists and community leaders keep close to their political contacts, and attempt to hold those in power accountable: 'We ask them what are the steps taken and advise them how to proceed' (Rajasekaran interview, 2020).

The strategies outlined above are not new to the Narikuravars; these are the same strategies I came across in early 2017, and were in place well before that:

The Narrikurovars have found it difficult to navigate this uncertain legal terrain and have been appealing to the principal Dravida political parties, the DMK and AIADMK. The latter, in turn, have pleaded with the central government, stating that 'the community leading a nomadic life was in a pathetic condition'. Since 2013, the Narrikurovars have focused their efforts on grassroots political mobilization and have been organizing several sit-ins and hunger strikes. This has increased awareness of the precarious state of the community and has led to efforts by the central government to amend the Constitution (Scheduled Tribes) Order of 1950 to include the Narrikurovar, Kurivikarran, and Malayelee Gounder among the STs. The bills were introduced in the Lok Sabha in December 2016 and await passage.

Dragomir, 2017

As a result of these long-lasting efforts, in late 2016 a bill awarding ST status to the Narikuravar (and two other communities), was introduced on the floor in the Lok Sabha. But 'no one raised their voice' (Rajasekaran interview, 2018) for the bill to be discussed, which is the necessary legal and political step for the legislation to be voted on. The bill's validity was weakened by the unfortunate timing of its introduction into the Indian Parliament, as at the same time the country was undergoing the sudden and dramatic process of demonetization initiated by Prime Minster Modi.[19] So, '*the bill lapsed*' Rajasekaran said in a quiet voice. When the law was not brought up for votes, and therefore did not pass, the Narikuravars kept appealing to people in government in Delhi: 'We went there to submit a request letter to consider our status. We went there, but they did not receive us. So now, we do not get to lobby also because of financial constraints, we can't cover the travel and expenses' (Rajasekaran interview, November 2020).

Struggles to date

In spite of their assiduous efforts not bearing fruit, the Narikuravar elites are not deterred, and expect to start the process again: 'With our effort, the bill was passed, but because politicians didn't do the work after that, we still don't have the ST status. It is still pending. We may even need to start the whole process again' (Rampa interview, 2020).

Listening to their uphill battle to obtain ST status, I looked closer into the underpinnings of the issue to understand the obstacles of their claim for justice, and probably unsurprisingly, I found several:

1. *Different aboriginals?* The Narikuravars' formal strives for justice have been focused on being recognized as Adivasi. The term Adivasi means: Aboriginal, original, tribal. In India, original communities are understood as inhabiting the sub-Indian continent before the Aryan invasions. They are thought to have a different life style, typically remote from mainstream society – secluded in jungles, forests or deserts. Due to their physical and cultural distance from other groups, they kept their traditional forms of life, lived outside mainstream religious, political and economic systems. As India has been creating its national creed, incorporating the Adivasi in the large national community meant allowing indigenous communities their right to live a different life.

However, as we have seen previously (see Chapter 2), the Narikuravars tell a different story of their community. They say that originally their community was urban, that they worked in the royal courts, serving in the royal military, but because of invaders they were forced to retreat into the forests. Here, they employed their weaponry skills, survived and kept moving from Maharashtra to the southern tip of India. This story comes at odds with the typical Adivasi histories, which are bound to the land, and make claims of indigeneity based on it.

2. *Nomadism.* As we have seen, the Narikuravar identify as nomads, which further weakens their claim as indigenous communities belonging to a specific land.

> Their precarious position is further complicated by their nomadism across rural and urban areas which runs against the criteria of 'geographical isolation' required for ST status. Additionally, as the Narrikurovar sell their products to the community at large, they might not display 'shyness of connect', which is another criterion. But since these criteria are not explicit, it is difficult for the community to formulate clear political demands.
>
> Dragomir, 2017

3. *Not all politicians are on board.* While the Narikuravars are pleading for support from different politicians, they are not successful in gathering constant help from those in power. As the struggle for obtaining ST status among local communities is fierce, politicians would be more inclined to side with other, competing communities from which they would garner more votes. This leads to a political friction that sidelines the Narikuravars'

efforts: 'There are internal and external differences, and some do not support this ST' [status for us] (Rajasekaran interview, 2020).

4. Linked to the above is the active denial of ST status for the Narikuravars. Other (ST) communities fight against this move. While the Narikuravars aim to obtain ST status so they do not to have to compete with more powerful communities over reserved seats, there are other communities who have ST status already, who do not want to have to share their reservations with yet another community, such as the Narikuravar. As a result, they mobilize politically against the Narikuravars being recognized as Adivasis, and lobby politicians against ST recognition of the Narikuravars: 'There are other communities, which are against [us] getting ST status. They block our ST lobbying' (Rajasekaran interview, 2020).

Thus, the Narikuravars do not have an orthodox argument for being recognized as Adivasi; they do not claim an indigenous history, and they do not fit perfectly the groups that are typically included in this categorization. Their claims are quite different, and they hinge on a social justice argument (i.e., because the community is underprivileged, they should get support from the government, so they can better themselves). And, in doing so, they push the limits of the reservation system in the name of historical discrimination and marginalization. These obstacles hinder Narikuravars' claims for recognition as Adivasi/ST. To be successful, the system of Indian reservations needs to undergo a rather drastic change, one in which reservations would be redefined to include the most vulnerable, and those who have been discriminated against for centuries.

Narikuravars as 'Gypsy': unofficial formal recognition strategies

To overcome their misrecognition, and to access resources, the Narikuravars employ an alternative technique. They often appropriate the other name with which they are referred by: 'Gypsy'. Over the past fifteen years, the Narikuravars have organized in different public forums, such as the 'Narikuravars Gypsy Association', and some folks from the community self-titled as the 'president of the Gypsy'. For example, in 2017 the Narikuravars from Trichy stated in the mission statement of the Narikuravar Education and Welfare Society (NEWS), established in 1990: 'Our mission: To bring about the social, economic, political and cultural enhancement of Narikuravar *Gypsies* [my emphasis], with focus on children, youth and women. Locally from within a Narikuravar *gypsy* [my emphasis] community, NEWS provides food, shelter and education for children from tribal backgrounds and works in five villages to alleviate poverty' (NEWS, social media, 2017).

While the 'Gypsy' denomination has pejorative connotations in the European context, within the Narikuravar context it becomes a way to recognition, a path to reach outside the community, and a possibility to network with the English-speaking groups. Their struggle is therefore not directed towards the label of 'Gypsy', which allowed for their marginalization within colonial rule, and today informally reinforces their peripheral position within the Indian hierarchy. For example, using this label, but employing it differently for the past three years, Rajasekaran created the 'Gipzys Development Society/ Tribal Society', establishing residential schools for the community.

The term 'Gypsy' is used to get international attention, and – while limited and precarious – their efforts pay-off. When India was hit by the second wave of the COVID-19 pandemic, the Narikuravars were in dire straits. Rajasekaran and Anuradha mobilized and organized crowd-funding campaigns on social media, which reached international networks using the English-colonial 'Gypsy' name: 'Second Wave Covid Appeal, Help Me To Provide Dry Ration, Milk And Sanitation Essentials To The Gypsy Families In India'.[20] These efforts need to be seen as forms of claiming the community's recognition, by re-articulating the term used by the colonial power to dominate and control them, into a form of (practical) recognition and empowerment.

Recognition: the Roma fight

The struggle for recognition of other communities labelled as 'Gypsy' in Romania has been engaged in a similar process of confronting misrecognition. Their formal struggles started years earlier, when Roma communities tackled discrimination by starting the process of changing their categorization from 'Gypsy'/'Țigan' to Roma. In Romania the name 'Gypsy'/'Țigan' has quite pejorative connotations, both within the social and political sphere (see Chapter 6). However, in spite of the fact that today there is a political recognition of the Roma identity within the Romanian Constitution, the term Roma is not uniformly accepted. To date, many people of Roma descent and/or belonging to

Roma communities would still prefer to self-identify as 'Gypsy' (see Chapter 3 and Chapter 6).

As with the Narikuravars, the Roma's recognition process has been decades in the making. In a similar manner, the Roma's fight for recognition has been interlinked with accessing redistribution of economic and social resources, and political representation.

Historical/political context

It is important to understand the Roma movement in its historical context: This is a movement that started a few decades ago and was actually getting attention under the Communist regime in Romania, and grew more during the first post-communist decade. The Roma formal activism, addressing systemic injustice in a transnational way, officially begun in 1971:

> The activity of the Comité International Tzigane, up until the First World Romani Congress in 1971, marked the first time in 400 years that Roma had travelled across state borders for political purposes of their own. Although the COMECON countries, apart from China, actively repressed emigration, there was a steady flow of Roma westwards; they benefited at that time from the status of being 'refugees from communism', nonetheless keeping in contact with Roma back home. Meanwhile, within the Soviet bloc, members of the Romani nomenklatura, who often travelled to Moscow for education and training, were able to present their contacts with western European Romani movements, as a possible alliance with helpful progressive forces.
>
> Acton, Roma Archive[21]

Within the emerging neo-liberal democracy in the 1990s, the Roma of Romania benefited (at least on paper) from assigned minority rights, similar to the Indian reservation system. While they are not as elaborate and extensive as those in South Asia, (in theory) Roma could access certain benefits like 'special places'/reservations [i.e., 'locuri speciale'] in education.[22] While limited and difficult to access, these developments contributed significantly to the creation of an intellectual elite of the Roma movement, who have been mobilizing politically ever since.

The newly formed elites have had a powerful impact on the recognition of the Roma identity, but their journey has been neither smooth nor an all(Roma)-embracing process. Ciprian Necula (interview, 2017) says that Roma leaders, like Nicolae Gheorghe, worried that NGOs will concentrate the Roma community's power, and that would lead to despotism, with Roma elites abusing their professional authority, and this might produce more damage than good to the overall Roma movement. To mitigate this, and to ensure the democratization of the process, Nicolae Gheorghe and others created Roma associations and working groups – which had civic means, and were civil society oriented.

Being 'Gypsy'/'Ţigan' in Romania

If for the Narikuravars, as we have seen above, the struggle for recognition has been concentrated on obtaining the ST status, for the Roma the recognition efforts have been focused on formally (and legally) establishing the 'Roma' term, and obliterating the 'Gypsy'/'Ţigan' one. According to Necula (2020), the term used to identify Roma was 'Gypsy'/'Ţigan', and was used in the documents of 1385 attesting the presence of Roma in the first Romanian area. The term 'Gypsy'/'Ţigan', Necula continues, is 'of Greek origin (αθιγγανοι, athinganoi – untouchable), and from the beginning became synonymous with being a slave. Throughout the years, 'the term "Ţigan" became synonymous with an inferior person. While the term had negative social connotations, it does not always have ethnic ones' (Necula, 2020: 526). For example, one can be 'Ţigan' in spite of their ethnicity – with 'Ţigan' being used as a pejorative adjective, rather than an ethnic marker.

As an alternative, according to Necula (2020), the term 'Rom' was used by Roma people to self-identify according to their language and tradition, long before it became a contested, political term employed by elites in their struggle for recognition.[23] Furthermore, Necula argues that Roma is the name they give themselves in Europe and beyond; any other name is foreign, and therefore imposed from outside, as a form of misrecognition. In a similar manner, Petre Matei (2012), cited by Necula (2020), explained that the problem of naming Roma as such did not exist in the period between the two world wars, because those labelled as 'Gypsies' did not – in spite of the nationalist fears among Romanians – define themselves by anti-Semitism. Thus, in the first half of the twentieth century Romanians were not necessarily hostile towards 'Gypsies'/'Roma'. The Romaphobia (McGarry, 2017), Necula further argues, started once Romania had seen a significant reduction in the number of Jews, and reoriented their hostility towards Roma in their political propaganda, and in re-defining Romanian nationalism (Necula, 2020: 527).[24]

In the second half of the last century, the term used to designate the Roma population in Romania became synonymous with 'black (or dark) people with bad habits' (Necula, 2020). As such, the term became a part of the Romanian vocabulary, where it also became a verb: 'A se ţigani', meaning 'to Gypsy', or to negotiate in bad humour. As an adjective, its meaning became cemented as an overall negative term to signify inferiority and uncivilization (Necula, 2020: 526).

The term 'Gypsy'/'Ţigan' became used both formally (in documents) and informally. After the fall of communism, in the 1990s we saw the emergence of a new Roma activism, mainly lead by Nicolae Gheorghe.[25] Under his leadership, the struggle for recognition of the Roma as different from 'Ţigan' was set in motion. Thirty years later, while the term is used by many Romani elites, and has become the official reference of the community, it does not have complete track within the communities, where many still argue for using 'Ţigan'. 'I don't say it with hatred or contempt, I know many gypsies who prefer to be called that', Necula mentions in reference to the well-known language tropes (Necula, 2020: 525).

While the term 'Roma' is currently in usage, its employment and meaning are still debated. The Memorandum No. D2.1092 of 2000 from the Minister of External Affairs, Petre Roman to the Prime Minister Mugur Isaraescu – responding to the campaign organized by a Roma NGO in 1950 – asked for an official change of the community from 'Ţigan'/'Gypsy' into 'Roma'. The campaign had reached both the national and international media, and was presented at international organizations. Recognizing the community's right to 'self-identify' in line with the international and national legislation, the memorandum proposed using the term Roma in all official correspondence of the Ministry, and the terms 'Roma/Gypsy', 'Roma/Ţigan', 'Roma and Sinti' for international communication in accordance with the name used by the international bodies. This was a glorified moment of success in addressing the misrecognition inflicted upon the community for centuries. Nevertheless, "Roma" has continued to be a contested term:

> Since 1989 and until now, there have been several Romanian parliamentarians who have submitted legislative initiatives to change the Roma ethnonym with the gypsy exonym in public affairs. Using a relatively unknown topic to Romanian citizens (including ethnic Roma), this generated heated debates on Roma crime, their international mobility, the confusion of Roma-Romanian in the European space, various global conspiracies to defame Romanians are induced by association with gypsies, therefore, in other words, speculate on political opportunities.
>
> Necula, 2020: 531

But in 2010, the term came under scrutiny again, and it was brought to the floor of the Romanian Parliament as a law that would make the official name of the community 'Ţigan'.[26] The law proposal was scrutinized and critically assessed by the activists of the NGO Romani CRISS, who argued the following:

> The word Roma is an ancient Romany word meaning 'human being' and has been the preferred designation of Roma civic organizations in Romania since 1919. We are aware that in Romania there is an unfortunate semantic confusion with the word Romania, but this can be overcome by goodwill, consultation and effective public communication. The word 'Ţigan', on the other hand, is associated in the collective memory of the Roma with the slavery that existed in Romania from 1385 to 1856, and also the forced deportations in WW2.
>
> Romani CRISS, 2010[27]

Just as in the case of the Narikuravars struggle for ST status, the law did not pass. But, different from the Indian community, the fact that the official recognition was a close call drew the attention of other Roma activists/scholars, such as Margareta Matache, who wrote: '"Gypsy" is a racialized and fixed contraction that has fed Roma oppression through their steady representations as thieves, uneducated, nomads and uncivilized. (...) The Gypsy identity is an outsider's view, and the boundaries between "us" (Gadje) and "them" (Roma) reflect essentially a superior–inferior hierarchy' (Matache, 2017).[28]

Along the same lines, Necula further argues that continuing using the term 'Ţigan', 'considering the socio-cultural connotations and political instrumentalization of the "Gypsy" exonym, regardless of the context, is romophobia' (Necula, 2020: 544). Accordingly, in the past decade, the term 'Roma' has been increasingly used both in legal documents and everyday language. While it is still not unanimously accepted (but what meanings are?), using the term Roma to identify communities has become a more visible occurrence.

Moreover, in Romania, as of 15 December 2020, after over forty years of striving for justice, racist acts against Roma became illegal, and punishable by a jail sentence. This is the result of a legal project that launched different measures for preventing and combating 'anti-Gypsism' that was adopted by the Romanian Parliament and was released for enforcement.[29] This is a strong legal stand, but of course this does not mean that 'anti-Gypsism' disappears overnight, as its enforcement is dependent on existent and long-lasting structures of power often reinforced in everyday life.

(II) Links to Redistribution

Recogntion and redistribtion are not separate, but as Fraser argues 'by understanding recognition as a question of status, and by examining its relations to economic class, one can take steps to mitigate, if not to fully solve, the displacement of struggles for redistribution; and by avoiding the identity model, one can begin to diminish, if not fully dispel, the dangerous tendency to reify the collective identities' (Fraser, 2000: 120). Thus, in understanding the struggle for recognition of the Roma and Narukuravars, we also need to undertand the practical, economic implications of obtaining their official recognition.

Narikuravar: need for redistribution and lack of funds

The Narikuravars understand that their recognition as Adivasi and ST is not done for symbolic reasons alone; this recognition is linked to tangible benefits that come in the form of reservations, helping them access redistribution. The Narikuravar elites I worked with over the years have been highly educated. In addition to their community language, they speak fluent formal Tamil and English. Their educational achievements award them a visible place within the society. Thus, the Narikuravar elites place a lot of emphasis on access to formal education, or lack thereof. However, besides those who used their education in the services of their community, creating NGOs and welfare funds, those with high-education degrees very rarely can find employment in their field. While finding sustainable employment is not uniquely difficult for the Narikuravars, in the case of their community there are additional burdens: Open discrimination and castism/racism, as they are not seen suitable for professional employment. Many times, the educated youth fail to get jobs, go back to the community, and try to make ends meet. Their unemployment comes under strict scrutiny by the community at large, disillusioned by the effect of the education. As a result, education might not be seen by all as a desirable path to be pursued by the youth.

The Narikuravars' limited access to resources is not unlike that of the other STs, whom – according to the Minority Rights Report – over 95 per cent still live in rural areas facing economic exploitation. This remains their most acute problem, because they depend on forest produce to survive.[30]

The Narikuravars are caught in a catch-22 process. To get their community recognized as an ST, and therefore access governmental programmes that help alleviate the poverty of their community, they need funds to pursue their education. To date, the community's life is marked by severe poverty, and even the elites are struggling to make ends meet. To continue the struggle and the demands to those in power is an expensive endeavour that takes money to cover logistics and to support their livelihood, which often the Narikuravars cannot afford. Referring to the struggle for ST status, Vijayasundaram explained the obstacles the Narikuravars face:

> In Modi's government, we got it [i.e., the petition] to the parliament again, but it never got passed. To try this again, we have to take it to the cabinet, and then the parliament. For this, we need to get to Delhi, and this needs funds. This is our only barrier. Once we get past this, we can guarantee a comfortable life. To help us get this, the state government isn't hesitating – we have support from the state. Even in the central government, they lend us an ear, but getting it through the right channels takes money and a strong team. We need to create a presence in Delhi, by going there several times, and we don't have the money for this.
>
> R. Vijayasundaram interview, 2020

The same issue is present when the Narikuravars look at gaining employment.

> We cannot go for jobs outside [of the community]. Once we get quotas, it would be easy for us to get jobs, so our education will be of use somehow. Everybody is working towards that. (. . .) Our college kids talked about how [their work] won't be acknowledged if we have gone to college. So, none of us can truly work anywhere. The only way we can get jobs is by changing our caste.
>
> Rampa interview, 2020

The Narrikuravars hope that achieving ST status would also help them with financial investments in their educational institutions: 'Right now, the governmental funds for NGOs are not sufficient – there are about 20,000 IRS per year/kids' education. This is not enough; so, we need other donors – private – to fulfill the multiple needs of our almost 350 kids' (Rajasekaran interview, 2020).

This process is due to the fact that to support their communities, the Narikuravars organize themselves into NGOs, try to fundraise as well as ask for support from the state. However, the global capitalist system is rather cruel on protecting vulnerable groups, whose traditional skills might not be competitive on the 'free' market. The Narikuravars are trying to address maldistribution by making and selling products. They look at capitalizing on their skills and start communal businesses, trying to sell their products.

In 2016, I invited Anuradha and Sekaran to a private school, where I was teaching over the summer. This was a high-end residential school, of English

Medium, in the state of Tamil Nadu. They kindly accepted my offer, and came here they presented their history, and interacted with children, parents, faculty and staff. They are both highly educated, have good command of English, hold graduate degrees, teach children in the community, and are ardent activists for Narikuravar rights. Their journey to the school was long, and took place in several overnight buses. Upon their arrival, they were enchanted to be at the school, jovial and ready to work with us. They also asked me if they could set up a stall, present and sell their hand-made jewellery. I spoke with the administrators, and we arranged for this to happen. After their presentation, Anuradha and Shekar did not take a minute of a break, but set up a stall inside the school, and displayed their products in the school library, further engaging everyone with stories of their community and explaining about the making of the display. Next morning, after breakfast, they went to work again. They set up a more public stall, and took photos of their customers. By evening, they came to me, and said they had sold every single item. They were so happy about it. I looked at them, and I was humbled by their tireless work, about how they were able to wear so many different hats simultaneously: How they had to fight for their community, while addressing personal struggles spurred by maldistribution. While their endeavours were successful, to be sustainable a systematic approach with programmes and interventions is needed so their (and the community's) economic mobility becomes a reality.

While often encouraged, the process of redistribution is limited. When the state fails to address their needs, the Narikuravars are left to their own device, and pushed into performing several concomitant roles, raising funds and awareness, providing services and pursuing their individual agenda. As we will see next with the Roma leaders, this often leaves people depleted, and – understandably so – often not able to completely fulfill all of their agenda.[31]

Roma: need for redistribution

As in the case of the Narikuravar community, official recognition enables its members to apply for rights and benefits, and address historical injustices, including the community's exceptionally high levels of exposure to physical violence,[32] social exclusion, discrimination and poverty.[33] These programs would enable the Narikuravars to enter the mainstream economy. Similarly, in their 2014 report, 'Diagnostics and Policy Advice for Supporting Roma Inclusion in Romania', the International Bank for Reconstruction and Development/The

World Bank, show that Roma have potential to participate in the overall Romanian economy, by contributing to the national revenue through their income taxes:[34]

> The labor earnings among Roma are significantly lower than for non-Roma. The surveys show that employed Roma earn only a fraction of the average earnings among the general population. As a result of low employment rates and low wages, the labor income of working age Roma men in Romania is estimated to be only 20 percent of that in the general population, and among Roma women, this is even lower: 12 percent.[35]

To help address these problems, as we have previously seen, the Roma have been allocated special seats for education, similar to the Indian reservations.[36] However, establishing who can and should have access to these rights is not an easy task, as the Roma identity is not officially, or legally acknowledged in any state documents. In other words, there is no official account of one's identity in legal documentation. In spite of the assiduous efforts of the Roma elites, at times the seats reserved for the Roma minority in higher education are not occupied.[37] This might be due to the lack of formal education, but it is also intrinsically linked to the 'segregation, the poor quality of primary education, etc. which push the Roma down, and they don't get to choose whether to go to high school or college or not' (Matache, 2021, personal correspondence). While good quality primary education would empower students to further their schooling, the shame associated with recognizing (officially) one's identity as Roma often acts as an obstacle. Furthermore, to apply for reservations, one has to establish their Roma identity through members of the community. This is a requirement that is not easily satisfied. For example, a written recommendation from a representative of a Roma civil, cultural or political organization, legally constituted, could attest for one's Roma identity.[38]

Thus, while these changes and 'reservations' are welcomed by the community, they are also acknowledged as limited: 'We will see differences in 10 to 15 years', said Damian Drăghici (Roma politician, representative in the European Parliament, and well-known pop-star) in a 2017 interview. He also added that, 'In education, transformations need to happen starting with access to kindergarten, through programmes, that would motivate Roma to attend. They also need to include social programmes, such as hygienic education.' Drăghici's suggestion acknowledges the double requirement for educational programmes: To be successful they need to be supported by other community programmes, and to be well-received by the Roma people.

But this is not the end of the sinuous road to accessing redistribution. An additional obstacle to accessing the reserved Roma seats is the reticence that many Roma have in being ethnically identified by authorities:

> It is not surprising that many Roma continue to see authorities as a threat. When they're asked to register their identity or to have their fingerprints taken the Roma people fear the worst. This is not difficult to understand, as we see how much of the contemporary 'anti-Gypsy'/'anti-Roma' rhetoric resembles the language used in Europe by the Nazis, Fascists, and Extremists alike.[39]

These hindrances bring into view how deeply entranced racism is in Romania, how historically rooted it is. It shows how we need to work on recognition and redistribution in tandem, to support access to programmes and ensure their success.

As Roma are well-known for their traditional skills, especially working with metal and crafts, some traditional Roma communities employ them to address maldistribution. In the Transylvanian village of Brăteiu, the Roma people are well-known for their crafts, working with copper pots and pans, and making jewellery. As in the case of the Narikuravars, they employ their skills and work tirelessly to promote their products. In the past years, they have been collaborating with a store/project in Bucharest called Mesteshukar Boutique,[40] where their products are displayed and sold in an elegant small elite shop in the middle of the country's capital, which caters to the taste of the newly formed hipster elite. In 2018, together with Ciprian Necula, we visited the village of Brăteiu. While driving, we could see the stalls along the road displaying hand-crafted objects. We stopped and talked to several Roma families, whose work was familiar to Necula. Everyone was very eager to share with us the history of their community, the uniqueness of their work, and showcase how the objects were made. The work is strenuous and labour intensive – but the Roma of Brăteiu are proud that they can carry forward these traditions, and that their village is well known across the country (and abroad). These engagements lead the Roma of Brăteiu to have economic successes; their brick houses stand tall as if piercing the sky; their living rooms are large and carefully ornated; their large courtyards host small farms; their workshops are filled with well-ordered and well-kept traditional tools and utensils; their properties are enclosed by high-metal fences, and well-made large gates. Nevertheless, in spite of this economic bonheur, the Roma of Brăteiu's life is not made easier. They are still confronted by systematic racism and discrimination. Moreover, their financial empowerment, which is at least partially due to the institutional support provided by collaborations, such as the Mesteshukar project, does not extend to other Roma communities.

In Ormeniş, for example, the Roma do not have marketable traditional skills that could be adapted to the globalized capitalist market, and – as other skills are often missing (due to lack of access to formal education) – the only form to address maldistribution is through state-supported empowerment programmes.[41]

Thus, just as in the case of the Narikuravars, lacking access to systematic programmes to support their economic mobility, makes the success of the Roma of Brăteiu be a mere outlier of a precarious economic development. It is also made clear that accessing economic mobility is necessary, but not sufficient to address systematic injustices, but it needs to be coupled with recognition and (as well we see next) with access to political representation.

It is nevertheless important to point out that access to economic resources is a double movement: One that starts from the state to the people, and the other from the people to the market. While the former aligns well with Nancy Fraser's theory of tripartite justice, the latter challenges it, showing how, in spite of their historical marginalization, the Roma and the Narikuravar communities have agency and, even when eclipsed from the acknowledgement and support of the state, they look for ways to empower themselves and affirm their place within society. This is not to imply that, when the state's presence is superfluous or unwarranted, that the responsibility should be delegated to the individual to find alternative ways of empowerment. But to combine these efforts, in order to make them both sustainable, and able to address systemic justice. It is nevertheless crucial to mention that context in which the Narikuravar and the Roma people are struggling to access economic access. Both Romania and India have been engaged in a strenuous process to align their economies along the neo-liberal creeds. Both countries share a history of community-oriented economy (at least in some states – in the case of India) that often comes at odds with the more recent strive of privatization. These systemic developments place communities like the Roma and the Narikuravar at its furthest margins, and make their support palatable as long as it provides profit. One could nevertheless imagine that a structural change within this economic approach would lead to a different position and access to economic resources for traditional nomadic communities.

(III) Works of Representation

To ensure recognition and redistribution, it is important to have a seat at the table, to have political representation. In other words, in addition to accessing redistribution and obtaining recognition, in order to ensure equitable access to rights, communities also need to have their political voices heard to dismantle 'existing disparities in participation, the asymmetries and the blocks placed by power, etc., and above all (...) identify those obstacles that are rooted in social relations' (Fraser, 2009).[42]

Narikuravar: representation, the quest for votes

Due to their traditional different life styles, Narikuravars have been able to maintain a good degree of self-governance including under colonial power.[43] Through Articles 330 and 332 of the Indian Constitution, those recognized as Adivasi have been provided with reserved seats in the House of People in Parliament, and also in the state and legislative assemblies. While this is seen as a positive measure, it is increasingly becoming a legal chore to fulfil 'constitutional formalities, [which are] failing to serve the STs' interests. Most Adivasi Members of Parliament (MPs) or Members of the Legislative Assembly (MLAs) belong to large national or mainstream parties, and are constrained by party ideologies and peer pressures.'[44] Therefore, it is often thought that the best Adivasi MPs could do is to bring issues to the floor, hoping to put pressure on other MPs to address their issues.

In the two houses of the Indian Parliament, the Lok Sabha and the Rajya Sabha, 7 per cent of the seats are reserved for STs. A similar representation is mirrored in the state assemblies, proportionally allocated by the number of (recognized) ST members.[45] This is a seemingly progressive approach to increase the political representation of historically marginalized groups, but in effect it rests on two assumptions: (1) that their minority representation has a political impact, which might not always be the case, as the numbers of ST representatives is small; (2) that all the Adivasi communities are recognized as STs, which is (as seen above) not always the case.

While the former is a more general deficit of representative democracies, the latter is an obstacle tied to the misrecognition of the Narikuravars as MBC, and not as ST. As a result, the Narikuravars have to compete with more powerful MBC communities to access their political reservations. This is an uphill battle that Narikuravars – to date – do not undertake. For now, they are focused on capitalizing on a small voting clout.

> If our community had a bigger population, if we had a bigger vote bank . . ., we would have more power over politicians to get this status. But our people are

spread across Tamil Nadu. In at least 200 different villages, there are people from the Narikuravar community. Only in a few areas are there big clusters, like 500 families. This makes it hard to gain power. The previous census was conducted on our community in 2008, and we do not know how the community has migrated from then. Those are the only statistics we have now. They still need to collect Narikuravar information from Tamil Nadu. We are even trying to ask for help from private donors, as these statistics might help us put our point across. What the government will see is the other types of communities under MBC [status], and question who should get the benefit of the status. We have poor home conditions, low education rates, and bad school accessibility. So, these disadvantages make them get comparatively lower marks. And economically, their bead products won't sell at all times of the year. Before that, when they hunted, that was banned by the government, they didn't have an alternative occupation. So, the youth started selling these as well.

Anuradha interview, 2018

The Narikuravars number only about 30,000 people (including children) in a state with a population over 84 million.[46] The state has been run by regional parties that often capitalize on their Tamilian identity (Swamy, 2019). Knowing that their vote bears little impact, the Narikuravar leaders often say that their community vote does not matter. They say this simply, and shrug their shoulders.

However, in 'the largest democracy of the world' (as India has been often called) everyone has the right to vote, even though exercising it is difficult. In 2016, according to *The Hindu* media outlet, in preparation for elections, local officials tried to address low voter turn-out, and brought 'a huge van with a model polling booth' into the Narikuravar 'settlement' in Puducherry to train locals on how to vote. While officers educated the community on the voting process, politicians were still slow to get involved: 'Even political parties have not knocked on our doors still, but these officers came to us with real-time polling system on the van. We learnt how to vote in the polling booth, and they also explained that we have the option of not voting for any of the candidates by exercising NOTA,' said Mallika, a Narikurava woman.[47]

Overall, the lack of importance of their political activity is often attributed to the small number of voters within the community. Additionally, being nomadic, the Narikuravars have a difficult time obtaining their voting cards, or the Aadhar cards,[48] which are the IDs needed to exercise their democratic right. This is mainly due to the fact that they have no fixed place of residence that is needed to obtain the card. As a result, even if some Narikuravars would be willing to vote, without the proper identification they cannot exercise this right.

This, in turn lowers the number of the votes[49] that one could garner from the community, lowering the chances that politicians would court them, and fight for the Narikuravar's ST status once elected.

Additionally, Rajasekaran told me that the Narikuravars do not have one unified political voice in Tamil Nadu. Rather, they 'generally vote based on their minds and hearts', said Rajasekaran explaining the community's political volatility. Typically, the Narikuravars vote for local political parties: 'They used to vote for AIADMK. This was because they felt seen'. Rajasekaran explained this choice, referring to Maruthur Gopalan Ramachandran's political leadership: 'He chose from the community for roles [in his films], and put the Narikuravars in songs. In the 1970s, people were interested in him; they felt that he is interested in them, and [that he] acted for us. When he started his own party, they voted for him, and then most followed this legacy, and voted for Ama-Jaylalitha' (Rajasekaran interview, 2018).

Since the passing of the mother of Tamil politics, Ama-Jaylalitha,[50] the Narikuravars divided their support: 'Now they are split between different parties. Whoever benefits them gets their votes. For example, the people who constructed a settlement got their votes. In Trichi, the DNK party also helped with housing. However, where Congress Party helped them, they received the votes. Thus, the Narikuravar votes are area dependent' (Rajasekaran interview, November 2020).

In my conversation with Rajasekaran, he explained that votes are granted on immediate satisfaction of their needs: 'During their reign of power if they help, people will go for them – they remember what they did for them'. This post factum voting support is equitable, but I was wondering if politicians reach out to the Narikuravars before election, and court them by giving small (but necessary) 'gifts', like rice, oil or sugar. Rajasekaran promptly reminded me that these 'gifts' are strictly forbidden by law. He laughs, and then he continues: 'But they are doing other malpractices. Monetary gains benefits,100–500 IRS [Indian Rupees] still in practice'. Considering this, I asked which party is more likely to ask for their support: 'Every local party approaches us', he says. 'Working with many parties in terms of strategies . . . TN politics is complicated, and usually the party AIADMK has only one vote in LS, but other parties have their votes. So, we need to work with all of them'.

Rajasekaran says this with no enthusiasm, and tells me that the national party like BJP, rarely reach out, as they know that the Narikuravars 'do not go for them'. However, even when they do, their political courtship is short-lived, because as soon as elections are over, so is the interest of politicians. Anuradha summarized the struggle:

We got help from the Ooty Research Centre, so that they could have a better look to prove that we are fully eligible for the status. But when the state government recommended it to the central, the bill lapsed in the Lok Sabha and Rajya Sabha. In 2016 or 2017, when it was Congress' last period [in power], we were supposed to be the topic of discussion, but the Telangana partition was more pressing then. This lapsed the bill, so it is still pending. That is the kind of thing we are still working on.

Anuradha interview, 2020

Their political activism is further hindered by the small number of politically active people in the community. Shankar, who has been politically active for the past thirty years, eloquently shared:

In a group of ten people, one person will be capable of assessing a situation and making decisions, another person will be able to do the same if he had thought it first, and two other people will get ready to experience it. So, among ten people, six will not be able to do much. What we are trying to do is to help these six people, because they do not know the way themselves. This does not make them less eligible, but it's just how the world treats them. These first four people will somehow find their ropes. The other six will not use the opportunity to grow, so they could benefit from things like the ST quota. This is the crux. All communities use the benefits of an ST for their whole lives. What we need is help for just one generation. We just want one period. The community just needs around fifteen years of support. At this time, one batch of kids can fully study, and start working. Once they have a steady income, they will focus on other things like saving money and helping his family. This is all we need. Fifteen years. And then they can take it from us and give it to others who need it more. By then, if I can buy a car and some respectable things, people will see past the community status and see that we are capable too. When my situation and educational background change, I don't need assistance anymore.

Shankar interview, 2020

These struggles persist across generations. Arun Kumar, who is 25 years old, shares Shankar's concerns:

Regarding this ST status, a single person cannot do anything, right? So, without a political influence, this will not succeed. Because they play a major role, we are currently researching what the best ways are to reach this connection with them. Here and there we still protest. In 2007 and 2008 Chennai, one lakh people gathered at my father's lead, and formed a chain from a famous statue up along the Marina Beach. And then, we organized a conference where some leaders could talk.

Arun Kumar interview, 2020

The Narikuravars understand that their journey to obtain political representation is not smooth or quick. That it is built on one political victory at a time.

> We need a few MPs and ministers who will listen to us, and speak about us. Even one or two ministers and a few IAS officers will be more than helpful. Right now, we are trying to build these connections. Let's see how it pans out. We just need to work harder and avoid those who were against our movement. Currently, we don't have these. People who already have this status tend to do this because they will have fewer quotas. The 1 per cent quota has not even been filled yet, but they think it will reduce their opportunities, so they will demotivate us. This is the situation we are trying to avoid. Even to buy land, if an ST member and an MBC member were trying to buy it for the same price, you can guess who will get the preference. But we have researched this in-depth, so we think we can avoid this.
>
> Vijayasundaram interview, 2020

This slow political development does not deter the Narikuravars: 'This is why we are confident, and sure that we will achieve this. If we can see success in our lifetimes, we will be satisfied, but the point is that it happens at some point' (Vijayasundaram interview, 2020).

Roma political representation

Different from the Narikuravars, who often depend on the goodwill of the other parties and political actors to push their agenda, since the 1990s, the Roma in Romania created the Roma Party, which was in theory (at least) independent and fighting for their community, but in practice it has been continuously in the shadow of other parties, 'selling the Roma votes'.[51] This led to the formal participation of Roma in politics, but with very little de-facto representation or decision power.

Nicoleta Bițu, in an interview in late 2020, said that often the Roma vote is based on their immediate needs, as they try to answer the stringent question of 'What do I need tomorrow?' This precarity gave space for many Roma elites to pursue their personal interests, and create unsavory alliances that did not necessarily support the overall Roma needs.[52] Thus, forgotten by elites, and used only for votes prior to elections, it is not surprising that in 2011, 'with a few notable exceptions, Roma [were] largely absent from the composition of elected bodies at local, regional, national and supranational levels. Roma participation in European parliaments is extremely limited. Only in the parliaments of a few countries in Central and South-Eastern Europe are there parliamentarians.'[53]

To respond to this lack of political agency of Roma communities, the Council of Europe's Commission for Human Rights,[54] in their 2011 report for the 'Human Rights for Roma and Nomads in Europe', advised to increase political engagements, pointing out that due to administrative obstacles and lack of identity documents or permanent residence, many Roma and nomads, alike the Narikuravars and other nomadic communities in India, are unable to vote. To address this limitation, the Council of Europe asks governments to 'repeal any laws and regulations that discriminate against the Roma minority in terms of political representation. Increased efforts are needed to encourage voter registration', and to involve women.[55] Moreover, the report says, the representation should not only be limited to the government, but needs to trickle down into the public life, which would be considerably improved when the Roma are visibly represented among civil servants, teachers and the police at local, regional and national level.

According to Roma scholars (Duminica interview, 2017), while in the 2011 census the Roma minority in Romania is about 3.3 per cent of the population,[56] in actuality the number is much larger, probably encompassing about 8 per cent of the Romanian population. The difference in census population size, scholars argue, is because many Roma are still afraid to officially recognize their ethnicity. And without this recognition is difficult to create a unified Roma political voice. Given the large number of Roma who are Romanian citizens with the right to vote in Romania and in the EU, Roma's participation in politics is seen as a potential force. This could make the Roma the largest political minority in Romania, with power to influence agenda, and everyday politics. However, to date the Roma's political presence has been limited:[57]

> Political representation remained (since 2004), with a small number of votes for the Roma Party (being represented by one MP) up to present.[58] (...) At local level, Roma are represented by over 250 local councillors and three municipal mayors. An organization was established to represent their interest, the Association of Local Elected Roma, whilst in the public institutions, according to an analysis of the National Contact Point, there are over 1,200 persons working as County Experts for Roma, Roma experts at local level and Roma education and health mediators.[59]

Thus, while the Narikuravars are struggling to get ST recognition through other political parties, the Roma have political representation through their ethnic Roma party (Partida Romilor/Roma Party)[60] since 1990.[61] While this was an important step in achieving social justice, Roma activists say this was not enough, as after Romania's accession to European Union membership, the Roma movement was not focused on obtaining political rights for the community, but changed from being a civil movement, to a service provider (Ciprian Necula interview, 2020). Typically supported by funds coming from the EU,[62] Roma NGOs worked directly with the community trying to supplement services that the state too often failed to provide. Some of them, like Romano Boutique[63] had tangible results, and created revenue that empowered members of the community, but others often failed to be self-sustainable. This is interpreted by Roma activists and leaders like Necula as follows: 'Maybe it was in the agenda of "others" that the Roma movement does not succeed; the Roma unified and strong would have posed a serious opposition. Especially for the other ethnic party. Like the UDMR[64] [Democratic Alliance of Hungarians in Romania]. Maybe it was easier to employ them as such, and make them the government machine', said Necula in 2020. Then, he reflected on his personal and activist trajectory: 'I also became a part of it', he confessed, 'I took the bait of the government!' He stops for few moments, and then continues: 'There were money to spend for the community, and we did it. But I realized that enough is enough! We can't replace the state. We should not do this, i.e. supplement state services. In a matter of years, we ended up running kindergartens, providing financial support etc. for the Roma people' (Necula interview, 2020).

Supporting the community has been a non-stop, arduous job, as Roma NGOs had to ensure the success of these strategies, while being buried in paperwork: 'We had to write 1000 pages of reports for the government to justify their programmes and funds; there was no time to mobilize politically, or to engage in other activities. As we were totally depended on donors and fundraising, we needed to implement the donor agenda', Necula continued. 'We were busy, so the Roma voices disappeared.' And he paused. The multiple burdens of the Roma (and Narikuravar) elites have been gargantuanesque (and tiresome), and one has to respect the focus, dedication and work of the elites, who work many times against all odds.

Strategies of community empowerment

As the Roma NGOs were struggling to comply with the programme requirements and provide services for the community, the 'Roma Party was trading votes!',

Necula (2020) says harshly. Roma politicians thought 'that the Roma NGOs got too much money from managing projects' (Necula interview, 2020). As a result, a schism between Roma civil society and its political actors was created, and some Roma politicians were even ready to 'disrupt the Roma civic movement; but fortunately, this has not happened. However', Necula continued, 'the Roma movement strived in spite of these obstacles, and reached a mature stage in which we say: "Enough is Enough" – is time to get back to the way it was programmed – back to Roma voices' (Necula interview, 2020).

Now, Necula says, the Roma movement aims to gain self-sufficiency and self-determination, but for this several steps need to be undertaken. First, the Roma need to organize as a political ethnic group, to define the 'we' of politics, and create a political dimension that unites. Necula says that the way in which Roma have been portrayed, especially by anthropologists, was by emphasizing the differences among them. For example, scholars would study a particular Roma community's tradition, emphasizing the extraordinary, the particular and the exotic. Their findings would then be extrapolated to the overall community, and Roma people would not see themselves in these descriptions, furthering the schisms among Roma communities. Instead of focusing on the cultural aspects, the political connections should be brought to the fore. This would lead to the second step, which is organizing the Roma around these goals. This, Necula admits, is a sensitive task, as 'the Roma were born too late for the nineteenth century nationalism, and too early for what is due to come', he nostalgically cites his mentor Nicolae Gheorghe. Thus, the urgency now is to organize the political platform for the Roma.

Different from the previous platforms, the Roma movement needs to transform victimhood into power and agency. Necula mentions that while changes have been small, the community has been incrementally getting better. Now these changes need to take a political format. The Roma could organize themselves politically, and vote for their own candidates, rather than simply supporting an agenda that is not theirs, in which they did not participate crafting.

As Rajasekaran mentioned when talking about the Narikuravars' votes being bought by unscrupulous politicians, Necula says that the Roma are often given election 'presents' (i.e., 'cadou') in the form of oil, sausages, etc. for a vote. In both countries, various political actors capitalize on the dire situation of those labelled as 'Gypsy', and give them 'food for one day', as Necula says. This explains the diverse Roma political engagements: 'Roma do not have a uniform vote. Whomever promises things.' Similarly, Nicoleta Bițu also explained how political candidates give food products in return for votes assuming that 'Roma do not plan long time, and live for tomorrow. Unfortunately, and sadly. Now, this practice is prohibited' (Bițu interview, 2020).

I often heard within the community that, 'Political parties just use us for political votes, but once they won, they would not support the Roma agenda because if they were to do that, they could lose their popular vote, and their appeal with the non-Roma.' Faced with this short-time memory of the political actors, Necula argues for political education: 'We need Roma to realize that politics is more than elections.' This would be possible by working with people at the grassroots level, supporting their participation at all levels of politics, and organizing them into a powerful political group. Necula says that for this project to be successful four dimensions need to be taken into account:

1. Community organizing: This would mean that Roma will become contributors with time and money.
2. Sustained campaigning: Media and door-to-door campaigns within Roma communities.
3. Advocacy at the local, national and international levels, which empowers people to act and support the Roma on the ground to ensure the success of their endeavours. This also includes expanding their networks, such as international Roma groups.
4. Gaining support from non-Roma: Working with national political figures, especially with the Liberal Democrats 'in pure sense', universities, researchers, and international institutions.

While developing these four dimensions, Necula insists the Roma need to keep their role as creators of programmes and projects, rather than follow an agenda that is not theirs. Following the others' political goals has been a disruption in the process of pursuing the potential of the Roma being organized. The Roma movement proposed by Necula implies mobilizing to define and pursue Roma rights. 'But not reacting', Necula explains. 'Reacting was the previous strategy that Roma leaders used. This was because of the political times in which they lived', Necula details to the historical context when 'being outside of structure of power was efficient' (Necula interview, 2020). But now, 'We need to get inside of the structures of power. We need to engage in a positive sabotage', also supports Nicoleta Bițu.

Dr. Nicoleta Bițu,[65] was the president of the Democratic Federation of Roma from Romania, and a member of the board of the European Roma Institute for Arts and Culture. A proud Roma, she has been tirelessly working in the field of human and women's rights for more than thirty years. She is a renowned feminist, activist and academic, who has worked at several NGOs: Romani CRISS, Open Society Foundation, the Council of Europe, the European Commission and Romano ButiQ.[66] Dr. Bițu, Nicoleta for friends, is a warm person, with large brown eyes and short dark hair; she speaks softly and with kindness. She is extremely articulate and very focused; her speech is precise and her thoughts are crystal clear. Her commitment to the Roma community's rights becomes apparent in the first few minutes of the conversation. She was the wife and life partner of Nicolae Gheorghe, and is the mother of two strong girls. Her work never stops: While taking care of the community, working and teaching, she is also always proud to support other Roma families.

We met in 2017 in her Bucharest apartment on a hot summer afternoon. We spoke again, over Zoom, in late 2020, while she was in London, where she passionately and compassionately shared with me: 'Roma need to be the drivers of the politics. This is the time for reflection and repositioning.' Bițu is dedicated to bigger changes in the Roma movement: 'We need to adopt difficult strategies.' She proposes memory as a strategy of engaging the history of the Roma, and participating in institution building, making sure that women are also included. In addition, like Necula's view, the Roma need to prepare for elections and to enter all levels of politics.

Also, like Necula, Bițu argued that ethnic representation is still needed in Romania: 'The critical rights are not yet achieved: we do not have collective rights – Roma museums, Romani language in schools are still goals that were not achieved. We are not yet there. So, ethnic discourse still appeals', Bițu argued, and continues to explain that this ethnic strategy needs to be employed until "we achieve political maturity". Until enough Roma people are politically trained, 'and then we can give up the ethnic party'. Until proper Roma representation is achieved, she argues, 'We need to fight more. Of course, this engagement with political power poses a danger. The danger is that if you are inside of power structures you might be eaten by them. You can get lost' (Bițu interview, 2020).

Overall, Romanian Roma activists and leaders, like Necula and Bițu, argue that the process of empowerment needs to include all Roma groups under one encompassing identity, which would be represented politically under their own terms, in their own voice, setting up their own agenda. For this to happen, the community needs specialized professional activists, who could dedicate their time to pursuing community work.

'Many of us are also tired,' says Nicoleta Bițu (2020). And she mentions that the work that needs is difficult to be done, while completing such diverse tasks. To this end, Necula argues that the Roma leaders need to create 'a political manifesto and outline what Roma want, and invite the candidates to discuss how they are going to address their ideas'. As outlined in the beginning of this chapter, the Roma manifesto places the Roma political demands in the 'room where it happens' (Hamilton).[67]

Conclusions: complex formal fights

The Narikuravars' and Roma's access to justice is intrinsically dependent on their (long fought-for, yet to be achieved) official recognition as a Schedule Tribe and as Roma. Thus, while spoke of in tandem, among recognition, representation and redistribution, we can see how recognition takes priority. For example, Rampa simply put it: 'If we had an ST status, we would have quotas' (Rampa interview, 2020). Recognition is thus important for the dignity of the community – but it also comes with the possibility to access economic resources, and participate in the redirection of resources. It is clear that only by working simultaneously on these three fronts, possibilities of overcoming structural injustice are created:

Community	Recognition	Redistribution	Representation
Narikuravar	ST status Use 'Gypsy' as form of recognition (esp. internationally)	Survival/'livelihood' state programmes and donations: funds for education	Working with political parties not in power
Roma	Roma rather than 'Gypsy'	Access to community funds – not only those distributed by the state	Aiming to control the political narrative and agenda: get seats in politics

At different stages of their social justice process, the Roma and the Narikuravars share many similarities in their formal practices. First, both communities in Romania and India work with and through the state to achieve recognition of their identity. This process is intimately linked to their access to programmes to economic (re)distribution and political representation. Second, both communities run NGOs, which work indefatigably to support their communities, and often do the job of the state, as Necula also complained. Third,

Roma and Narikuravars have been used by other parties to curry favour for elections, but they are currently engaged in changing this situation. Fourth, to date, members of the two communities (while sharing community bonds) are not unified to vote according to their ethnic interests. Fifth, in spite of their efforts, the Roma and Narikuravars are still the victims of historical persecution, struggling to survive and provide education, healthcare and livelihood for their community.

In spite of these similarities, the Roma and the Narikuravars have their different paths, which need to be accommodated in the larger political context they inhabit. First, there is a different access to higher education: While some of the Romanian Roma have been integrated in the main education system for decades,[68] the Narikuravars had limited (at best) access to formal education. As a result of their efforts, over the past three decades the Roma activists have created in Romania a group of committed, educated and very active community leaders. However, to date, in the Narikuravar community, the group of the educated activists and formal leaders is small, as many Narikuravars are struggling to survive.

Second, while the Roma are united under a common identity across the continents, and have expanded their networks across Europe and beyond to fight for their common rights, the Narikuravars are still struggling to organize within their community. As they are not yet recognized as Adivasi, they cannot officially ally themselves with other Adivasi communities and form networks that would empower their access to social justice. The Narikuravars find themselves in a catch-22 situation, because groups often compete for limited resources/reservations, so other ST communities might not be ready or willing to engage and support the Narikuravars' struggle to obtain ST status. To access this status, a major change needs to be created and implemented at the level of political discourse, one that re-imagines the Indian reservation system in the light of the contemporary context, historical precedents and future developments.

Third, the two communities establish their identity on different mobility/ nomadic principles. Many Roma aim to distance themselves from their history of nomadism; often Roma activists and scholars speak of their mobility as a historical hapenstance, and present themselves as sedentary. Differently, the Narikuravars embrace their nomadic tradition, and use it as part of their identity and in their claims for rights and justice.

Fourth, they are in different stages of their empowerment processes. While Narikuravars have been struggling for the past thirty years to obtain Schedule Tribe (ST) status, as well as education for the community, they struggle financially and hope to develop small businesses that would empower their access to health care, safe water and food. Roma communities have a more complex agenda and one that has been changing over the past decades, with different segments adopting different goals and strategies. However, what they have in common is the belief that they all need to be more pro-active in their agenda, rather than reactive. They have been establishing themselves as a social/ethnic group, and now they would like to take more of a leadership role in politics, and drive the overall agenda. This is done in parallel with understanding that most members of the community are still in great need of satisfying their basic needs for housing, safety, health care and education.

Overall, in spite of the differences, both communities advocate for an increase in professional activism. They are aware that to achieve this: 'Development of sustainable, reliable and accountable knowledge depends on many factors. Among them are the professionalization of activism and its embedding in relatively stable and secure funding structures. Some of the disputes about the adequacy, competence and reliability of activist networks and social movements begin here' (Van Baar, 2013).

This could be coupled with understanding the community, as Necula suggested (2020), on political principles rather than ethnic ones. Accordingly, the efforts should be focused on: 'The articulation of Roma [and Narikuravar] as a political identity rather than as specific ethnic groups per se. A political identity is unhindered by the reaction and production of an essentialist Romani [and Adivasi] ethnicity (by the majority) and instead emphasizes Roma political agency' (McGarry, 2017: 37).

To formally access social justice from the place of historical marginalization is neither easy, nor quick. People dedicate their entire life to produce small, long-lasting changes. Facing the perils of discrimination and the obstacles of systemic racism, which at times seem insurmountable, people in both Roma and Narikuravar communities, leaders and community member alike, in spite of being tired, engage – as we will see in the next chapter – in informal practices of justice.

Informal Practices of Aiming for Justice

Rajasekaran often told me the detailed story of their actions once the bill for their ST status reached the Indian Parliament:

> It lapsed because none of the Tamil Nadu MPs were ready to raise their voices to support Narikuravars. So, we decided to inform the government that we are waiting to get our rights. We decided to make the announcement through rallies and [a] hunger strike. We tried to reach several MPs from Tamil Nadu in Chennai and Delhi. First, we decided to have a hunger strike in Delhi at Jantar Mantar on 4th December 2015. We had a fifty people mixed age group there; children and fifteen women were also there.

He recalls the long days:

> It was hard. We felt really bad. We travelled to Delhi by train with the children, women and aged people too. We didn't have a proper shelter. There was a winter time when the parliament organized its session. We did not even have blankets; we are new to Delhi during the winter time, so we don't have a good blanket. Children suffered; women suffered a lot. [...] when we decided to meet to some MPs we had to get up in the early morning during the winter session, and we had to go, meet the people at their residence or office, where they could be available. So, we were ready, the children, women, were hoping to get support, because this were our rights. The strike was conducted at Jantar Mantar from the morning to end of the day, five or six o'clock in the evening.

The political use of hunger strike is legendary in India. Often the (symbolic and visual) site of hunger-strike-politics is Jantar Mantar,[1] a place used by many communities to stage their public protest, organize hunger strikes and get the attention of the media, and of the politicians: 'Through the hunger strike we raise our voices and address the media. And tell them we need to get the ST status.' But for fifty people to travel and stay in the nation's capital is not easy; it is costly and difficult to manage: 'It's really hard to stay in Delhi for very long period. We don't have any money. To go to Delhi the organizers have to get some funds from the *people. [Funds being limited,] we were not able to get proper food, shelter, and amenities. This was it, was really, really very hard time to talk to the people in charge. So, we have decided to come back.'*

Their perfomative acts yield some results: 'Then, 25th of May 2016, the BJP-led cabinet ministers approved Narikuravar community to be included among Scheduled Tribes. They have given the bill number 325 for 2016. The bill title is that constitution Schedule Caste and Scheduled Tribes order Amendment Bill 2016.'

While important, this was only the first step in an arduous and complicated political and legal process. As mentioned earlier, the bill was officially instituted, but it was not discussed on the Lok Sabha floor. And the Narikuravars know this. They are politically knowledgeable, aware of the complex political processes:

> *We know it is a very long run. So, we have decided to follow up and meet all the MPs from Tamil Nadu and the Tribal Minister, and even we tried to get all the support from the Honourable speaker of Lok Sabha, Dr. Tambi Durai. So, after our hunger strike, we made the Honourable Tribal Affairs Minister, and went to meet the Minister Honourable Pond Radha MP at his residence.*

Seeing no further results, Rajasekaran and other Narikuravars organized again and tried to get the attention of the government to their community issues. So they returned to Delhi:

> *Two or two and a half, three years of BJP-led government passed and nothing happened. We, the organizers, I Rajasekaran, and Mr. Jaishankar, Mr. Makaishwaran and Sudeep from Khushnagri had decided to go back to Delhi in late March 2017. This time we stayed almost one month there to get the attention of people, to lobby. We travelled daily to meet Tribal Minister, we tried to meet the Radhakrishnan, Member of Parliament and some other MPs from Tamil Nadu. We met several members of parliament at Delhi, but the parliament session came to end, and right now the bill was lapsed again.*

In spite of these set-backs, the Narikuravars are not deterred in their struggle, and are committed to use all political means at their disposal to further their rights:

> *Still, we are looking for the opportunity to meet the government officials and secretaries, member of Parliament's to convey our request to include Narikuravar community in ST status. In 2019, the new government was formed and we were hopeful. But immediately, due to Corona effect, we couldn't go back to Delhi or Chennai, to meet the MPs and the secretaries. So, now we are just planning to go*

*back again to restart our work to convey our request to include Narikuravar
community in Scheduled Tribe status.*

Introduction

In the previous chapter, we saw how formal practices aimed at accessing justice
are mainly conducted at the level of the elites. However, forms of resistance to
discrimination and asserting one's place in society, in hope of achieving social
justice, are neither limited at that level, nor are they done only in formal ways.
This chapter looks at the three aspects of justice as outlined by Fraser, namely
recognition, redistribution and representation, and outlines the practices that
take place at the level of the community, in more informal ways.

(I) The Struggle for Recognition

As we have seen throughout this book, both Narikuravar and Roma communities
have been struggling with misrecognition. How different Roma and Narikuravars
decide to purse their recognition depends on their local and community histories,
contexts, tools available and personal experiences. While their elites and leaders in
Romania and India fight to pursue an agenda of official recognition as Roma or
ST, at the community level folks find different strategies of empowerment.

Recognition: Narikuravars, from ST or 'Gypsy'

As I started my research in India, people in Tamil Nadu engaged rapidly and told
me that they know 'Gypsies', and that they have been seeing them since they were
children. The Narikuravars are seen as nomads, as tribals 'roaming around', as
'Gypsy', and 'impure'. Often, I heard stories about the Narikuravar hunting tradition,
that they eat meat, which is considered impure. Moreover, it is believed that their
impurity is transmissible. While anecdotal, the ways in which the Narikuravars are
described point out the dynamics that exist within the society, and showcase the
marginal places that are often allocated to the Narikuravars: 'Ideas of purity/
impurity were present all over Hindu society for centuries: In domestic, as well as
public life, in exchange for food or water, in practicing occupations, in kinship and

marriage, in religious action and belief, in temples and monasteries, and in a myriad different contexts and situations' (Shah, 2007: 355).

Coming into contact with the Narikuravars, and other lower-cast Adivasis, tribal communities are seen as a possible dangers of 'contamination', which would make one 'impure'. Therefore, keeping distance from them is thought to be best strategy. While officially in India the caste system and its implications of purity have become illegal, in practice these hierarchies of castism persist.

These caste-based dynamics were visible when I was trying to find translators who would accompany me into the Narikuravar community. While most of the people were willing to help, as time came closer to our trip, many times they cancelled under different pretexts, from children being sick, to grandmothers not keeping well, and to disappearing all-together. When we were in the community, my translators were polite and helpful, but often tried to keep away from the people we were working with. Through their body language, the physical distance that they maintained from the Narikuravars, they continuously signalled that they were not equal, that they were not from the same community, that they were – unmistakably so – not Narikuravar.

Outsiders of the community call them Natoti, or Nadodi, நாடோடி in Tamil. As a result, the place that is allocated for them, often based on racist and essentialist tropes, is marginal and inferior. It is not surprising that Narikuravars find ways to redefine and adjust. This translates into an avid daily struggle against practices of misrecognition. Faced with these discriminatory practices, Narikuravars often turn to other identity markers. As we have seen in the previous chapters, they know that they are associated with the English term 'Gypsy' and, as this word is not historically or socially relevant to them, they use it to empower themselves, and to create recognition outside of their local and state communities.

The label 'Gypsy', a term used negatively against the Narikuravars, has become one way for them to positively identify, and make claims of recognition. For example, Rajasekaran's social media reads: 'Rajasekaran Selvam Looking forward [to receiving] your support to bring out positive change in *gypsy children* education and development' (Facebook, January 2021). In 2020, in the middle of the global pandemic lockdown, Rajasekaran posted a video of volunteers distributing milk to the community with the caption: 'Regular #Milk supply to the children and families *of Gypsy* and Tribal in various villages of Tamil Nadu. We #Grateful for the supporters to made this possible' (my emphasis).

Using the label 'Gypsy' in their social media is mostly employed as a means to ask for international financial support. Thus, it is important to understand this as an instrumentalization of their identity, not limited to a symbolic recognition, but one that potentially improves their social and economic outcomes, thus linked to redistribution and representation.

This identification leads to crystallizing their identity, and helps them promote their image as a community separated from others. However, this is not the only way in which they show their identification. Rajasekaran, Anuradha and Sugan, the Narikuravar folks whom I have been connected with on social media for the past four years, also post during local, state and national celebrations. They post photographs of themselves, with their family and larger community, showing their commitment to their local, and even to the national identity. For example, for the past four years Sugan, who is an ardent fan of Rajinikanth[2] ('Tamil movie superstar' as Sugan always says in a proud booming voice), populates his social media pages with the actor's image and actions. Showing his commitment to the nation, Sugan also changed his main photo to be incorporated in a frame that claims support for the national Indian military. They all regularly post on Republic Day, signaling their membership in the larger Indian nation.

As a result, while the Narikuravars strive to identify as ST, Adivasi and 'Gypsy', and in this way carve out their place within society, they also want to make their recognition a part of the larger community – and informally further their complex, different and complementary identities at once.

Roma in Romania: ambiguity of identity

The fact that we can identify simultaneously with multiple identities is not particular to the Narikuravar communities who are tribal, Adivasi, STs and 'Gypsies', as well as Indians. Similarly, the Roma in Romania operate concomitantly within the local and national identities, and navigate the tension between the label 'Gypsy' and Roma. As we have seen previously, the Roma elites have been officially struggling through formal means to have their identity recognized as Roma, different from 'Gypsy'. While this label gained currency, both at the national and international level, in communities the term is not uniformly embraced.

Fighting against their 'Gypsy'/'Țigan' misrecognition, the Romanian Roma leaders and elites have been engaging in complex formal processes. As a result of their work, within Romania – at least – at the level of the elite, the term Roma is predominantly accepted. However, when I worked in Ormeniş, and I asked the people about their identity, they often proudly told me they were 'Ṭigan'. When I asked what Roma community they are from, they mostly shrugged their shoulders or they reluctantly called themselves 'Vătraş', or 'Căldărari', and 'Romanizat' (meaning Romanian-ized Roma those who have been present next to Romanian households).

Lucica, who was 50 years old and studied up to 4th standard, was one of the people of Ormeniş who identified as 'Ṭigan'. Once, while I was travelling with her by car with her son, daughter-in-law and little granddaughter, we were talking about their process of migration, and she was telling me about her experience in Germany, where she migrated a few years back, with her husband and her son. Down memory lane, she was gladly sharing her recollections:

> I was also cleaning there, in a house like a villa! I went to work 2–3 times a week. The lady of the house was paying me, and she also gave us clothes; mostly blouses. Oh, how we enjoyed them [she says smiling]. As soon as we received the clothes, we went home, and put them in the washing machine, and then we dressed with them! One day the lady showed me her long skirts. Those skirts were not like our Gypsy ones, but they had aprons attached, which were like ours. I also cleaned for her sister-in-law. They liked the way I work [she said proudly]. So, one day, this lady's husband told me: 'Tiganoi!' pointing to himself. And I answered: 'Me to!' [she laughs]. He liked it [she repeats in excitement], he says: 'Me too!' meaning he was a Gypsy!

Her son Raul interjected while driving and minding the road: 'They were from somewhere in India, they were not Germans. That is why they said that they are Gypsies!' Lucica continued: 'Raul [i.e., her son] told me I shouldn't say I'm a Gypsy. But why not?!' she asked rhetorically. Her proud identification as 'Ṭigan' was one that she was familiar with, one that she understood as a part of herself. However, for her young son, this labelling was problematic. Raul shared with us that he was aware that the moment when they would be identified as 'Ṭigan' or 'Gypsy', their employment with this family in Germany might be in peril, so he suggested his mother keeps this identification to herself. Raul said that he prefers 'Roma' to 'Gypsy', as the latter has negative connotations that often lead to blatant discrimination. Faced with racist practices, it is rather easy to see how Raul, and others, would feel very uncomfortable with the 'Gypsy' label, and would rather not be identified as such.

Other folks in the Ormeniş community were not only proud to be seen as 'Ţigan', but also refuted the 'Roma' terminology as a creation from the people who are outside of their own community. Sometimes, even within the same community, the terms Roma and 'Ţigan' coexist, with people of the same family claiming their identity differently.

The people's community identification came to the fore when I was interviewing them about discrimination. The people would tell me that they are not ashamed to be seen a 'Ţigan'. But, they continued to tell me, this came with practices of exclusion and discrimination. In 2018, when I went to Sibiu with Ciprian Necula, we spent the entire day in the Brăteiu community of traditional Roma, who identify as 'Căldărari'. The Căldărari are a proud Roma group, a community well known locally and internationally. As seen earlier, they are exquisite copper masters of jewellery and pot making. They are traditional Roma, which means (among other things) that they keep their traditional clothes, and that their identity is visible. When the evening came, Necula and I were trying to find a hotel in the neighbourhood, and our hosts took us to one nearby. As Necula and I entered the reception area, our hosts were walking behind, slowly coming out of their car. We asked for rooms and the receptionist started telling us about different accommodations, when our friends entered the hotel. On seeing them, the receptionist (a young Romanian girl) stopped her search and looked puzzled. Our Roma friends came and started talking to us, and hearing this the receptionist said abruptly that she did not have any rooms.

In response to this racist act, the Roma man leaned over the desk of the receptionist, and politely explained: 'The rooms are not for us. We are not staying in this hotel. This is only for them', and he pointed to us. To this the receptionist politely said, 'Oh ... ok', and she kept typing, then she turned to us and said, 'I have two rooms.' Necula and I looked at each other, talked briefly, and refused the offer, moving to another hotel – where probably practices of discrimination were blatant as well, but we did not come across them. The Căldărari family was a proud family, who took great care in their traditional dressing, and who also informally asserted their Roma identity and demanded recognition, even when faced with blatant forms of discrimination. But they have this too often!

How communities identify, and how they use the labels that are imposed on them, differ based on context and preferences. Beyond victimization, their choices need to be seen as modes of resistance, empowerment and ways to address injustice. Their practices show how communities like the Roma and Narikuravars take ownership of recognition, creating and re-creating taxonomy and meaning to access justice.

(II) Redistribution: Migration and Capitalizing on their Racialized Image

Both Roma and Narikuravars inhabit and operate through the contemporary socio-political-economic trends marked by globalization within a neo-liberal framework:

> Since the end of the Cold War, there has been a reduction in local production, and the privatization of social services, like education and health, have increased. Hospitals are giving way to private nursing homes and privately-run schools are mushrooming. Many goods and services are affordable only by the elites. The gradual retreat of the Indian state from these and other such social sectors leads to the withdrawal of benefits from ordinary people. This could further aggravate existing tensions. Both the trends, of liberalization – giving freedom to domestic capital for the privatizing of the economy – and of globalization – breaking barriers in the march of foreign capital – do not lead to a balanced investment in all parts of the country, but rather to the pockets of the developed regions which bring quick returns. The regions where most of the Adivasis live are left out of this process. Indeed the liberalization is likely to increase their hardship. Disparities are likely to widen, and poor regions like Chathisgarh, Jharkhand, western Orissa and parts of the North-East are likely to become poorer.
>
> Minority Rights Group International, 1998: 13

Today, many people whom I worked with from the Roma and the Narikuravar communities are dependent on state help, of the financial aid that is given to them on a regular basis. However, the financial support of the state is often insufficient to make ends meet, and they have to find ways to provide for themselves. Thus, when the state fails to make sufficient financial provisions to support their survival, and when employment in their area is not available also due to discriminatory practice, those labelled as 'Gypsy' in Romania and India who were a part of this study (mainly) employ different means to survive, which fall into two categories: Migration/movement and using the (often racist) stereotypes to empower themselves.

While we see many Narikuravars and Roma fostering their identity, taking pride in their family and community heritage, and investing in preserving it, we also see others, especially those of the new(er) generations, moving towards a different understanding of their traditions and belonging. This is of course not new, neither is this unique to the Roma or Narikuravar communities. These communities, like all others, are caught in a process of change, in which they have partial agency, but mostly depend on larger structures of power, which are complex, multilayered and perpetually transforming.

What makes the situation of the communities labelled as 'Gypsy' different is the way they are understood and described in literature, science and politics, as static communities caught in time immemorial, unwilling to change and therefore suffering from their own traditions. However, the changes from one generation to the next are rapid and significant.

Mobility as a form of access to both to redistribution

The situation of the Narikuravar youth is no different from that of other indigenous communities, who:

> In the last decade [i.e., 2000s], large numbers of indigenous youth from the uplands of Northeast India have migrated to metropolitan cities across the country. Many end up in the new service sector, getting jobs in high-end restaurants, shopping malls and spas. (...) Young indigenous migrants seem to be on a journey without a fixed destination, struggling to make out what and where home is. We refer to this as wayfinding: A journey without a map or pathway to follow, with no clear destination or end point, but rather a form of movement in which the traveller constantly adjusts direction, seeking out new places and possibilities as he or she is moving on.
>
> Karlsson and Kikon, 2017: 447, 449

Similarly, in the Narikuravar community, middle-aged and older folks are committed to their traditions, and look within their community to make things happen, while the younger Narikuravars have their eyes on other horizons. No different from many other youths of their age across the world, they want to have employment with a stable income, and access to modern/technological goods that would make their life rather similar to their peers. They are excited about owning the products of modernization: Video games, TVs, jeans and the latest models of phones. This entails entering formal, neoliberal economic structures, so they often seek employment, and (want to) move to factory sites.

While half a world apart, the Narikuravars' views and situation are no different from those of the Roma, who, faced with dire employment prospects, often plan their movement along the lines of 'push-pull' migration theories.[3] Thus, like many other migrants, the Roma and the Narikuravars' movement is often motivated by hopes of economic advancement. While their ancestors mostly travelled within groups, engaged in a community-based travel, today the process of migration takes place one individual at a time. Many of the Narikuravars and Roma people I have interviewed told me that they often try to find employment abroad. The Narikuravars strive to go to Singapore and Malaysia, and the Roma to Western European Union countries.

The Narikuravars need to overcome strict legal hurdles. They need to obtain travel documents, i.e. passports, which require them to have a national/local identification that in turn requires a stable address, a document that for Narikuravars might not be easy to prove. Moreover, once the passport is obtained, they need to have the permission to travel abroad, the visa authorization. Furthermore, to obtain a work or business permit is a lengthy and complex endeavour, which many do not undertake. For the Romanian Roma, once Romania became an EU member their travel requirements diminished, with Romanian citizens no longer being required to have a visa to travel or work. However, as Romania is not a part of the Schengen agreement,[4] Romanian citizens need a form of valid national identification when travelling abroad. Nevertheless, while Romanians' free movement within the EU is protected by law, Roma migration is still a complex and difficult endeavour:

> Roma EU citizens also face particular challenges when exercising the right to freedom of movement. These challenges, and solutions for integrating Roma migrants, were actively discussed in 2015, particularly at events on East–West cooperation in both municipalities of origin and municipalities of destination. Such discussions build on the emphasis of the Council's 2013 Recommendation on effective Roma integration measures in the Member States, which highlights that: 'In the context of intra-Union mobility, it is necessary to respect the right to free movement of the citizens of the Union and the conditions for its exercise [...] while also seeking to improve the living conditions of Roma and pursuing measures to promote their economic and social integration in their Member States of origin as well as their Member States of residence'.
>
> European Union Agency for Fundamental Rights Report 2016

The challenges encountered by Roma migrants have been researched, however those of the Narikuravars and other Adivasi/Indian mobile communities have not been studied (to date), and are therefore unknown. It does not take super powers to understand that the Narikuravar/Adivasi presence in Singapore or Malaysia is significant, and that they are often seen as 'problematic' migrants.

In my interviews in the Narikuravar community, they often shared that they 'travelled abroad for business'. They follow the other Indians migrants, and go near the Hindu temples, trying to sell jewellery. As they are targeting a small migrant community, which often is composed of low-wage labours, their selling and profit margin tends to be slim. The Narikuravars also shared that they usually live in common spaces, sharing basic accommodation with other Indians, and that they often have to run and hide from the police and other official bodies, who are chasing them due to their lack of migration documents. Facing these perils made Narikuravars aware of the complex logistics they need to navigate, but these vicissitudes do not deter them from wanting to migrate abroad, as a way to better their economic conditions.

Thus, I suggest that we need to see labour migration as striving for redistribution, as a form of accessing economic means that are not available within the country or place of origin.[5] The Roma from Ormeniş, due to their proximity to the Hungarian community in the village, often speak Hungarian, so they try to find work in neighbouring Hungary. They told me that they become seasonal agricultural workers, and they go and 'pick-up sparanghel' (i.e. asparagus). Most of them find their own seasonal work through networks of friends, relatives and acquaintances, and in spite of facing difficult living conditions, as well as discriminatory practices (not unlike other migrants from Transylvania), many of the Roma from Ormeniş think this is a worthwhile endeavour.

It is mostly men who work abroad, sometimes women, and if the children are old enough, they also bring them along. The 'West' (i.e. 'Occidentul') is imagined as a better place. Those who brave adventure, and/or those who have family or friends willing to help, sometimes find Germany and Italy as desirable migration destinations. Here, they live usually among other migrants, and get hired as daily labourers. However, Roma migrants (like other migrants) do not aim to enter the black market of daily wagers, but hope to obtain contracts abroad. Many would like to work full-time in factories, or in agriculture, as contracts would provide them with a more stable source of income.[6]

Faced with many economic difficulties back home, many of the Roma youth – especially male – from Ormeniş, like many Romanians and other Eastern/ Central Europeans who migrate abroad, are eager to embrace any job to make ends meet and send money back home:[7]

> Migrant Roma live a transnational existence. Their migration is not 'completed', they maintain connections with their relatives and friends in the locality of

origin, creating a continuous flow of people, goods, and knowledge between the different places of migration and back home. Migration offers potential for upward social mobility for the Roma families involved, who either move out of ethically segregated communities or enhance their social, economic or cultural status.

László Fosztó, Stefánia Toma and Cătălina Tesăr, 2017[8]

The eagerness of the Roma and Narikuravars to find formal, stable employment within the larger society comes at odds with the stereotypes about their lack of work ethics and their assumed willingness to engage in the informal economy. But these myths were dismantled, as the people I interviewed during my fieldwork were very interested in working abroad, and committed to finding ways to access employment opportunities; they often asked me if I knew people abroad who might be interested in hiring them.

When I was conducting interviews with Romanian Roma women migrants in Bavaria, Germany, I approached many whom I met while they were in the street, and near churches, begging. They were often chased away by the police and by the clergy – who came out and yelled at the Roma in front of their parishioners right after the Sunday mass. The Roma usually retreated for a few minutes, and then came back. When I talked to them over coffee and soda, they told me that they were looking for work, that they always try to find something, but it is hard as they do not have an official German address, and therefore they could not be accounted for in the labour department.[9] Sometimes they work in temporary jobs, which gives them a small income, but does not allow them to survive. As a result, they supplement it by coming and begging at the Romanian church during the weekends. Some of the people I talked to shared with me that they had family back home, usually young children, who were left in the care of elderly parents who need money to make ends meet. Thus, their meager income needed to become part of their remittances.[10] While remittances have been recognized as a mode of redistribution, and of empowering different communities, when it comes to Roma people, alternative or informal practices of employment – such as begging – are not yet accounted for, and often criminalized. We need to see begging as an alternative, informal employment strategy, one which has its labour rules (timing, schedulling, zoning, practice, skills) and an integral part of the globalized neo-liberal economy, and not as a devious criminal practice of those who refuse engagement with the larger society, and disrespect its rules.[11] Rather, we need to analyse this phenomena in close encounters with people within the communities, to ensure that they do not fall victim of the crime circles of human trafficking,[12] and to understand the obstacles that they encounter when attempting to enter the formal labour market.[13]

Capitalizing on their racialized image

Not always migrating or moving is an option. Many times, those in the most dire situations are unable to migrate.[14] As we have previously seen,[15] faced with discrimination and racism, living in poverty with very little opportunities to streamline their situation and formal access redistribution, many of the Adivasi/ Narikuravars and Roma resort to creating small business ventures.

While they were traditionally hunters, the Narikuravars had to change their profession when the Indian government passed the law protecting animals in the forests.[16] As such, they had to re-specialize, and started making beads, which they sell in the nearby Hindu temples (see Chapter 2). Many times, the majority of people in Tamil Nadu also refer to them as the 'bead-people': 'Narikoravan is a nomadic tribe involved in the making of "rudrasksha malai" and other such long chains, rosary beads which have been historically part of temple economies. Their products find great demand among pilgrims who travel to Sabarimala Ayyappa Temple in Pathanamthita, Kerala.'[17]

Their craftmanship is well regarded; Tamilians often told me that they might take home some of these beads, that they are nice, 'hand-made' and 'natural'. This image of the Narikuravar products is supported by essentializing stereotypes, which assume that Narikuravars are a tribe secluded from the modern world, that they are somehow caught in the *ilo-tempore*, in a cycle where time stops, where they live only by their ancestral (sic!) practices. As a result of this stereotype, the Narikuravars are assumed to have access to ancient techniques of jewellery making, and to materials that are not (supposedly) 'contaminated' by modernity or technological transformation. Thus, people often expect the beads to be authentic, natural and hand-made. And many times, they are. The Narikuravars shared with me that they try to get cheap raw material, and travel a great length to procure it. They work hard with the raw materials and transform them into jewellery.

However, different from the stereotype that assumes that 'tribals' will go to the forest to procure materials, the Narikuravars actually travel to urban areas where they buy them in bulk from distributors. These materials are often not even of Indian origin, but they might be man-made in China. Nevertheless, they 'pass through' the Narikuravars hands, and through racist/essentializing imagination, and as a result are seen as unique, natural and valuable crafts.

When I visited the Narikuravar villages near Mettupalayam, people would come to greet us; they would talk to us and make bead-strings. Without looking down, their hands moved quickly, with strict precision, transforming copper into necklaces. Their necklaces are typically 'mala' – 108 plus one of beads used in Hindu and Buddhist traditions as prayer beads. They are popular and traditionally used in India. They also make 'fancy beads', which are more colourful, made of plastic and other materials, and – while they maintain the same mala-like pattern – they have variations that could be used for adornments alone, rather than for religious practices.

But the most sought-after malas are the 'Rudraksha'. The beads used for them are typically found 'in the Western Ghats in South India, but the best quality ones come from a certain altitude in the Himalayas because somehow the soil, atmosphere, and everything influences it. These seeds have a very unique vibration.'[18] Rudraksha needs to be entirely natural, and made out of rare material hard to find. Due to their rarity, they cost a considerable sum of money (from about $30 to $150).

In my first visit to the Narikuravar community in the 'settlement' next to Mettupalayam, during a meeting with Mr. Raja, the 'president of the Gypsy', he was telling me the story of his family, and took me inside of his house. The back room was dark, and had a metal armoire on one of the walls. On top of it, there was a large pile of Rudrakshas. It looked like they would be at least two-hundred malas. This would amount to a small fortune, so I stopped, and asked if I could photograph them. He nodded, and stroke a pose for me next to the beads. Knowing how difficult it is to get them, I asked if he went to pick them himself. The translator translated my query, and the president looked confused. Then he pointed to the malas again, I nodded, and he firmly stated: 'They are imported from China!'

I smiled and moved forward. Mr. Raja made the situation clear: The Narikuravars are good business people. They understand the market, what is needed, and what brings profit. They also understand how others see them, and are able to capitalize on their image of 'beads people'. As the majority of the population exoticizes them, creating the image of them being caught in the past, the natural, traditional people who are not tainted by modern technological developments, the Narikuravars use these tropes to empower themselves. It is true that the Narikuravars work hard to make the beads, but their process is not as old and traditional, or as natural as it is typically imagined. It is rather reflective of the modern market endeavours: Travelling to find a cheap material, engaging in labour division that addresses strenuous processes of sorting and making the beads, and marketing for which in addition to standing in markets and in front of temples, they also use social media.[19]

The Narikuravars understand how laborious the process is, and therefore are looking to minimize the cost and labour production, and maximize their profit. It is therefore easier and more profitable to buy beads in bulk from China, and sell them. And, while they do that, they capitalize on the racist image that has been constructed about them as sage-aboriginals, not assimilated in the capitalist/modern market. The Narikuravars successfully employ this image to have access to better financial means, to redistribution.

Mr. Raja's entrepreneurship was not unique. When I was asking the community leaders what would they need to make their community life better, often they would tell me: A machine that will make their beads, so they do not have to make them manually. Getting the machine that would make the products with more ease is expensive, and the community needs to put their resources together to get it. In the meantime, they try to organize as best they can, with several men of the community travelling for long distances to get better prices for their beads, and women creating small cooperatives where they sort and align the beads. However, as the reason why people are interested in buying their products is due to their natural, hand-made allure, their marketing might not include transparent modes of production. These endeavours are small, but also follow the principles of the market, showing how the Narikuravars are in effect adaptable and aware of market strategies, and are willing to engage in them to better their overall situation.

Similarly, Roma communities also capitalize on their essentialized and racist stereotypes to access redistribution. For example, Ciprian Necula shared with me a story from his childhood:

> For the people in my grandpa's village I was 'fierar de tei' [i.e. linden blacksmith] – meaning the first male born. Thus, it was thought that I have magic powers. If I worked with iron, the tools I made could prevent evil eye with it. So, an old lady came to me, asking me to make these iron tools [he says smiling]. I tried really hard – but I was not really successful. However, my uncle made them in 3 minutes. And I only polished them and gave them to the old lady. She was happy with my work! This made me very popular – many asked me to make their utensils, and of course my uncle was happy as we could make money, [get] bread, wine etc. So, I performed the role of the first born 'Fierar' a lot – for 12 years. But, actually, my uncle was doing the work. So, we were capitalizing on the myth.
>
> Necula interview, 2017

Capitalizing on the myth that the Roma have extraordinary powers able to influence one's life is not new. Roma women have been seen as possible witches, able to curse and un-do curses for a long time. These myths and stereotypes become embodied in the global neo-liberal market dynamics that take grandiose forms. For example, the cult of the public Roma witches grew strongly in the first two decades of the new millennium. Powerful Roma witches like Mama Omida,[20] and others capitalized on the mystique associated with Roma women, and built empires working with spells.[21] They are now a part of the Romanian labour (un-taxed to date) market, which engages the larger Romanian community, and gives stable employment for many Roma women. They all capitalize on the image of the Roma woman: Long hair, with distinguishable traditional clothing, etc.[22] Moreover, these practices also empower women in the Roma community to access power and privilege within their community, and outside in the larger society to gain agency and occupy positions that otherwise they cannot access.

Of course, not all the stories of their empowerment through racialized and essentialized images are stories of empowerment via identity trickery. As presented earlier, the Roma in Brăteiu, Sibiu, capitalize on their traditional 'Gypsy' (as they prefer to be called) image as skilful masters of copper and iron to sell their products on the international markets. They manually create objects and jewellery of exquisite refinement, and have become well-known across the country and abroad for their skills and high artistic standards.[23] In spite of recent technological development, the people of Brăteiu do their work manually, crafting objects of unique value. They are very proud of their traditions and work, and they showcase it to outsiders.

In India, being called 'Gypsy' and known for their hunting skills, Narikuravars have been employed by the municipality of Chennai to help with their 'pigeon problem' in the airport. In 2016, Chennai's airport was facing a dire issue of pests in the form of pigeons: 'The pigeons would find a way inside the terminal and steal (. . .) food', admits an airport official. 'Or worse: Defecate on it' ('Gypsies vs Pigeons: How Chennai airport deals with feathered menace', *Hindustan Times*, 15 June 2016).[24] To address this issue, the airport authorities reached out to the Narikuravars in the vicinity, who were asked to take care of the issue:

'We were told that passengers complained a lot about the pigeons', says R Babu, one of the three Narikuravars who was hired by the airport from their settlement in Kotturpuram. 'So we dealt with the problem by luring them onto the ground with seed and catching them in our nets, before releasing them beyond the airport's boundaries', he adds.

The 50-year-old agreed to go work at the airport because of the guarantee of three-square meals a day. 'We worked there for a week and got decent food and Rs 300–400, which is better than most days,' Babu, who usually helps his wife in making colourful bead necklaces to sell, says.

'We were picked because we know how to catch the birds without killing them,' agrees another Narikuravar, who did not wish to be named. 'But some local TV channel took photos of us with the pigeons in our nets. Ever since then we've been getting complaints from welfare groups like Blue Cross. But we didn't harm a single bird,' the 38-year-old swears.

The feathered menace was a regular sore point for passengers at the airport, especially those who decided to get a meal while waiting for their flight.

Hindustan Times, 15 June 2016[25]

While this is a positive engagement of the Narikuravars' traditional skills for the good of the community, this endeavour needs further unpacking. First, in spite of their traditional skills being illegal now, they are appreciated by the larger community and by the authorities. Second, the Narikuravars are still being described as close to animals, as the *Hindustan Times'* reporter says in their title 'Gypsies vs Pigeons: How Chennai airport deals with feathered menace', capitalizing on a play of words that suggest that 'Gypsies' are typically the menace that confronts people. '"We had already tried and exhausted all possibilities," says a senior airport official. "We turned to the Narikuravar community because they have the skill to not only catch the birds but do so without killing them." This is the first time that an airport authority has contracted a Scheduled Tribe group for what essentially amounts to pest maintenance' (Ibid.).

Third, being known as a 'Gypsy' with particular skills that others do not have, also allows the Narikuravars to capitalize and access certain forms of employment and business ventures. When the COVID-19 pandemic hit South Asia, the state of Tamil Nadu went into a prolonged lockdown, which also included no public movement, and limited access to temples. Moreover, as the economy was strictly limited, people were not interested in buying the products that the Narikuravars typically offered. As a result, the Narikuravars' economic means were dramatically affected and curtailed. When I asked Anuradha how they were coping with the crisis, she told me that they were making a new concoction of a health mix drink that was supposed to boost one's immune system, and prevent the spread of COVID-19. To increase their sales, the Narikuravars capitalized [again] on another image that the people have about them:[26] As the community supposedly 'jungle people', or forest tribes, they are supposed to know the forests well, and to employ their knowledge of traditional medicine to address illnesses. However,

While the Narikuravars' 'healing practices and epistemologies' are legendary, and the Narikuravars healers well known in Tamil Nadu, the women in our study, both in rural and urban areas, used and preferred allopathic doctors and medicine (Alex, 2009). Most women said they do not use natural medicine, but many said: 'I do not use to follow our traditional practice. But I have heard people say it usually works' (Rekha, 29).

Dragomir and Zafiu, 2019: 71

Dragomir and Zafiu's (2019) study revealed that many Narikuravars:

Did not use formal medical services to address chronic and non-urgent ailments. But the reality of the community does not perfectly overlap with its images still vivid in the minds and imagination of the people of Tamil Nadu. Narikuravars know the images and also know that they are inaccurate. Thus, Narikuravar women showed no knowledge of traditional practices; that maybe their ancestors did, but they do not use them and that they typically resort to allopathy to address ailments.[27]

Facing multiple perils during the COVID-19 pandemic, the Narikuravars, adapted again, using their image as knowledgeable people of traditional herbs coming from the forest. So, Anuradha's family created a health-care mixed drink. As the Narikuravars are known (or imagined to be) picking their products from the forest, they are expected to have 'pure' products in their mixture. They use this image to their advantage but, they told me, they actually ordered the products, i.e. ginger, cardamon, clove, etc., in bulk (again) from urban distributors. They prepared the mixture, and sold it in markets.

These informal processes are used by both the Narikuravars and Roma to access economic means, when the state fails them. Both Roma and Narikuravar are able to capitalize on the racist myths about their community, and use them as tools of empowerment, and access to redistribution, adapting to stereotypes.

(III) Representation: Alternative Public Demands to Power

The same sinuous road that the Roma and the Narikuravars often have to take to access their social and economic rights is needed to navigate politics. Here, it becomes obvious that the term 'informal' might be insufficient, as it might not entirely capture the way in which the Narikuravars and the Roma navigate the political realm. In what follows, I will detail the practices used to overcome their marginalization and discrimination. Unlike recognition and redistribution processes, which could be rather informal or formal, representation – in its very nature – is a formal process, implying activity in the political sphere.

To have their voices represented in politics, the Roma and Narikuravars work at the level of civil society. As they are typically excluded from the political process, and paid attention to only when there are elections, those labelled as 'Gypsy' are rarely included in the decision-making process at community level.

The Roma organize a public march at Târgu Mureş

In January 2020, Dorin Florea, the mayor of Târgu Mureş, one of the largest cities in Transylvania/Romania, declared that the state should screen would-be parents for stable jobs, financial resources, age and education levels, and even remove children from families who do not fit the criteria. 'I don't think we should boost demographics at any cost',[28] the mayor said. Moreover, he continued: 'There are many underprivileged families in Romania, I am … talking about people able to work, who don't want to work, and who are having children with the sole purpose of having a source of income. This environment generates high crime rates, (school) drop-outs, lack of an education' (US News, 22 January 2021).[29]

This was (rightfully) seen as a direct attack on the Roma communities, which often are perceived as lacking the economic and social means to care for their children: 'Asked to clarify what he meant, Florea later told online news publication HotNews.ro that "Gypsies are a serious problem for Romania and we're pretending we're not seeing it"' (Ibid.). In response to this, Aresel (the Roma lead civil society platform) mobilized its supporters, and together with other Roma (and Roma-supporting) civil society groups, organized a march in Târgu Mureş, demanding that the mayor be penalized:

> Today is a historic day. The Roma, for the first time in the last 30 years, take to the streets to express their point of view, because such statements as those of Mayor Daniel Florea are not correct in the 21st century, in Romania. It is a firm position that we have, in which we sanction such statements, which lead to chauvinism, we call it electoral Nazism. The reason why the mayor made these statements was to take the votes of the Romanians through this latent racism that is behind the heads of every Romanian. It is a subject that we approach every four years, we upset and manipulate people, we use it for personal gain. I don't think Mr. Florea

is as racist as he says, but it's irrelevant. The political act he has done here is one of civil war, an act of incitement to hatred between ethnic groups, and this must be sanctioned and we must make sure that this gentleman will no longer run. We want him to apologize and we want him to resign.

Nicu Dumitru, from Platforma Aresel[30]

As a result, more than one hundred people, most of them Roma, protested in front of Târgu Mureș city hall, chanting 'Resignation', 'Shame on you', demanding the mayor's resignation from office. Discussing the event, Necula explained how this came into being. He acknowledged that the percentage of Roma in the county of Mureș is very high, estimated at 15–20 per cent of the population. Thus, Necula mentioned, it is important to understand that – if united – the Roma could have political clout, and could influence local politics in and beyond local elections. Târgu Mureș has about 135,000 ethnically diverse inhabitants. Officially, at the county (Mureș) level the ethnic structure as of 20 October 2011 was as follows: 'Romanians 50.35 percent, Hungarians 36.5 percent, Roma 8.5 percent, Germans 0.3 percent and other ethnic groups 4.35 percent.'[31]

Necula's reflection acknowledged the unspoken political dynamics of the locality, which has a large Hungarian community that has been mobilizing throughout the past three decades (since the fall of the communist regime) under one party: UDMR [i.e., The Democratic Alliance of Hungarians in Romania]. UDMR has been well organized, ethnically aligned, winning elections and accessing power, and able to impose its agenda at both the local and national level. While both Hungarians and Roma are the largest ethnic communities in Romania, they typically see themselves as competitors rather than possible allies. Thus, Necula's comments about the Roma political clout implicitly refers to that of the other minorities – which is especially important in an ethnically diverse (and at times tensed) city and county like Mureș.[32] While some Roma leaders argue that the Roma minority might be numerically comparable with the Hungarians in the country (overall 8 per cent or more), they acknowledge that the lack of unification of Roma, and their weak organization at the political level considerably diminishes the Roma political viability. In localities like Târgu Mureș, the Roma could play an important political role as their votes might be able to break the election tie between the Romanian and Hungarian parties.

However, this cannot be achieved without the Roma coming and voting together, along ethnic lines (like the Hungarians): 'It is important to unite them and fight racism for everyone. There is a commonality of experience of being a Roma, and we have to focus on what they have in common', explained Necula, and added: 'Yes, there is diversity among the Roma, but we need to work on the unity' (Necula interview, 2020).

Necula argues that the events from early 2020 in Târgu Mureș were an example of (alternative) community organizing: 'We organized, we followed suit, and we marched.' The Roma marches made waves in the local political arena and also (while to a much smaller scale) reverberated on the national and international stage.

Their public display of political power yielded results: 'The anti-discrimination watchdog found Florea infringed on the right to dignity of an ethnic minority and fined him 10,000 lei ($2,320)' (US News, 22 January 2021).[33] Necula commented: 'We got the mayor fired. He lost the Roma votes in the upcoming election.' And he further explained: 'Because the mayor refused to come to talk to us, the Roma mobilized and voted with the opposition, with the Hungarian candidate, who became the mayor. He came and thanked the Roma for the votes.' This political success empowered the Roma leaders to further unify the community. Necula says: 'We worked at creating a political manifesto and outline what Roma want too, and invited the candidates to discuss how are they going to address their ideas' (Necula interview, 2020). Thus, while not accessing political power through formal means, like setting the agenda, running for elections, creating and implementing policies, the mobilization of the Roma 'in the streets' of Târgu Mureș yielded a political result, and empowered the community's work.

Similarly, as seen earlier, the Narikuravars, when facing obstacles in obtaining their ST status and therefore not being able to access recognition and redistribution, engaged in alternative practices of representation.

> Nearly 50 Narikuravar women, children and men, under the banner of Tamil Nadu Narikoravan (A) Kuruvikaran Welfare Federation (TNKWF), travelled to Delhi all the way from Tamil Nadu. For over two weeks (starting from the first week of December 2015) they lived in tiny lodge in Paharganj area of New Delhi to meet MPs and Union Ministers. They also staged a hunger strike on 4th December 2015 at Jantar Mantar. The Union government ensured that the bill would be enacted, without any delay.
>
> Round Table India, 2016[34]

The Narikuravars' actions outlined in the beginning of this chapter by Rajasekaran, while visible, lead to a very limited outcome:

> Outside a tiny chapel at the centre of the settlement, Shanmuga is slumped onto a grey plastic chair, pensive. One of the local Narikurava leaders, he details his painstaking crusade for the bill to be passed. 'For me, growing up in a small

settlement in Trichy to making recurrent visits to Delhi for strikes and protests – I saw how the world saw our people. They admired our colour, our culture and our mysticism. But that's where it ended. Whether opportunities were afforded to us, they didn't care.'[35]

New News Minute, 1 June 2016

Just as in the Roma case, the mobilization of the Narikuravars in the public sphere yielded results: By using democratic practices, they received attention to their claims. But for their representation to fully take place, their presence needs to be formalized, and they need to be given seats at the tables where decisions are taken.

Conclusion

The Roma's and Narikuravar's informal striving for justice is relentless and fought on multiple fronts:

Community	Recognition	Redistribution	Representation – alternative ways to access political power
Narikuravar	'Gypsy'	Migration Assuming 'Gypsy' identity	March to Delhi and hunger strikes
Roma	'Gypsy' ambivalence	Begging, etc. Migration	March Târgu Mureş

Their elites work continuously, under extraordinarily difficult circumstances, with no financial gain, overcoming geographical and weather impediments, to support their community and ensure that their rights are respected. Their work is remarkable, and nothing – not even a global pandemic – deters their focus and their striving.

In both cases, we see the Roma and Narikuravars engaged in active demands for justice. They are not working against the state, as is often thought to be the *modus operandi* of those labelled as 'Gypsy', but through the state's mechanisms they develop processes to gain visibility and have their voices heard. These are different from resistance practices to an oppressive system (Scott, 1985; Chandra, 2015[36]). They are active engagements with social justice. As Mitchell argues-these forms of political protests:

Rather than challenging state sovereignty, such political actions are in effect, further reifying the state's authority in their explicit recognition of the state's ability to intervene, adjudicate, and hear complaints, and that the goal of such actions is not to humiliate state officials but rather to gain an audience with them.

Mitchell, 2012: 5

Thus, through these seemingly protest interventions in politics, the Roma and Narikuravar communities are striving to 'hail the state' (Mitchell, 2012), asking to be included in its policies. Facing denial of their rights and discrimination, they engage in practices, which at first glance might look like forms of resistance, but they are in effect complex processes of inclusion, and requests for rights and justice: 'We don't want to scare away people', said Geetha [Narikuravar]. 'The truth is, we're all trying to be like them' (New News Minute, 15 June 2016).

9

Conclusions

Harish Rajavendiran is a 13-year-old boy. He is slim, tall, with big dark eyes and a white strike of hair on his forehead, making his dark hair brighter. He wears his hair well-trimmed and styled, and has a small earing in his left ear. I had met Harish when has was less than ten, and saw him grow into a lovely young man. One day, I sat down with him and his friend in the public space of their 'settlement', chatting under the blasting Tamil sun.

'I am proud to be a Narikuravar', he tells me, smiling. 'I like to be here. My school is in Mettupalayam. I get there in school bus, with my friend Vassu', Harish says, pointing to Vassu, and taking him under his arm. 'We are both in 7th Standard.' They then tell me about their future plans. Vassu wants to be a Software Engineer, and Harish an Airport Engineer: 'I like to fly and airplanes. And I want to work in Africa or America.'

'Are you interested in hunting?' I ask, thinking of the traditional Narikuravar community customs. The boys respond immediately in one voice: 'No!' Vassu adds with a grimace: 'I don't like it.'

'Have you ever tried?' I softly challenge him. 'No', he replies. 'But, I prefer to be a software engineer. I like computers. In school we have computers, and we learn about them', he says, highlighting how the education that the boys undertake yields results. 'Tamil Nadu government, Jayalalitha is providing free laptops for the students', he proudly says. 'It's a very big thing.'

'Jayalalitha is no longer, right?' I push back, referring to the recent changes in the Tamilian politics. He nods in agreement, and then makes his political predictions: 'No. But she will be back.' I smile back at them.

Harish's father, Sugan, comes along and tells us: 'Both boys like the school, and they did not complain of not being respected in their school. This makes a difference', Sugan adds. He continues by telling us about the process: 'We send our children better prepared. We take more care of their dress and neatness than the other children', he says, implicitly refering to the stereotypes that Narikuravars are 'unkempt'.

'When I grow up', Harish says, 'I am not going stay here; I'm going to the town to learn there. Then, I'll stay there' – he points his finger to a far-away place – 'in a big city, and I'll come for maybe two to three days here.'

'We like the city', complements Vassu. 'It is better. And there is no hunting in the city', he reminds me of my rather naïve question. I smile, and the boys take me for a walk into the 'settlement', introducing me to the others: Old folks and their young friends, showing me their temple, and their houses.

near Mettupalayam, 2016

Overview

The Roma and Narikuravar communities live in different geographical areas, under different governments, have diverse cultural, religious and linguistic practices. The comparison of their process of accessing justice has been by default unequal. While the Roma in Romania have been undergoing a strict process of assimilation (especially during communism – Necula, 2020), the Narikuravars and other Adivasi communities in India have been maintaining their community traditions for a longer time. Also, while the Romanian Roma have an established elite, economically, politically and socially visible, the Narikuravars have an emergent elite whose work on the ground and at the political level is of tremendous magnitude, especially considering the limited number of people involved.

In spite of these differences, the communities share a history of nomadism/ mobility that has often been criminalized, and a long-lasting systemic experience of being subjected to racist discriminatory practices with others refering to them as 'Gypsy'. Faced with historical and systematic injustice that has been denying them access to basic human rights such as housing, schooling, safety, etc., the two communities have been working incessantly in their own ways to access their rights.

As we have seen in Chapter 5, 'Our Justice', both communities have been practicing traditional forms of justice: Panchayat and Kriss. Their tribunals have been rather flexible, not quite formal, composed of the elder men. The selection of the justices is typically done based on the power and prestige one holds, and women are typically excluded (older women sometimes have a role, but even in these exceptional cases their position is minimal). The goal of these traditional judicial bodies has been to reach peace within the community.

The long-lasting justice practices are linked to their nomadic lifestyle, which often situated them apart from other systems. However, as their mobility has been diminishing, so have their traditional justice systems. Their Panchayat and Kriss have been (partially) replaced by the justice of the larger community, and often by policing practices of control and punishment. As a result, mostly private matters, such as marriages and personal relations now remain regulated through traditional forms of justice. Moreover, in communities like the Roma of Ormeniş, Kriss is a part of the Roma past, with most people in the village not being aware of these practices at all. As policing and larger justice systems are swallowing up more and more territory, it is probably to be expected that these traditional forms of justice would be a thing of the past within one generation.

In lieu of traditions, new forms of justice following the axis defined by Fraser have been taking shape: Recognition, redistribution and representation. As we have seen, the Roma and the Narikuravars engage fiercely in formal and informal practices of social justice, through which they can claim their rights.

Practices of recognition

As their discrimination and historical marginalization are based on their misrecognition as 'Gypsy', the Narikuravars and Roma are working on redefining their identity in their own terms. These efforts are aligned with the goal of obtaining the ST status for the Narikuravar, and for the Roma to be recognized as equals, (typically) as 'Roma'. The Narikuravars have been engaging for the past thirty years in formal and informal practices to have their official legal status changed. They organize petitions, mobilize in voting, spread awareness within their community and go on hunger strikes in the country's capital. The Roma in Romania organize international campaigns, change legislation at the national level, and petition for their recognition as Roma. Thus, both communities engage in laborious processes that include developing legal measures and processes of affirmation in their daily lives. However, their processes are ambivalent, as on the ground the people in the communities labelled as 'Gypsy' still employ the term, while infusing it with different meanings, and articulate it in a way that empowers their identity. Roma in Ormeniş often articulate 'Gypsy' as a self-identity, with pride while referring to their community and traditions. The Narikuravars employ 'Gypsy' to make themselves known to the international community, and forge international ties. To date, these different meanings and references coexist, empowering communities to voice their truth, but also to make them the target of racist and differential behaviour.

Practices of redistribution

When the Roma and Narikuravar identities are misrecognized, there are dire consequences for their access to resources. This impedes their access to distribution.

In Romania, Roma are recognized as a national minority by the state; however, at the level of the community many do not assume this identity, especially when it comes to state benefits, such as educational programmes. In Tamil Nadu, the Narikuravars fall under the Most Backward Class (MBC) category, and as a result they have to compete with larger, better prepared communities for reservations and state programmes. Different from the Roma in Romania, they recognize themselves as Adivasi, or Scheduled Tribe (ST) at the level of the community, but they are not legally recognized as such by the state, which further impedes their access to resources. These limitations, coupled with structural racism and discrimination practices, curtail their access to social and economic mobility.

Faced with these limitations, both Narikuravars and Roma employ alternative means to better their economic standing. They often move, or migrate, in search of business and employment. The Narikuravars migrate internally and also go to Singapore and Malaysia. The Roma from Ormeniş consistently try to get employment in the nearby town of Braşov, but when this fails they migrate to Hungary and to Western European countries.

In both communities, there are further alternatives to access redistribution, and that is turning the essentialized, exoticized stereotypes used by others to define them into a profitable outcome. In Romania, some Roma women employ witchcraft and begging as means to assert their social and economic independence. The Roma also make use of their traditional skills, as in the village of Brăteiu, to access larger markets. In India, the Narikuravars use their image of 'bead' and 'jungle' people to create businesses that make use of these images, but in turn they employ modern business techniques, such as buying raw products in bulk from urban areas, or importing them from China. These practices need to be seen as informal and alternative employment practices that allow them to make needs meet and access economic rights that otherwise are inaccessible to them.

Practices of representation

While these three axes of justice are analysed here individually, they are in effect intertwined and interdependent. For Roma and Narikuravars to be recognized, they need to have political clout in changing laws and ensuring implementation of programmes. Political participation is further tied to having the economic means (both in terms of time and funding) to access the political sphere. Thus, while recognition of their identity seems to be primordial, the glue that makes (or breaks) everything is their political participation.

In both communities, leaders often said that political participation is scarce, that elites carry multiple burdens, and often have to work at the grassroots level to address vital problems of the communities, and have little time to engage in (re)creating their political agency. Thus, they often become service providers for their communities, replacing the parsimonious and (purposefully) estranged state. The Roma and Narikuravar elites understand that an organized political strategy is key to ensuring that their truth is spoken, and their voices heard.

But, for now, they also know that their communities have little political power, as they are small voting group (Narikuravars), geographically dispersed (Narikuravars and Roma) and politically divided (Narikuravars and Roma). In turn politicians, hungry for large numbers of votes, rarely pay attention to Roma or Narikuravars. If they receive any consideration, it is short-lived, right before elections, and present in tangible forms (typically food or cash) – but promises are quickly forgotten. This is mostly because of the limited clout that the Roma and Narikuravars have, but also because politicians do not want to be associated with the so called 'Gypsy issues' for fear of alienating their base.

Aware of these hurdles, the Roma mobilize politically and engage in different means of creating their own platform, which would empower them to have a (significant) saying in creating the overall political agenda. The Narikuravars (for now) aim differently; they hope to forge stable relationships with those in power, and ensure that they are taken into account when political decisions are made. While engaged in different strategies, both communities, in spite of the myth that claims that those labelled as 'Gypsy', like the Roma and Narikuravars, resist the state and do not want to engage, are in effect actively and continuously asking for their inclusion, demanding policies to be mindful of their existence and needs. In other words, both Roma and Narikuravars are 'hailing the state' (Mitchell, 2012), aiming to be included in state policies, while managing the dignity of their identity.

Their struggle is decolonial work. To access justice, Roma and Narikuravar people need to expose and dismantle gripping structures of power. This is a colossal task that requires undoing of power, 'knowledge, spirituality, and thought, structures that are clearly intertwined with and constitutive of global capitalism and Western modernity' (Mignolo, 2018: 22).

Internal hierarchies

We typically speak of the Roma and Narikuravars' access to justice, but it is critical nevertheless to underline that – as with any other communities – diversity and hierarchies are always at work. The voices of the Roma and the Narikuravars in this study are selected voices. They are often those of elites, and many times they are those of males, who are close to the majoritarian population, and therefore to power. While the diversity of Roma has often been discussed, and widely acknowledged, the diversity of the Narikuravars got less attention. Throughout this book, I have tried to address this insufficiency in the approach, but to a limited outcome. Thus, we need to underline that these findings pertain to the groups I worked with, and also that certain people's preferences might have come to the fore.

Furthermore, we need to acknowledge that in this process, class and especially gender differences are not neglectable. While the gender divide of those who share a tradition of nomadism does not follow with precision the lines of the settled communities, we have seen how women in Roma and Narikuravar communities often find themselves at the intersection of gender, class and ethnicity, often being discriminated against from many perspectives (Crenshaw et al., 1996). While this work has not been analysing the role of LGBTQ+ identity, it is foreseeable that the situation would probably not be improved in these (sub)communities. These internal hierarchies often limit access to power, and these dynamics replicate within communities. It is thus paramount to address them in tandem with the larger community issues.

Changes: on the move

'Before, we kept moving from place to place', Sugan tells me in 2017. 'We didn't have a permanent place to stay. But, finally we came here', he says, referring to the 'settlement' near Mettupalayam, 'and stayed for permanent. We now own houses, and banks are ready to give loans and support us. We own properties and vehicles, and are providing for ourselves. If you don't have proper residency, no one will support', he adds, explaining the reasons in the attitude change from the banks.

'We got our respect after we made our homes and settled here', he emphasizes, referring to the new sedentarization process. 'If we keep migrating, obviously we won't get respect. Because in the past we only stayed in place for 2–3 years and go.'

'Before these 30 years, when you were migrating from place to place, how did the people and government see you, and now how are they seeing you?' I tried to clarify.

'Government didn't care about us. People too, they were like: "They are Naadodigal [i.e., vagabonds]. They will be here today, and gone tomorrow." So, we didn't get any respect in the past; nothing like we are getting now', he says proudly, highlighting the transformations of his community within one generation.

In Romania the changes are not that different: 'My uncle – who is the last "Fierar" [Iron Roma] – has 12 kids', Necula starts his family story. 'He is 42 years old, he is married with Romanian', he specifies, 'but she is a "Fierar" – she uses the hammer! When my grandpa wanted to marry, he had to pass a labour exam. My grandma was not even home when this happened. "Let's go in the workshop to see", the maternal grandfather said. He made my dad perform to see that he is good enough to support a family. Of course, today there is no need to do that. Many "Fierari" do not even know to hold the hammer', he says, smiling. 'Overall, we do no longer care that much about the group cohesion; now we care about the individuals in the group. Individuals are more important than the group. "Fierari" had the same experience as Romanians', Necula says, articulating the generational transformation (Ciprian Necula interview, 2017).

My work for this book, which started from the premise of the traditional mobility as a basis of struggle for justice for the Roma and Narikuravars, revealed that these communities are in the midst of dramatic transformations, they are on the move. It is just a different move. Of course, Roma and Narikuravar practices and customs, like those of other communities, have always been changing. However, while these changes tend to be progressive and take several generations, in these historically nomadic communities the changes have been dramatic. Within a generation or less, the traditional forms of employment and their traditional practices of justice have often been forgotten, or used as symbolic means of achieving justice.

Their transformations are uneven and unequal, with certain members adjusting to the new conditions more successfully than others. Nevertheless, the path is clear, they are moving away from traditional forms of living and access to justice, and assimilating into the larger society: Romanian, Indian or global. These changes are often lamented by traditionalists and essentialists, who describe and exoticize these communities as being caught in time immemorial, not changing, but being stuck in their own ways. However, the Roma and Narikuravar people I work with have been resilient; they have been adjusting, adapting and successful in making ends meet in their struggle for justice, often within unjust systems.

Labelled as a 'Gypsy'

As stated throughout this book, there are many differences between communities that are labelled as 'Gypsy' around the world. They might have a common ancestral past, but this has been forgotten by the communities, and used typically by outsiders – scholars and researchers. They are also sometimes used by people in communities to make claims for justice at the national level in Romania and at the international level in India.

Both communities share a history of nomadism, but they also share a history of states continuously policing them and trying to forcibly settle them. They share a history of persecution, of marginalization and of oppression over centuries, under various forms of government. The emergence of the centralized state in the 1600s started draconic practices of settlements (Dragomir, 2019) and taxation for those who were labelled as 'nomads'. As colonialization took place, by the 1700s the term 'nomad' was interlinked with that of 'Gypsy' and exported into India, where it took grip of the South Asian sub-continent through practices of surveillance and sedentarization. What it is important to understand is that this criminalization of nomadism actually was a criminalization of mobility, one that legitimized racism and discrimination. It transformed the 'nomad' into a 'vagrant' and 'undesirable'. This is the long-haul of criminalization, which we see today, when migrants, refugees and asylum seekers fall into this paradigm, and are regarded as a 'danger' to the receiving society. Furthermore, this view also enabled the creation of systems of criminalization of those who move.

As the South Asian sub-continent had a long-lasting pre-colonial history of accommodating movement, the colonial efforts were only partially successful, and communities – like the Narikuravar – could negotiate their (lack of) place in the society. Dramatic changes in nomadism came in the twentieth century with dictatorial governments enforcing extermination of those who were deemed as 'undesirable', and those seen as 'nomads' and 'Gypsy' were a part of them. In India, the practice of sedentarization brought by the colonial powers was absorbed and practiced after independence in an effort to 'civilize' the indigenous 'tribes' and to create a unified nation.

In Eastern Europe, Romania especially, communism controlled the country's inhabitants, and was able to make Roma nomadism a part of the lost history for most communities. Through draconic policing measures, everyone's 'place' in society was heavily accounted for. By now, nomadism was not only criminal, illegal and frowned upon, but was also a part of the mythical past of the Romanian Roma. The late twentieth and early twenty-first century saw the re-emergence of neoliberalism and capitalism across the world, and that led to an increase in 'freedom' for those who had practiced mobility in the past. Now, their pattern of nomadism became 'dynamics of migration'. But, different from their traditions, where mobility was community based, now we see individual forms of migration, with communities being broken up and different members of the same group remaining behind in their permanent 'settlement'.

Where states, governments and colonialists have failed in sedentarizing, and bringing to heel those who traditionally moved, the neoliberal market succeeded in bringing about change. In search for limited state benefits and for stable forms of access to health care, schooling and employment, that would allow their social and economic accession, those who were traditionally nomadic 'gave in' and applied for permanent residency cards, like the AADHAR in India or 'buletin' in Romania. The new generation of Roma and Narikuravars tend to be semi-nomadic (at best), while most are actually sedentarized. Moreover, with the exception of those migrating for work, most Narikuravars and Roma understand themselves as 'settled'.

The success of those who criminalized movement has been long lasting. Being associated with nomadism is considered an 'essentialization' and often an 'insult' for the Roma and Narikuravars. If being a nomad is a negative term, one that could lead to exclusion and even criminalization, it is understandable that one does not want to be associated with it. This consequence not only impacts those labelled as 'Gypsy', but people on the move everywhere. If we criminalize movement, if we regard mobility as a negative trait or characteristic, we cannot expect to have fair and just migration policies. Those labelled as 'Gypsy' have been at the forefront of this struggle; they were also the canaries, signalling the practices of racism, injustice and discrimination that would be inflicted on all those who define sedentarization and challenge the state's boundaries.

Instead of refusing the connection with nomadism for traditionally mobile communities, I suggest a more radical approach, one that re-establishes the dignity of those who move, and which understands that one's life might not be identified with a given territory, artificially marked by those in power. This is the legacy for the future that those who move, like the Roma and the Narikuravars, bring to us today. It needs to be honoured.

Notes

Chapter 1

1 These forms of engagement with injustice are explained within decolonial scholarship as 're-existence'. Citing Adolo Alban Achinte (2008), Mignolo and Walsh state that: 'Re-existence, [is] understood as "the redefining and re-signifying of life in conditions of dignity." It is the resurgence and insurgence of re-existence today that open and engage venues and paths of decolonial conviviality, venues and paths that take us beyond, while at the same time undoing, the singularity and linearity of the West' (Mignolo and Walsh, 2018: 3).

2 http://www.icare.to/article.php?id=32114&lang=en; accessed 20 May 2021.

3 https://fxb.harvard.edu/2017/06/19/dear-gadje-non-romani-scholars/, 2017; accessed 20 May 2021.

4 Also see Matras 2004.

5 https://fxb.harvard.edu/2017/06/19/dear-gadje-non-romani-scholars/; accessed 20 May 2021.

6 http://socialjustice.nic.in/writereaddata/UploadFile/NCDNT2008-v1%20(1).pdf; accessed 13 February 2021.

7 The issue of defining nomadism as different from semi-nomadism is a legal matter in India. Thus, NCDNSNT 2008 argues that: 'we should not be distinguishing nomadic from semi-nomadic communities, since the measures of development and compensatory discrimination we suggest are for all of them. In other words, we are not proposing different sets of benefits for nomadic and semi-nomadic communities respectively. If the benefits and positive measures are going to be the same for them, there is no point in struggling with the issue of separating nomadic from semi-nomadic communities, for in reality, they cannot be separated in the way some theoretically-inclined scholars have tried to do. The list can be prepared by collating the following sources:

1. The Census of India, 1931, which gives a list of nomadic communities, under the rubric of "wandering communities."

2. The People of India Project, which provides short ethnographic sketches on 4,635 communities. A close reading of the volumes of this project will help us in identifying nomadic communities or communities that had a traditional nomadic background; may be a century ago, they were leading a fully nomadic or semi-nomadic existence.

3. The list of nomadic and semi-nomadic communities provided by different states and union territories of India.

4. The list of nomadic and semi-nomadic communities prepared on the basis of the field survey undertaken by members of the Commission.

5. The representations made by different communities claiming to be traditionally nomadic.' http://socialjustice.nic.in/writereaddata/UploadFile/NCDNT2008-v1%20(1).pdf

8 Nevertheless, the committee is also firm in making the distinction between habitually nomadic groups and migrating individuals, especially labour migrants: 'Nomadic communities are perpetually moving, for their occupation demands it. They do not leave their areas temporarily because of poverty, crop failure, or some natural calamity. They are also not shifting cultivators. In fact, nomadic communities are not food producers. They are usually engaged in other non-agricultural occupations. Hence, it would be wrong to characterize either seasonal migrants or shifting cultivators as nomads. For us, nomadism is a way of life, and therefore, is not a common metaphor for all kinds of mobile people who move from one place to another for earning their livelihood.' http://socialjustice.nic.in/writereaddata/UploadFile/NCDNT2008-v1%20(1).pdf; accessed 13 February 2021.

9 https://socialjustice.nic.in/writereaddata/UploadFile/NCDNT2008-v1%20(1).pdf; accessed 25 September 2021.

10 'The Roma in many ways comprise a most unusual ethnic group not only in Eastern Europe but also in the larger global sense. The uniqueness of the gypsies lies in the fact that they are a transnational, non-territorial based people who do not have a "home state" to provide a heaven or extended protection toward them' (Barany, 2002: 1–2). Furthermore, Barany states that, while not making any references to any historical or geographical data, states that: 'Romani groups moved north from the southern Balkans to present day Bulgaria, Romania, and Yugoslavia, some settling along the ways, others migrating further to Central Europe and beyond' (2002: 9).

11 Racism is understood here: 'As a system of structuring opportunity and assigning value based on the social interpretation of how one looks (which is what we call "race"), that unfairly disadvantages some individuals and communities, unfairly advantages other individuals and communities, and saps the strength of the whole society through the waste of human resources' (Jones, 2018: 231).

12 Along similar lines, *Critical Romani Studies*, the journal published by the Central European University, aims: 'To transform not only Romani Studies but also account for past injustices that have suppressed the voices of racialized minorities. Borrowing hooks' terminology, the Journal strives to contribute to an "education of critical consciousness", which in turn may transform the culture of domination in academia and beyond' (Bogdan et al., 2018: 5).

13 For example, in her analysis of W. E. B. Du Bois' work, Collins shows how the intersection of the paradigms of race, class and nation create social hierarchies that in turn shape one's access to 'status, poverty, and power' (Collins, 2000: 42).

14 https://newleftreview.org/II/3/nancy-fraser-rethinking-recognition; accessed 22 March 2018.

15 'Interview with Nancy Fraser: Justice as Redistribution, Recognition and Representation', https://mronline.org/2009/05/16/interview-with-nancy-fraser-justice-as-redistribution-recognition-and-representation/; accessed 22 March 2018.

16 I employ the term 'interview' in a loose format to denote the interactions, face to face, over phone/communication apps, or email that I had over numerous years with the participants in this study.

17 Teju Cole, 'When the camera was a weapon of imperialism and when it still is', *New York Times*. https://www.nytimes.com/2019/02/06/magazine/when-the-camera-was-a-weapon-of-imperialism-and-when-it-still-is.html: accessed 1 December 2021.

18 Nevertheless, to avoid the objectification of the communities, I do not directly use the images, but use them to support analysis, and to ensure detail accuracy.

19 https://elephant.art/ayana-v-jackson-how-has-the-camera-been-a-tool-for-colonialism/; accessed 20 May 2021.

20 Thorough out the years, this work has been greatly supported by many people - including students, with whom I conducted research.

Chapter 2

1 The presence of the Narikuravars in the south of India takes casual racist undertones: 'Tamilnadu is a home to various categories of gypsies, and among them the nomadic tribes or gypsy named as Koravar (or) Narikoravan (or) Kuruvikaran stands in the forefront. The occupation of Narikoravar community is mostly hunting jackals and other wild animals. Later, due to the government ban on possession of fire arms, the Narikoravar community changed their occupation to selling handicrafts.' (Chandru and Thrimalaisamy, 2019: 150).

2 Sometimes the Narikuravars are described as a part of a larger group, the Kuravars or Korwas, and their origin is traced as such: 'Hill Korwas are a branch of Mundas, a branch of Astro-Asiatic sub-family of Austric family of tribes of Chhotanagpur, which is the central habitation place of many aboriginal tribes in India. It is said that Hill Korwas moved westward to the Khudia region of Jashpur State (at present Jashpur district of Chhattisgarh) from Chhotanagpur at a date which cannot be fixed and are the original settlers in the Khudia region of Jashpur, when it consisted of virgin forests. From Khudia, in due course of time, they migrated further to adjoining regions (Srivastava, 2007). There was a certain group among the Korwas, tagged as a

criminal class, that used to be involved in committing theft, robbery, etc. in the forested regions. They were called the "Wild Hill Tribe". When their activities started increasing, the landlords of Khudia allotted lands for livelihood to them, to settle them peacefully. The group stepping down from the hills and settling in the villages was called "Dehari Korwas", and those who remained on the hills and did not leave shifting cultivation, maintaining their nomad and wild life with primitive culture were called "Pahari Korwas" or Hill Korwas (CGTRI, 2016). These groups of Hill Korwas settled down in the high mountains and deep forests, and started living by Jhum cultivation, occupying jungle land and resources. High mountains, thereby, became their native place and habitation. They all claimed descent from Khudia Rani (a deity of Hill Korwa, seated in a cave) and Khudia as their native country and looked upon landlords of Khudia region as their Head' (Das, 2020: 89). However, no specific study on the origin of the Narikuravar has been conducted to date, and their origin is based on their oral history.

3   Water scarcity is one of the issues confronting many communities in India, and the Narikuravars are faced with this problem on a regular basis. The problem became acute during the COVID-19 crisis of 2020, when washing hands and ensuring one's hygiene became a matter of survival (see Dragomir, 2020).

4   The Narikuravar community in the Tiruvallur district, Tamil Nadu, struggle for ownership over the land the government donated them. 'Their story of "great hope" began in 1963, when the then Member of Parliament donated 45 acres of land to the Narikuravar community to set up a colony at Karudalapuram village at Orakkad near Sholavaram. The colony was inaugurated on February 26, 1964, by then finance minister M. Bhaktavatsalam. Like in many other situations, the allocated land was a "dilapidated structure". Things went smooth until one P. Raghupathi, who incidentally also faced several criminal cases over the years, managed to register a transfer of patta for nearly 15 acres of the Bhoodan land in the name of a society registered as the South India Schedule Tribes Welfare Association. However currently they are being told that the local MP Govindarajulu by mistake donated the government land as Bhoodan Movement land to the Narikuravars' (*Land shark gobbles up Bhoodan gift in Tiruvallur*, 17 July 2016: http://www.nyoooz.com/chennai/543530/land-shark-gobbles-up-bhoodan-gift-in-tiruvallur; accessed February, 2017).

5   https://casi.sas.upenn.edu/iit/cristinaioanadragomir; accessed 11 February 2021.

6   https://www.thehindubusinessline.com/opinion/columns/from-the-viewsroom/children-of-a-lesser-god/article8650874.ece; accessed 11 February 2021.

7   https://casi.sas.upenn.edu/iit/cristinaioanadragomir; accessed 11 February 2021.

8   https://www.firstpost.com/india/land-pirates-of-tamil-nadu-that-history-forgot-6707351.html; accessed 7 February 2021.

9   'Close to 200 communities, mostly nomadic, were notified by the British government as "criminal tribes" through a notorious piece of legislation called the Criminal

Tribes Act, 1871 The rationale behind the Act was the European view that all *gypsies* [my emphasis] are criminals, and following that logic, all Indian nomadic communities were also believed to be potential criminals. For this reason, there is a large overlap between communities that were declared criminal tribes and those that were nomadic. The Criminal Tribes Act, 1871 identified the following six categories as belonging to "criminal tribes":

i.   Petty traders who used to carry their merchandise on the back of animals and supplied villages with varied items like salt, forest produce, etc.

ii. Communities that entertained the public through performing arts. Among these were musicians, dancers, singers, storytellers, acrobats, gymnasts, puppeteers and tightrope walkers.

iii. Communities that entertained the public with the help of performing animals such as bears, monkeys, snakes, owls, birds, etc.

iv. Pastoral groups, and the hunting, gathering, shifting cultivator communities within forests that traded not just in forest produce but in animals as well. They were also herders, and traded in meat or milk products with outlying villagers.

v.   Artisan communities that worked with bamboo, iron, clay etc. and made and repaired a variety of useful articles, implements and artifacts. They traded or sold them to settled villagers.

vi. Nomadic individuals who subsisted on charity, or were paid in kind for "spiritual" services rendered to traditional Indian society. Such sadhus, fakirs, religious mendicants, fortune tellers, genealogists and traditional faith healers had a low but legitimate place in the social hierarchy of settled people. Some carried medicinal herbs and provided healing services as well.'

National Advisory Council Working Group on Denotified and Nomadic Tribes, https://nomadsgroup.files.wordpress.com/2010/04/dnt_draft.pdf; accessed 12 February 2021

10 https://www.firstpost.com/india/land-pirates-of-tamil-nadu-that-history-forgot-6707351.html; accessed 7 February 2021.

11 The categorization 'Criminal Tribe' was also envisioned by the British as 'emancipatory', as in able to transform the tribes with 'criminal' tendencies into good citizens of the empire: 'The Reformatory measures taken by the British administration through the Criminal Tribes Act was the establishment of Reclamation to the Criminal Tribes or Denotified Tribes. The British Government wanted to change the character and outlook of the Criminal Tribes in general for elevating their status on par with other people. The introduction of a reclamation scheme for the Koravars formed the major initiative of the administration for effecting social mobility and fraternity. The Reclamation for Koravars emphasized the need to make the Korava criminals thoroughly unpopular with the members of their own community, to provide them with an alternative occupation, so as to make them

economically independent of crime and at the same time to divert the energies of the younger generation devoid of their parental habits' (Neela and Ambrosia, 2015: 44).

12 This has been historically imposed through colonial epistemology: 'The British colonizers' survey reports and documents became the source of invaluable information about such region and at the same time a tool for their continuous expansion of colonial administration. However, by using official machinery and tour for collecting data they bypassed the ethical consideration of research. Their writings in many ways ended up contorting tribes as being synonymous with being backward, uncivilized and barbarous. (Zilpao, 1; https://www.academia.edu/6505077/tribes_and_Tribal_Studies_in_North_East_India_Deconstructing_the_Politics_of_Colonial_Methodology).

13 For example, according to Bhengra et al. (Minority Rights Group International, 1998: 6) accounting for the criminalized tribes has not been accurate, because a considerable number of non-Adivasi communities have been included in the STs list. Some poor communities are demanding ST status due to the policy of reserved places for STs in higher education and in state-sector employment. Non-recognition or 'de-listing' of genuine Adivasi communities is an additional aspect of the population picture. Many believe that arbitrariness and political expediency are often factors in determining the recognition or non-recognition of Adivasis as STs.

14 According to the Habitual Offenders Act (1956) '"Habitual offender" means a person— (a) who, during any continuous period of five years, whether before or after the commencement of this Act, has been convicted and sentenced to imprisonment more than twice on account of any one or more of the offences mentioned in the Schedule to this Act committed on different occasions and not constituting parts of same transaction; and (3) "registered person" means a person registered under this Act as a habitual offender; (4) "prescribed" means prescribed by rules made under this Act; (5) words and expressions used but not defined in this Act shall have the meanings assigned to them in the Code. 3. Registration of habitual offenders.—The Government may direct the District Magistrate to make or cause to be made a register of habitual offenders within his district. 4. Restriction on registration.—No person shall be registered under this Act if more than six months have elapsed since the expiration of the sentence of imprisonment relating to his last conviction. 5. Procedure in making register.—Upon receiving a direction under section 3, the District Magistrate shall publish a notice in the prescribed manner calling upon habitual offenders [etc.]' (Habitual Offenders – Control and Reform – Act 1956, Act No. XI of 1956, https://www.indiacode.nic.in/bitstream/123456789/4911/1/habitual_offenders_act.pdf).

15 The Prevention of Cruelty to Animals Act came into effect in 1960. It has been articulated under various formats over the years, and in 1972 India's Wildlife Protection Act (i.e. Act No. 52 of 1972) was passed regulating sanctuaries, national parks and zoos among other protected locations, and aims to curb illegal trade in wildlife and derivate parts (https://www.animallaw.info/statute/wildlife-protection-

act-1972; accessed 28 December 2020). As a result of this legislation, the Narikuravars, tradition of hunting (with) jackals has become illegal as well.

16 https://casi.sas.upenn.edu/iit/cristinaioanadragomir; accessed 11 February 2021.

17 http://www.thehindu.com/news/national/tamil-nadu/forest-department-grapples-with-clandestine-trade-in-monitor-lizards/article8299720.ece; accessed 1 June 2021.

18 http://timesofindia.indiatimes.com/articleshow/80619650.cms?utm_source=contentofinterest&utm_medium=text&utm_campaign=cppst; accessed 7 February 2021; also see '12 Narikuravars held for killing jackal by stuffing explosive inside meat' (June 2020), https://www.newindianexpress.com/states/tamil-nadu/2020/jun/09/12-narikuravars-held-for-killing-jackal-by-stuffing-explosive-inside-meat-2154011.html; accessed 7 February 2021.

19 https://casi.sas.upenn.edu/iit/cr istinaioanadragomir; accessed 11 February 2021.

20 https://www.firstpost.com/india/land-pirates-of-tamil-nadu-that-history-forgot-6707351.html; accessed 7 February 2021.

21 For more details on the Narikuravar rituals, their preparation and dynamics, see Dragomir 2019, 'Gendered Practices as Rituals of Knowledge'.

22 https://indianexpress.com/article/explained/jallikattu-tamil-nadu-assembly-election-bjp-congress-7148150/, 18 January 2021; accessed 12 February 2021.

23 'As adivasis become increasingly visible as subjects in debates around conversion, identity, indigeneity, and development, the field of "Adivasi Studies", centered on the subject of the adivasi, becomes increasingly relevant. As a newly emerging field, it engages with archaeology, anthropology, agrarian history, environmental history, subaltern studies, indigenous studies, aboriginal studies, and developmental economics but adds to these debates that are specific to the Indian context. This essay discusses some of the imperatives that make a revisit to the field of Adivasi Studies compelling. It engages with the ongoing dialogue amongst those who write the adivasis into the larger project of history-writing, and sets out the markers of the field of Adivasi Studies from a historian's perspective. It reflects as much some of the dilemmas that one faces while engaging with the field of Adivasi Studies' (Dasgupta, 2018: 1). For more information on 'understanding and critiquing Subaltern Studies' rediscovery of the "primitive" tribal subject in the forests of Middle India', see Chandra, 2016: https://podcasts.ox.ac.uk/rediscovering-primitive-adivasi-histories-and-after-subaltern-studies; accessed 23 December 2021.

24 The terminology is still a contentious site; the terms 'Adivasi', 'tribe', 'Scheduled Tribe' and 'Indigenous People' are 'often conflated in common parlance. Since these terms are neologisms and are products of distinct genealogies (Karlsson and Subba, 2006), for academics and non-academics, the choice of which nomenclature to use is usually a careful, political one. (…) Tribe, particularly from the mid-nineteenth century, is primarily seen in colonial records as a stage in an evolutionary schema, a type of society that was different from caste societies, and marked by primitivism and

backwardness. (. . .) For academics like Damodaran, colonial discourse, rather than conjuring imaginary landscapes, analysed real landscape differences: the colonial stereotype of a simple tribal people who needed protection against exploitation thus had a historical basis (Damodaran, 2006, p. 44). Others like Devalle, Skaria and Guha (Devalle, 1992; Guha, 1999; Skaria, 1997), emphasize the hitherto fluid and interconnected relationships between social groups in the pre-colonial and early colonial period which were erased with the idea of tribe' (Dasgupta, 2018: 3).

25 'While the Order declared 212 tribes located in 14 states as Adivasis, the Government of India today identifies 533 tribes. To many therefore, any aggregate analysis of Adivasis is meaningless because it cannot capture the uniqueness that defines tribal groups' (Das and Mehta, 2012: 1).

26 'The term "adivasi," translatable as "original inhabitants," came into use for the first time in 1938 in a political context, with the formation of the Adivasi Sabha in Jharkhand (Hardiman, 1987, p. 15; Bosu Mullick, 2003, pp. iv–xvii). By claiming for themselves a long tradition of "insurgency" against colonial rule for their rights over land and against economic exploitation in postcolonial times, adivasis enjoy, in the language of Banerjee, "a kind of political hyper-visibility – a hyper-visibility quite disproportionate to their numbers" (Banerjee, 2016: 140). Adivasi, as a term, is distinct from Scheduled Tribes; as Xaxa has argued, adivasis, through bonds of emotion, view themselves as belonging to the same community irrespective of whether a group or a segment of it is listed or not in the constitution as "Scheduled Tribe" (Xaxa, 1999, p. 3595). Yet, paradoxically, in demographically enumerating the adivasi population, references are made to available data on Scheduled Tribes (see, for example, Shah et al., 2018). Moreover, while tribal communities confined to the Fifth Schedule areas in eastern, central, western and southern India identify themselves with the politically assertive term "adivasi," for those living in the north-eastern part of India and governed by the Sixth Schedule of the Indian constitution, the category of Scheduled Tribe or tribe is acceptable in the pan-Indian context' (Dasgupta, 2018: 2).

27 Typically, Adivasi studies have been emerging from anthropology, which led to a cultural, traditional investigation. Only in recent years has this been challenged (Behera, 2019).

28 The hierarchical structure of the Indian society is thought by some authors as a part of the plurality of the Indian system, in which different communities are allocated their just place. 'Pluralism in Hindu society is the result of a peaceful consistence among minority groups; it did not come about as a result of violent conflict aimed at achieving social change. (Unfortunately, a certain group of Western and Indian scholars insist on emphasizing conflict, which serves the agenda of vote-bank politics.) Under colonial rule, European colonizers did impose their canonized texts and theories on those whom they conquered. Worse, they completely liquidated indigenous peoples and, with them, their rich and valuable traditions of knowledge. They saw the natives as "tribals". Today's scholars have superimposed the same

structure dichotomy in the vain hope of understanding India through divisive and conflict-ridden categories, and there has been a concerted effort to show that learned dharmic traditions are hegemonic and oppressive to the "real" natives of India, but in India, the so-called tribals (characterized by rural life and informal knowledge systems) have always coexisted in harmony with formalized dharma systems' (Malhotra and Dasa Babaji, 2020: 244).

29 https://openknowledge.worldbank.org/bitstream/handle/10986/26335/114157-BRI-India-PSE-Adivasis-Brief-PUBLIC.pdf?sequence=1&isAllowed=y; accessed 1 May 2021.

30 Internationally, the rights of the indigenous communities have been coming under recognition for the past twenty years: 'Some states have even "come to recognize the multi-ethnic and multi-cultural character of their national societies and the need for respecting this diversity for political stability and social progress". India is not a signatory, however, to the revised ILO Convention no. 169 which essentially removes the earlier assimilationist approach of Convention no. 107. A draft UN Declaration of the Rights of Indigenous Peoples has been formulated and a "Permanent Forum" on indigenous peoples within the UN is contemplated. Although India has been among the first to declare its intentions with regard to the protection and promotion of the natural rights of Adivasis, its actions have sharply differed with these declarations. The recognition of Adivasis as indigenous peoples would enable the Indian government to develop and translate the evolving principles and norms at the international level into practice in accordance with the aspirations of the Adivasis' (Minority Rights Group International, 1998: 13).

31 In 2016, according to the Government of India as per the 'Status of Inclusion of Denotified, Nomadic and Semi-Nomadic Tribes among Scheduled Castes/ Scheduled Tribes/ Other Backward Classes', National Commission for Denotified, Nomadic and Semi-Nomadic Tribes of the Ministry of Social Justice and Empowerment, 2016, the Attur Kilnad Koravars and Attur Meland Koravars were Koravars as Denotified Communities, who are OBC; none of them are recorded as ST and the Narikuravars are not mentioned.

32 https://uidai.gov.in/; accessed 13 February 2021.

33 https://www.globalsecurity.org/military/world/india/caste-dnt.htm; accessed 13 February 2021.

34 https://nomadsgroup.files.wordpress.com/2010/04/dnt_draft.pdf; accessed 12 February 2021.

35 https://www.yamunaflaherty.com/stories/2018/4/10/narikuravargypsies; accessed 12 February 2021.

36 Next to 'tribal people, women and other marginal sections of Indian society' in the first two decades of the twenty-first century the Dalit studies have been emerging. This has been connected to the attention that was paid to 'the persistence of practices

that sustain caste inequality and its relationship with the unraveling of modernity in India' (Ramnarayan and Satyanarayana, 2016: ix).

37 The Adivasi's uneven development is remarked by scholars, who argue that 'existing policy regimes have not improved the status of DNT and NT. They continue to be denied effective voice, are forced to live in poor conditions and suffer from an inter-generational neglect that deprives them of real and viable opportunities for social and economic mobility despite the fact that formal education remains a core aspiration among them, for the large part unrealised' (Kannabiran et al., 2018: 102).

38 The Narikuravar community is not the only Adivasi group that has been undergoing drastic transformation: 'While tribal identity should be preserved, tribals should develop in their own way without hindrance. For a tribal group like Hill Korwas with distinct life and processes, integration must be sharply differentiated from assimilation which means complete loss of cultural identity for them. Each group must be able to uphold its cultural heritage with dignity and sense of achievement. Integration is a dynamic and continuous process which necessarily involves give and take by the various sections of the national communities – this process could never be complete. Without taking the tribal ethos and sentiments into account, no development initiative might succeed. Need of education, healthcare amenities, decent livelihood and living are felt even at the most interior parts and by most vulnerable groups. Modern means are to be co-opted with modern ways of reaching out to the vulnerable to cater their needs within their cultural ambit and distinct identities' (Das, 2020: 95–6).

Chapter 3

1 Like the situation of the Narikuravars in India, the Roma in Toflea (researched by Necula in 'Studiu de Diversitate', work in progress) live in similar, rather dire, conditions: 'Most Roma living in the valley do not own property documents on their house or land, and pay taxes based on the registration in the Agricultural Register. Regarding the living conditions, the mayor's office estimates that approximately 13% of the total households in the commune have less than 15.33 sqm/person. Most overcrowded homes belong to Roma people. Priority for all those who have overcrowded homes and in an advanced state of degradation is to build one or two rooms with the hall. Next to most of the small houses there is either a foundation already made or the brick stored' (Necula in 'Studiu de Diversitate', work in progress).

2 Just as in the case of Indian communities, the Roma research conducted before the twenty-first century was almost entirely done by outsiders, who used an objectification, essentializing and exoticization of the community, producing questionable quality of the scholarly work and politicized writings, often supporting discriminatory views, which frequently muffled community voices. Many studies

describe the Roma community from outside (McDowell, 1970; Matras, 2014/2015), speculate about where they come from (Shashi, 1990; Hancock, 1991), outline their history (Crowe, 1996; Stewart, 1997; Petcut, 2016; Marushiakova and Popov, 2021), describe the Roma along overgeneralizing lines (Fonseca, 1996) and deplore their dire situation and how they are marginalized (Pons, 1995; Barany, 2002). Many of these works attempt to dismantle some preconceived (and usually negative) views that potential readers might hold about the Roma, might run short in accomplishing this goal and often end up reiterating many of the clichés that essentialize the communities. While notable works have been breaking the mould over the years (Hancock, 1991), new voices have emerged in the field of Romani (critical) studies questioning the colonizing perspective previously employed, 'reclaiming Romani-ness' (Costache, 2018) and affirming Roma voices. More recently, scholars have been focusing on the Romani peoples' segregation in urban European spaces (Picker, 2017), on how neoliberal governmentality affected the integration of Roma in Europe (Voiculescu, 2016), about striving for social justice (Rostas and Ryder, 2014), about public policy and Roma inclusion (Anan et al., 2014; Anton et al., 2014), on EU policies regarding Roma (Rostas, 2019), on how discrimination and phobia regarding the Roma community still persists (McGarry, 2017), on how the Roma community has been accessing human rights (Bhabha et al., 2017), on Romani history/slavery (Chiriac, 2020), Romani politics under the communist regime (Necula, work in progress), about Romani women mobilization (Corradi, 2017; Kóczé et al., 2018; D'Agostino, 2019) to name only a few. Important works have also been designed as activist scholarship, aiming to directly empower the community (Gheorghe, 2016). Moreover, Surdu's book, *Those Who Count*, adopts a different view, and instead of researching the Roma, he analyses how research about this community has been developing, highlighting the data and praxis that is currently available for analysis.

3   Thomas Acton, 'Migration and the Roma', https://www.romarchive.eu/en/roma-civil-rights-movement/migration-and-roma/; accessed 21 February 2021.

4   Similarly, Hancock, says that: 'The presence of Shina and (possibly) Burushaski items in Romani suggest that the Ancestors of the Roma crossed a significant expanse of the western Himalayas in leaving the Indian subcontinent. These words are the primary evidence which can be employed in reconstructing the early migrations of the Roma across the Karakoram and Hindu Kush ranges and into Persian-speaking territories' (Hancock, 2002: 10).

5   *On Romani Origins and Identity,* Ian Hancock, https://radoc.net/radoc.php?doc=art_b_history_origins&lang=es&articles=true; accessed 21 February 2021.

6   https://www.youtube.com/watch?v=LDQRyzKBRpY; accessed 21 February 2021.

7   Across Europe, especially in England, from the seventeenth century onwards nomads came under the strict scrutiny of the state, and both their movement and behaviour were criminalized. In pre-colonial India, nomads were overall better

accommodated within the overall society, but nomadism was at times associated with criminal behaviour. However, once colonialist ruling brought its stereotypes and legal mechanisms, all nomadic communities of South Asia came under strict surveillance and became severely criminalized (Dragomir, 2019).

8   From 1949 onwards, the Roma have been described as a 'social problem' within the official documents of the Romanian Workers' Party and, according to Necula: 'The new [communist] regime applied a double measure to the Roma. Sedentary Roma, in the process of assimilation, became part of the system, they no longer needed special attention, except for reparative measures to "lift" and combat prejudice of bourgeois origin against them' (Necula, work in progress).

9   Similarly, in his detailed review of the diversity of Roma communities, Necula ('Studiu de Diversitate', work in progress) distinguishes specific details between different community characteristics based on their profession, for example '*Argintari/ Silversmiths* (goldsmiths), who traditionally make ornaments of precious metals. They came from among the princely slaves (property of the ruler and then of the state) and practiced their craft nomadically. *Boldenii*, also identified as florists, deal with the sale of decorative plants, especially flowers, with the making of ornaments and floral arrangements. The Boldeni live mainly in Bucharest and self-identify with the traditions specific to their community, different from other Roma, especially regarding the central role of women in the family's economy. *Căldărari* lived a nomadic way of life, traveling in wheeled carts and living in large tents, intended to house and forge; they settled in the 1970s and live in compact groups adhering to a strict set of rules. This group of Roma is recognized as the most conservative of Roma cultural traditions and practices: they proudly use the Romani language, the traditional dress, etc. (. . .) *Fierari* (blacksmiths, sometimes laity): process of hot metal (iron, steel, etc.) from which they make agricultural tools, horseshoes, carts, etc. The old deeds and documents are frequently mentioned when they were called by lords or boyars (even by the rebellious peasants) to make tools and weapons. They were among the first Roma to sedentarize. (. . .) *Lautarii* are musicians, recognized in all historical periods for their artistic mastery. They developed an identity discourse that places them at the top of the pyramid compared to other Roma: "Roma elite", "Roma aristocrats", etc. Lautarii are spread all over Romania, some of them still speak and sing in the Romani language and practice a culture specific to the fiddler Roma, including in the recruitment policies of the group members. (Necula, 'Studiu de Diversitate', work in progress).

10 These definitions are rather controversial, with 'Rudari' for example being thought not to be Roma, but Romanians who shared similar economic and educational characteristics with other Roma communities.

11 As a result, the European Parliament rapport of 2020 remarked that: 'The [current] framework highlights the diversity inherent in the general term "Roma", but does not

recognize the diversity within populations of Roma origin. The term "Roma" or the double term "Sinti and Roma", used in EU policies and discussions, does not reflect the heterogeneous nature of this minority, so that some people of Roma origin, such as those belonging to the communities of Kalè, Manouche, Lovara, Rissende, boys, taming, caldaras, romanichel or sinti, feel excluded or not taken into account. The Roma represent only one of the populations with Roma origins in Europe.' As a result, the rapport recommends that: 'Using the name of a group to talk about other groups in EU policies and discussions is a practice often criticized by members of these communities. Therefore, the post-2020 policy for equality and inclusion of people of Roma origin should take into account, in priority areas, the internal heterogeneity of this community, ensuring that no one is left out, including those who do not have an ethnic context, such as the Ashkali, the Balkan Egyptians or the nomads, but who are stigmatized as "gypsies". In addition, it would be logical for the term referring to all groups to be "population of Roma origin" [or "Roma" in the broadest sense – translator's note].' https://www.europarl.europa.eu/doceo/document/A-9-2020-0147_RO.pdf; accessed 13 August 2021.

12 The term 'Gypsy' in English, 'Gitano' in Spanish, 'Gitan' in French and 'Țigani', is considered to come from the word 'Egyptian', because the Roma are originally from Egypt. In other sources, Neacșu claims that the name 'Tigan' comes from the Greek word 'athiganos/athiganoy'. Hcih sigiens 'pagan', 'eretic', 'Untouchable' or 'Impure' (Grigore et al., 2007: 9).

13 'Several Roma, including children, have been killed in attacks this year involving firearms, gasoline bombs and hand grenades. Roma activists blame right-wing groups, which appear to have grown in strength as the economic crisis has deepened across much of Eastern Europe' (Eric Westervelt, 2009, *Wave Of Violence Strikes Eastern Europe's Gypsies*, https://www.npr.org/templates/story/story.php?storyId =112460670; accessed 25 February 2021).

14 *Dear Gadje (non-Romani) Scholars*, https://fxb.harvard.edu/2017/06/19/dear-gadje-non-romani-scholars/; accessed 21 March 2018.

15 https://fxb.harvard.edu/dear-gadje-non-romani-scholars/; accessed 17 November 2017.

16 For more information see: https://centerforjustice.columbia.edu/content/roma-peoples-project; accessed 23 December 2021.

17 Activists and Roma scholars also declare that it is not politically salient for those currently in power to have all the Roma declare themselves as such, as this would increase the unity of the community, and would pose a political threat to current leaders who benefit greatly from Romani voters supporting different leaders, mainly 'Gadje' ones. As Hungarian voters overwhelmingly cast their vote based on the candidate's ethnicity, the Hungarian political leaders are powerful players in Romanian politics, participating in important national decision-making processes. Differently,

Roma vote for political candidates whom they are familiar with, and are usually courted by politicians briefly before elections, and then ignored after they get elected.

18 As a result of this sensitive identification, some scholars (Ladanyi and Szelenyi, 2001; Surdu, 2016) argue that identification should consist of a triple procedure: (1) the subjects self-identify as Roma; (2) the experts place categorizations based on their previous interactions with the population under scrutiny; and (3) accepting that the field operators that make ethnic identifications are socially accredited (Surdu, 2016: 61). This approach, while lengthy and uncertain and complicates fieldwork, would reveal the stereotypical identification of the Roma, allowing both for the voice of the community to be heard and for the external identifications to be brought to light. Moreover, as Surdu (2016) argues, this would lead to an epistemological transformation of the Roma subject from an independent variable (one that is unchangeable, one that could explain variety and change to other variables) to a dependent one (a variable or category that is changing depending on the three processes outlined above).

19 Similarly, according to Necula ('Studiu de Diversitate', work in progress), discussing the Spoitori Roma community in Calafat (southern Romania), schooling 'is seen as a form of social emancipation: "In our family, the children are at school, in kindergarten. For example, my daughter is in the 5th grade, she only takes 9 and 10 and her niece is the same. The little one is 5 years old, she is in kindergarten now." Necula details that the Roma see education as a possibility to make future plans: 'Well, I want to leave her at school, now it depends on her how smart she wants to be. I want to let her finish everything, to come out with a job, with something. She says she wants to be a doctor, a nurse, a lawyer, it depends on her what she wants.' Necula's study cites one of his Roma female participants, aged 37, who graduated 10 classes.

20 In the same vein, Roma in the other parts of Romania are also 'aware that changes take time, perhaps with the change of generations. He notes that the community is more open and modernized and that the main factor has been access to information through television and the Internet.' Similarly, in Cetate, Ursari stated that the main factor of change is the possibility to work locally. 'This would solve many of their problems, including economic mobility and hard work in agriculture, in European countries: "Give us a job, work and have something to live on. Look, let's go during the day, let it be a hoe of corn, sunflower, beets, look, let's have something to work on"' (Necula, 'Studiu de Diversitate', work in progress).

Chapter 4

1 UNICEF, https://www.unicef.org/Educatie_romi.pdf; accessed 22 March 2021.

2 Buzescu, 2012: 'Roma palaces', in *National Geographic*, https://www.youtube.com/watch?v=iTVCjvTU274; accessed 20 March 2021.

3 Those labelled as 'Gypsy' fall through the scholarly and mediatic cracks; they are the middle-class Roma, those who have careers, and develop their lives in connection to the larger society (as we will see in the story of Roma and Narikuravar women below).

4 In their 2009 work, Kóczé and Popa highlight how research and policies from Central and Eastern Europe (CEE) claim their specific attention on the situation of Roma women in the analysis and in the design of solutions, in effect they rarely take an intersectional outlook, and in return create 'anti-discrimination policies [that] are not sufficient to address various forms of intersecting inequalities in social policies' (Kóczé and Popa, 2009: 13; https://cps.ceu.edu/sites/cps.ceu.edu/files/cps-policy-study-missing-intersectionality-2009.pdf; accessed 19 March 2021).

5 Oprea (2012) and Schultz (2012) argue that to address violence against Roma women we need to understand that it takes place 'in complex ways that vary widely across Roma communities—from intra-group forms such as domestic psychological and physical abuse and harmful practices that are often labeled "cultural traditions"' (Kóczé and Popa, 2009: 13), and that this will need an intersectional approach at all levels, from policy making to implementation. Furthermore, scholars (Schultz, 2012), also bring to the fore the difficulty of creating an intersectional feminist movement unanimously accepted as a 'large number of women activists pursued a very progressive Romani women's rights agenda in Central and Eastern Europe over the past decade and that not all of them have chosen to call themselves feminists. The defining characteristic of this agenda was to question Romani gender politics and thus, in some senses, Romani tradition. Other Romani women activists prioritized anti-Romani racism but would support Romani women's rights in specific instances. It would be inappropriate for me to label all of this activity as feminist. (Schultz, 2012: 37).

6 For example, in 'the Report Discrimination and the Roma Community 2016, out of a total of 154 cases, 149 Roma women were identified as victims of racial or ethnic discrimination. This information, along with further information given by FSG staff and the experience of Roma women who have approached the FSG, shows the importance of analysing how interrelated forms of discrimination such as discrimination on the basis of gender and racial or ethnic discrimination operate together, in order to work towards eradicating discrimination against Roma people' (Ruz, 2019: 4–5; https://www.gitanos.org/upload/22/65/GUIDE_ON_INTERSECTIONAL_DISCRIMINATION_-_ROMA_WOMEN_-_FSG_33444_.pdf; accessed 19 March 2021).

7 However, the specific obstacles faced by women who are also members of specific communities and 'castes', especially Dalits, has been interrogated: 'Female disadvantage is well documented and finds its rationale, as does the caste system, in Hindu law books (Deshpande 2002). It plays out in several spheres of economic and social life: women's lower labor force participation and wages relative to men, poorer health and

education outcomes, less voice in the political or general public arena, and less access
to markets. In an infamously Indian pattern, we find that, in terms of sex ratios, India
lags behind many countries at the same income level. This represents stark testimony
of female disadvantage and the disincentive for parents to have daughters, although
there may be evidence of an incipient turnaround in some parts of India (Das Gupta,
Chung, and Shuzhuo 2009). Yet, when girls and women do survive, they do better
today than did the girls and women of the generation of their mothers, which is
another way of saying that key indicators of gender equality are improving if one
discounts the "missing women" (Sen 1992). The absolute levels of the indicators,
however, continue to be poor, especially for Dalit and Adivasi women, who suffer
from multiple disadvantages' (World Bank, 2011: 23). The connection between gender
and community/'caste', is still not fully pursued in understanding structural
inequalities in South Asia. However, incipient efforts have been made by the World
Bank which in 2011 mentioned (in passing) that 'Adivasi, Dalit, and Muslim women
tend to show much poorer outcomes than other women [in India]' (World Bank,
2011: 24; https://openknowledge.worldbank.org/handle/10986/2289).

8 See also Fonseca, 1996: 130.

9 https://www.worldbank.org/en/news/immersive-story/2017/08/22/educating-girls-
    ending-child-marriage; accessed 14 May 2021.

10 In his 'Studiu de Diversitate', Necula interviewed Roma from different communities and
    found that school, marriage and gender dynamics are a great part of the societal
    concerns for the Roma: 'The fact that the girls are married at a very young age, leads to
    their retirement from the school system at a fairly young age of 10–11 years. Thus, the
    dropout rate among girls from the family of spoilers is very high', said one of his
    interviewees. 'Ursari of the Cetate consider that the pride of any family that has a
    daughter is the honor of the girl. There is nothing more important than the honor the
    girl does to her family. Not even the girl's school education. Because the family considers
    that outside influences are a risk regarding the preservation of the face's purity, the
    parents withdraw her from school, around the age of 12, and prepare her for life.'

11 'Drepturile Omului pentru Romi și Nomazi în Europa', https://www.coe.int/t/
    commissioner/source/prems/RomaTravellersExtraits_ROM.pdf; accessed 19 March
    2021.

12 In 2006, the Human Rights Watch declared that: 'The divisive caste system – in
    operation throughout India – Old and "New", together with inequitable gender
    attitudes, sits at the heart of the wide-ranging human rights abuses experienced by
    Dalit or "outcaste" women. Discriminatory and cruel, inhuman, and degrading
    treatment of over 165 million people in India has been justified on the basis of caste
    … Despite, as Navi Pillay, United Nations High Commissioner for Human Rights
    states, India's "far-reaching constitutional guarantees and laws which prohibit
    caste-based discrimination", Dalit women are the victims of a collision of deep-

rooted gender and caste discrimination, resulting in wide ranging exploitation. They are "oppressed by the broader Indian society, men from their own community and also their own husbands and male members in the family" [UN]. Practices like the Devadasi system (where girls as young as 12 years of age are dedicated to the Hindu goddess Yellamma and sold into prostitution); honour killings; sexual abuse including rape; appalling working conditions; and limited access to basic services such as water, sanitation and employment are commonplace.' https://www.hrw.org/report/2007/02/12/hidden-apartheid/caste-discrimination-against-indias-untouchables; accessed 17 March 2021.

13 The Narikuravar girls and women's situation is therefore comparable to that of other Adivasi/ST communities across India who share a nomadic tradition. According to the National Advisory Council Working Group on Denotified and Nomadic Tribes 2011: 'Child labour: NCPCR should have a special focus on the children of DNTs who are more prone to child labour.' Also: 'Trafficking of women and children: State Commissions on Women should focus on women and girl children of DNTs who are victims of large scale trafficking due to loss of livelihoods. Alternative employment should be provided for such women to make them less vulnerable to trafficking. Women and girls: DNT women should be given priority while providing loans, training, asset building, land distribution, etc. Women among DNT communities are economically active and are frequently the only breadwinners for the entire family. Special attention should be paid by MCWD to health, education and protection of the girl child.' https://nomadsgroup.files.wordpress.com/2010/04/dnt_draft.pdf; accessed 9 March 2021.

14 http://www.errc.org/roma-rights-journal/romani-women-in-romani-and-majority-societies; accessed 18 March 2021.

15 Limited opportunities for women and girls across India, across communities, geography and 'caste' leads to gender-based inequalities. A World Bank study of 2011 showed that: 'Less than half of Indian women receive complete antenatal care, and 60 percent of all childbirths take place at home. A majority of the women who give birth at home feel it is not necessary to deliver in a formal medical facility. The public health system has agonized over the low demand for maternal health services; cultural and behavioral factors have been blamed (see Basu, 1990). Medical practitioners often cite ignorance as the reason for the poor outcomes among women (Khandare, 2004). It is true that, among the women who gave birth at home, a majority felt that to give birth in a medical facility was not necessary. However, the low demand for health care may also be triggered by gaps in supply, the inability to reach a health center in the moment of need, and the lack of information on whether the health centers would be open' (World Bank, 2011: 25, https://openknowledge.worldbank.org/handle/10986/2289).

16 Across India, because of high dowry rates, daughters are at times perceived as a net loss in economic terms. However, now the trends are slightly changing, where families

with sons have to import daughters-in-law from across the country, blecoring state and caste lines. Nevertheless, whether these trends will have longer-term consequences is yet to be determined (Kaur, 2013). According to the World Bank (2011: 25, https://openknowledge.worldbank.org/handle/10986/2289), childbearing remains a high-risk event, with Indian women facing a 1 in 70 risk of dying in childbirth.

17 In his work, Matras over-generalizes the gender relationships within the Roma communities: 'Women tend to engage in economic activities that bring them in contact indiscriminately with a wide general public rather than with selected, particular networks of trade associates' (Matras, 2014: 46). 'While women maintain the control over work organization by the daughters and daughters-in-law, men retain the symbolic power of decision over the household as a whole, and the role of representing the household towards the outside world, be it in negotiation with others or in ceremonial functions such as attendance at funerals' (Ibid., 51).

18 For example, looking at Lambadi/Banajra communities in Andhra Pradesh, Naik (1996) states that in spite of many changes, especially in their nomadism, many community members are still seasonal migrants, and they maintained specific customs and traditions, especially in terms of their gender dynamics, permitting both monogamy and polygamy. And overall, the community follow more patrilineal society.

19 While I have observed that within the community women were portrayed as empowered, as having more rights than other women from neighbouring communities, outsiders often describe them as victims: 'Narikoravar women have always taken a background role – subordinate to the figure of men as the "bread winner", and were "shut away" in their family home. Compared with women of other communities, the Narikoravar women have more responsibilities imposed on them that resists their self-development. The plight of these women is mainly due to their upbringing in their family and culture. The nomadic nature of their culture poses an obstacle for them to make a permanent income for their livelihood. They are economically poor and have engaged in self entrepreneurial business for their livelihood like selling fancy items, grocery items, making soft toys, ornaments and beads, etc. Even though they have an ability and skill in entrepreneurship business, they lack in upgrading their skills with technological enhancement' (Chandru and Thirumalaisamy, 2019: 150).

20 World Bank, 2011, https://openknowledge.worldbank.org/handle/10986/2289; accessed 19 March 2021.

21 Furthermore, the World Bank class the current situation as 'muddy waters', because of 'an income effect or a discouraged worker effect? The literature on women's labor force participation, particularly in developed countries, indicates that women's employment decisions are often contingent upon the employment status and earnings of husbands (see Cohen and Bianchi 1999). Das (2006) finds that the education and wages of husbands do lower the probability of employment among

women' (World Bank 2011: 28, https://openknowledge.worldbank.org/handle/ 10986/2289; accessed 16 May 2021).

22 Not all women from the Roma and Narikuravar communities are in dire economic upheaval. Just as in other communities, certain individuals are able to succeed, sometimes against all odds. The Roma communities in Romania, including those of Ormeniş, have several examples of powerful, successful women. In Ormeniş, Anca is a teacher with an MA degree in education, who has been wining international awards and accolades. There is also a Roma nurse (whom I have not met) that everyone proudly referred to. In India, a few Narikuravar women like Anuradha and Jayachitra are thriving and creating a path for themselves, and many others are coming in the future.

23 The Narikuravar situation is like that of other women in the Adivasi and ST communities, and 'Female labor force participation rates have remained low. (...) SC and ST women participate more in the labor force out of necessity; the latter mostly take up self-employment in agriculture, while SC women undertake casual labor.' This is typically connected to the community's traditions: 'The cultural mores and values of status and seclusion in the region; this may prevent higher-status households from allowing women to work or demand jobs. Family honor in most parts of India, for instance, requires that women be restricted to the home, thus affecting the ability of women to work outside the home (Chen 1995)' (World Bank, 2011: 28).

24 World Bank, 2011: 31, https://openknowledge.worldbank.org/handle/10986/2289.

25 https://openknowledge.worldbank.org/handle/10986/2289; accessed 14 May 2021.

26 https://www.unwomen.org/en/what-we-do/ending-violence-against-women/ facts-and-figures#notes; accessed 18 March 2021.

27 https://evaw-global-database.unwomen.org/en/countries/asia/india#1; source: International Institute for Population Sciences (IIPS) and ICF, 2017. National Family Health Survey (NFHS-4), India, 2015–16: India. Mumbai: IIPS.

28 Ibid.

29 https://evaw-global-database.unwomen.org/en/countries/europe/romania#1; source: European Union Agency for Fundamental Rights, 2014. Violence against Women: An EU-wide Survey. Luxembourg: Publications Office of the European Union.

30 Ibid.

31 Ibid.

32 This is not to say that the Roma women's political movement in Eastern Europe in general and in Romania in particular does not have a long history. Angéla Kóczé, in her article 'The Building Blocks of the Romani Women's Movement in Europe', presents the long-lasting Romani women's activism, starting from the 1920s, going through the Second World War and Holocaust, continuing during communism until today. https:// www.romarchive.eu/en/roma-civil-rights-movement/building-blocks-romani-

womens-movement-,europe/ (accessed 16 May 2021). Also, Kóczé et al. in *The Romani Women's Movement* (2019) explain the role that Romani women played in politics, especially in shaping equality-related discourses, policies and political movements.

33 https://aresel.ro/en/about-us; accessed 24 December 2021.

34 Next to Aresel, there is Eromnja (https://e-romnja.ro/; accessed 8 August 2021), a Roma apolitical and non-profit feminist organization that fights for the rights of Roma girls and women, and which tries to address these gender imbalances of power and engage women and girls from the Roma community in formal and informal acts of justice. Also see Kóczé et al., 2018; Rostas, 2009; Rostas and Rövid, 2015.

35 For more information about the LGBTQI Roma movements see 'The experiences of Romani LGBTIQ people: queer(y)(ing) Roma' (Fremlova, 2017).

36 http://www.errc.org/roma-rights-journal/romani-women-in-romani-and-majority-societies; accessed 18 March 2021.

37 Barany similarly challenged (while rather essentializing the typical gender dichotomy assumed within traditional communities such as the Roma): 'Although traditional Romani society is male-dominated, females prior to and after child-bearing associate with their male counterparts more freely. Women are expected to be men and are ordinarily held in higher esteem more' (Barany, 2002: 14).

38 See also Fonseca, 1996: 12.

39 These stories were part of a mixed media project titled 'Women Beyond Borders', which showcased the self-images (i.e., women took the image of themselves or decided on their image) of Narikuravar and Roma migrant women. The work was originally presented at Berlin Silent Green Kulturquartier in 2019 (https://www.zeit-stiftung.de/f/alumnioverviewbox/Beyond%20Borders/Flyer%20Beyond%20Borders.pdf; accessed 8 August 2021).

Chapter 5

1 'Indigenous knowledge reaches into time immemorial and has continued as an unbroken strand in spite of national policies aimed at completely assimilating Indigenous peoples. It continues to operate in the social consciousness of Indigenous peoples and in their everyday lives, even if it is not recognised as "law" by the undiscerning' (Zuni-Cruz 2020: 315).

2 The study further reveals, that 'Roma are subjected, disproportionately, to arbitrary detention measures. The Commissioner considers that the excessive use of force by the police in this area must cease; concrete measures must be taken to prevent the arbitrary detention of Roma. Other steps need to be taken to improve the relationship of trust between Roma and nomadic communities on the one hand and the police on the other, such as the recruitment of Roma in the police, or the recruitment and

training of Roma mediators to cooperate with the police.' https://www.coe.int/t/
commissioner/source/prems/RomaTravellersExtraits_ROM.pdf; 2011: 6–7.

3   The field research in Romania and India on traditional forms of justice, has been
supported by teams of translators and research assistants.

4   While Panchayats of the nomadic communities are legally recognized (Extension to
Scheduled Areas Act, 1996, PESA) (see Krishnan, 2019; Pal, 2000), they are often
thought to be 'hindering their integration', and to be one of the causes of the so called
'backwardness' (Gandhi and Sundar, 2019), which needs to be abolished in the name
of development.

5   I use Kriss here in this spelling, but the spelling differs from region to region and
amongst authors, etc. For example, in Romania it is Criss or Cris, while in the UK it
is Kris, Kriss or kriss. As forms of traditional Roma justice vary, so does their name.
So, knowing this but hoping to make the analysis easier to follow, I decided on the
use of Kriss as the name that is typically recognized to refer to the traditional Roma
justice system.

6   Barany (2002) argues that there are two forms of justice in the Roma systems:
'Divano', an informal mediation procedure which has been typically engaged in
conflict resolution that rectifies minor grievances, and 'kriss', 'the ultimate source of
law and order in a traditional Romani community is the kris, which solves criminal,
moral, civil and religious disputes through the participation of judges. In contrast
with divano, the rulings of the kris are final and binding. (...) The judges are always
male, as are the traditional leaders (baro, voivode, etc.) of Romani communities: the
selection of the leaders is usually based on earned respect, but they also need to be of
relatively advanced age (i.e., they should have grandchildren) and to command
authority in their bailiwick' (Barany, 2002: 14). See also Fonseca, 1996: 283.

7   Similarly, Tal Correm (Work in Progress) explains that: 'The problem with
communal councils is that even though they are elective, they are liable to infringe
on human rights of minorities, especially Dalits and women. They would, in other
words, perpetuate the social hierarchy that aggravates inequality. This was true in
Gandhi's times as well as today.' (Tal Correm, 'From Force to Political Power: Frantz
Fanon, M. K. Gandhi, and Hannah Arendt on Violence, Political Action, and Ethics'.
PhD diss., Temple University, 2014: 202).

8   However, according to Davidd Friedman: 'There are at least three different ways in
which a community can enforce its own legal system despite the superior access to
force of the legal system of the state within whose territory it is located. One is by
delegation; the state legal system subcontracts the job of enforcing legal rules on the
members of the community to the communal authority, and delegates some of its
authority for the purpose. Gypsy communities in the past have claimed and may
perhaps have possessed such delegated authority, but contemporary communities, with
very minor exceptions, do not.' http://www.daviddfriedman.com/Academic/Course_
Pages/legal_systems_very_different_12/Book_Draft/Systems/GypsyLaw.html.

9 https://www.merriam-webster.com/dictionary/panchayat; accessed 23 April 2021.

10 While Roma communities are diverse, the virginity of the girl on the night of marriage has been brought up as one of the traditions across Roma communities in Romania (Necula, 'Studiu de Diversitate', work in progress). However, it was also mentioned that these traditions, which were still in place about 30–40 years ago, now are no longer prevalent in the Roma communities.

11 Dasgupta (2018) quotes Xaxa as 'the term "Scheduled Tribe", distinct from the word "tribe" but drawn from "many of the parameters through which the colonial category of tribe was structured, is a legal and constitutional category. It is rooted in the state's concern to address the issue of the protection, welfare and development of the tribal population" (Xaxa, 2016, p. 15). Post-independent India, as Xaxa pointed out, has been more concerned with the identification of these communities than with their definition. Thus, they created the criteria for identification: "geographical isolation, simple technology, backwardness, the practice of animism, differences in language or physical features—were neither clearly formulated nor systematically applied" (Xaxa, 1999, p. 3589)'; in Dasgupta, 2018: 3.

Chapter 6

1 https://www.nytimes.com/2010/09/07/opinion/07iht-edzaretsky.html; accessed 27 May 2021.

2 https://www.nytimes.com/2012/06/22/opinion/global-agenda-magazine-the-gypsy-in-me.html; accessed 11 March 2021.

3 https://cutra.ro/povesti-si-lectii-din-colonia-scolii-romanesti/?fbclid=IwAR0zB0t9E GN5Lz9WT7nDUMHmrxD4VfSjBPF2FBLrjJER5NcbDmjVrOTwtV0; accessed 27 December 2020.

4 These forms of racism, against the Roma in Europe while at no avail, have been extensively documented. For example, according to the Fundamental Rights Report 2016, European Union Agency for Fundamental Rights: 'The 2015 Eurobarometer survey on discrimination shows that ethnic origin remains the most prevalent ground of discrimination. Results concerning Roma indicate that anti-Gypsyism is widespread: the percentage of respondents who would feel comfortable working with someone with a minority ethnic origin drops to 63% for a Roma person, compared with 83% for a "black" or "Asian" person and 94% for a "white" person.' Similarly, the Fundamental Rights Report 2019, European Union Agency for Fundamental Rights (p. 111): 'The European Commission evaluated the EU Framework for National Roma Integration Strategies. The evaluation assesses the policy, legal and funding instruments that have been aligned and mobilised since 2011 and explores ways to develop the EU framework and feed into the targeted and mainstream EU policy, legal and funding instruments after 2020 in the light of the

Council Recommendation of December 2013, focusing on the fundamental right to equal treatment and non-discrimination, in particular in relation to access to employment, education, housing and health'. The PEW Research Center 2019 presented similar data: 'Of the minority groups tested on the survey, Roma stand out for the negative sentiments expressed toward them. In 10 of the 16 countries polled, half or more have an unfavorable view of Roma. The strongest such anti-Roma sentiment is in Italy, where roughly eight-in-ten (83%) say they have unfavorable views of Roma' (PEW, 2019; also see Rostas and Danka, 2012).

5   See http://miris.eurac.edu/mugs2/do/blob.pdf?type=pdf&serial=1131546418406; accessed 13 August 2021.

6   However, the situation of the Roma is not identical across Europe: 'From a legal point of view, the Romany community is still not regarded as an ethnic or national minority group in every member state, and thus it does not enjoy the rights pertaining to this status in all of the countries concerned. Roma must be treated as an ethnic or national minority group in every member state, and their minority rights must be guaranteed. The Framework Convention for the Protection of National Minorities and the European Charter for Regional or Minority Languages exist and must be applied' (http://assembly.coe.int/nw/xml/XRef/Xref-XML2HTML-en.asp?fileid=16999; accessed 13 August 2021; also see Tsekos, 2002; Cierco, 2017).

7   http://www.romanicriss.org/Romii%20si%20Conventia%20Cadru%20pentru%20 Protectia%20Minoritatilor%20Nationale.pdf; accessed 13 August 2021.

8   https://www.europarl.europa.eu/doceo/document/A-9-2020-0147_RO.pdf; accessed 13 August 2021.

9   The Amit Thorat and Omkar Joshi study, *The Continuing Practice of Untouchability in India: Patterns and Mitigating Influences*, in 2015 revealed that '27 per cent of India still practices untouchability, with 30 per cent of households in rural and 20 per cent in urban areas accepting the practice. The 33 per cent of poorer Indians by income practice untouchability while 23 per cent of the rich do. The report mentioned that 40–49 per cent of households in the Hindi belt in North India accepted the practice, while Southern India accounted for 17 per cent. While literates showed 30 per cent practice, higher education did not bring it down much (24 per cent)' (Vundru, 2021: https://www.tribuneindia.com/news/comment/the-scourge-of-untouchability-continues-70718; accessed 5 January 2021).

10 According to the Human Rights Watch: 'India's caste system is perhaps the world's longest surviving social hierarchy. A defining feature of Hinduism, caste encompasses a complex ordering of social groups on the basis of ritual purity. A person is considered a member of the caste into which he or she is born and remains within that caste until death, although the particular ranking of that caste may vary among regions and over time. Differences in status are traditionally justified by the religious doctrine of karma, a belief that one's place in life is determined by one's

deeds in previous lifetimes.' https://www.hrw.org/reports/2001/globalcaste/
caste0801-03.htm; accessed 14 March 2021.

11 'Exclusion from Hindu temples has been the most publicized, if not the most onerous,
single aspect of untouchability' (Galanter, cited by Ghosh, 2018), https://ohrh.law.ox.
ac.uk/the-sabarimala-temple-ban-an-untouchable-rule/; accessed 5 January 2021.

12 https://www.newindianexpress.com/states/tamil-nadu/2020/jun/09/12-
narikuravars-held-for-killing-jackal-by-stuffing-explosive-inside-meat-2154011.
html; accessed 7 February 2021.

13 For example, in their work 'Housed Gypsies and Travellers in the UK: Work,
Exclusion and Adaptation', David Smith and Margaret Greenfield argue that:
'Gypsies and Travellers are one of the most excluded black and minority ethnic
(BME) communities in the UK across numerous domains. Despite the increased
policy focus on levels of unemployment and economic inactivity among BME
groups in recent years, little attention has been paid to the economic position of
Gypsies and Travellers, not least because there is a lack of systematic data on the
employment status and working patterns of these communities. Few of the
programmes set up to tackle unemployment specifically target this population and,
anecdotally, a mismatch exists in relation to mainstream back-to-work programmes
and community needs. This article considers a series of related studies that explore
the accommodation histories and adaptive strategies utilised by housed Gypsies and
Travellers across four locations in southern England. One strand of these studies is
concerned with employment opportunities and practices following the transition
into housing. We draw on these findings to discuss the role of cultural adaptations in
mediating the wider socioeconomic context and how recourse to collective
responses helps to shape economic and labour market outcomes for members of this
group' (Smith and Greenfield, 2012: 48).

14 https://www.worldbank.org/content/dam/Worldbank/document/eca/romania/
OutputEN.pdf, p. 31; accessed 11 March 2021.

15 https://www.coe.int/t/commissioner/source/prems/RomaTravellersExtraits_ROM.
pdf; accessed 11 March 2021.

16 https://www.coe.int/t/commissioner/source/prems/RomaTravellersExtraits_ROM.pdf.

17 In India the National Advisory Council Working Group on Denotified and Nomadic
Tribes 2011 declared that: 'Shelter and infrastructure development programmes: A)
Conduct a nation-wide survey of DNT settlements whether temporary or
permanent. This could form the basis for introducing a suitable shelter programme
for houseless DNTs. B) Free or subsidized housing may be provided to eligible DNT
households in a phased manner – adopting special measures like Rajasthan's Gadaria
Lohar community housing scheme. C) Given the high incidence of homelessness
among DNTs, a proportion of the current outlay for Indira Awaas Yojana could be
earmarked for DNTs during the XII. DNTs could be assisted financially to construct

dwelling units by receiving priority under the on-going housing programmes of the Central Government. D) Homeless nomadic fishing communities could be resettled, as far as possible, close to the dams and reservoirs, so they can continue their traditional occupation. E) An Integrated Infrastructural Development Programme could be specially designed to provide basic amenities such as roads, schools, electricity, drinking water, community centres, etc. in the existing settlements of nomadic and denotified tribes.' https://nomadsgroup.files.wordpress.com/2010/04/dnt_draft.pdf; accessed 12 March 2021.

18 'Interventions in the housing sector, of similar importance for improving living conditions, need to take account of the heterogeneity of housing conditions. There is no one-size-fits-all approach, and housing assistance needs to be expanded beyond "social housing". By broadening the menu of options with such measures as infrastructure upgrading, legalization of property titles, home improvement and housing microfinance, interventions could be made more cost-efficient, equitable, sustainable, and suitable to the needs of Roma population' (World Bank, 2014, https://www.worldbank.org/content/dam/Worldbank/document/eca/romania/OutputEN.pdf).

19 https://www.coe.int/t/commissioner/source/prems/RomaTravellersExtraits_ROM.pdf.

20 Under-five mortality rates among tribal children remain startlingly high at about 96 deaths per 1,000 live births in 2005 compared with 74 among all children (Das and Mehta, 2012: 2).

21 The World Bank report of 2014 concluded that: 'Addressing the health challenges of the Roma is crucial for improving basic living conditions, and requires cross-cutting efforts. Improving the dire health outcomes among the Romanian Roma requires policy measures on a number of fronts, including initiatives in other sectors such as education and housing, and need to be complemented by broader reforms in the healthcare system. The prevention of risky behaviors, including improvement of diets among the Roma deserves priority concern, along with increasing access to, and usage of prenatal and early childhood healthcare. Roma families' health status is likely to benefit from the removal of financial barriers, both with respect to healthy diets and with respect to preventative check-ups and other healthcare visits; as well as a clear policy focus and reliance on the Roma health mediator program to improve service delivery and awareness raising at the local level' (https://www.worldbank.org/content/dam/Worldbank/document/eca/romania/OutputEN.pdf; accessed 14 August 2021.

22 http://documents1.worldbank.org/curated/en/857771468260645048/pdf/613140PUB0pove158344B09780821386903.pdf; accessed 14 March 2021.

23 The Narikuravars' situation is like other Adivasi communities, who were criminalized under colonial rule. According to the National Advisory Council Working Group on

Denotified and Nomadic Tribes 2011, The Mahatma Gandhi National Rural Employment Guarantee Act of 2005, the Ministry of Rural Development, Government of India (MGNREGA): 'Concerned panchayats must be made responsible for implementing MGNREGA for the benefit of DNT communities. The requirement for permanent address should be made flexible. Wage employment under MGNREGA should be provided on priority to the homeless. Opening of a bank account or a post office account for disbursement of MGNREGA wages should be made possible even for those with temporary habitations, or for homeless DNTs' (https://www.nrega.nic.in/netnrega/mgnrega_new/Nrega_home.aspx; accessed 17 February 2021).

24 http://www.errc.org/roma-rights-journal/systemic-exclusion-of-roma-from-employment; accessed 11 February 2021.

25 Ibid.

26 'The problems that hinder the inclusion of Roma in the labor market are numerous and they result in an almost complete exclusion of Roma and nomads from civilized labor in Europe. Endemic discrimination, combined with insufficient education, seems to nullify the effect of emerging employment policies on Roma and nomads. Despite positive efforts in some countries, unemployment among Roma and nomads in Europe is invariably at a significantly higher level than among non-Roma. In a number of countries, Roma and nomads are denied employment – on discriminatory grounds related to ethnicity or the perception of association with Roma or nomadic groups or communities. Experiences in Europe also show that employed Roma are more likely to be discriminated against in the workplace. Discrimination also affects educated Roma, who are prevented from progressing. Across Europe, although perceptions of discrimination are widespread, data are lacking, in part because discrimination in the labor market is often hidden. Racial and ethnic discrimination in the labor market is in breach of the European Social Charter and the European Union's Gender Equality Directive. Measures to address unemployment among Roma and nomads must include assistance to victims of discrimination when they claim their rights' (https://www.coe.int/t/commissioner/source/prems/RomaTravellersExtraits_ROM.pdf).

27 http://www.cdep.ro/pls/parlam/structura2015.mp?idm=170&cam=2&leg=2016; accessed 13 March 2021.

28 https://www.romaniajournal.ro/politics/there-are-too-many-gypsies-in-the-government-who-said-that/; accessed 13 March 2021.

29 https://www.europarl.europa.eu/meps/en/124786/DAMIAN_DRAGHICI/history/8#detailedcardmep; accessed 13 March 2021.

30 Similar denials of discrimination have been encountered in Hungary during fieldwork about the Roma and their relationship with local autonomy. This research, conducted by Kai Shafft and Roland Ferkovik, was presented at the *Opre Khetanes*

IV Concert and Conference on Romani (Gypsy) Musics and Cultures at the University of New York in March 2016. Ferkovik mentioned that while interviewing in a school in rural Hungary, he asked one of the Roma leaders in the community if he experienced discrimination. To the researcher's surprise he said no. Ferkovik was astonished because the interview took place in a segregated school, attended solely by Roma children. Ferkovik thus argues that discrimination is 'the normal' in Roma communities, and that the Romani people grew so accustomed to it that they are both surprised and glad when someone does not insult them: 'We have a Jobbik mayor so Jobbik leadership of the town but still we have not experienced any harm or insult to the Roma not at all. We have suffered no harm' (Schafft and Ferkovik, 2016). The Hungarian Roma denied their discrimination, while they admitted that the village mayor does not invest in developing the necessary infrastructure in the Roma part of the village: 'He comes down to take a look, but nothing has been established. For instance, in the Gypsy quarter where we live and where we have been living since 1951 at the edge of the town, there have been no public utility undertakings since 1951, no concrete roads or asphalt roads have been established. When there is rain, we are walking in mud up to our knees' (Ibid.). During Skype conversations, Ferkovik confirmed his analysis that the Roma in Hungary internalize the narrative created about them and are aware of negative consequences of challenging it, and often prefer not to contest it.

31 https://www.europarl.europa.eu/factsheets/en/sheet/146/the-protection-of-fundamental-rights-in-the-eu; accessed 27 May 2021.

32 Ibid.

33 https://openknowledge.worldbank.org/bitstream/handle/10986/26335/114157-BRI-India-PSE-Adivasis-Brief-PUBLIC.pdf?sequence=1&isAllowed=y; accessed 2 October 2021.

Chapter 7

1 https://petitie.aresel.ro/aresel-manifest; accessed 16 January 2020.

2 https://newleftreview.org/II/3/nancy-fraser-rethinking-recognition; accessed 22 March 2018.

3 This is not to say that Roma or Narikuravar identity is completely endogenous to the communities, or that their members do not have agency over them. The topic of agency over one's identity is intensely debated by Surdu (2016), who on the one hand argues that the 'Gypsy' label is an external construction, and Mirga (2017), who on the other hand pleads for understanding the Roma as an ethnic identity, similar to other ones, internally constructed. While important, this debate is beyond the scope of this study that looks at the social movements aiming at attaining social justice.

4   http://www.bcmbcmw.tn.gov.in/bclist.htm; accessed 28 May 2021.

5   Reservations are envisioned as positive discrimination: 'Positive discrimination
    along with developmental interventions, and capacity and asset building, was
    considered essential to this social engineering. For achieving a state of social and
    economic equality, the builders of modern India have undertaken certain measures
    right from the time of Independence' (National Commission for Denotified,
    Nomadic and Semi-nomadic Tribes, Ministry of Social Justice and Empowerment,
    Government of India, 2008: 1). It is apparent from the observations of the above
    Committees or Commissions that the conditions of the Denotified, Nomadic and
    Semi-Nomadic Tribes or Communities are deplorable and deserve a separate and
    special treatment so that their lot can be improved. This is essential for bringing this
    very large section of downtrodden citizens of India into the ambit of development
    and to confer upon them the dignity of citizenship with all its appended social,
    cultural, economic and political rights on par with the others (Ibid., 7).

6   http://www.bcmbcmw.tn.gov.in/; accessed 12 December 2020.

7   Assigning ST status is not a regular, streamline process of recognition. Accordingly,
    'article 342 of the Constitution lays down the power by which the state can specify a
    people for scheduling'. Moreover, 'scheduling can be arbitrarily applied, and that
    additionally, only a part of a group may be scheduled. For example, the Kurdmis of
    Jharkhand, a group whose language family is Dravidian, the same as that of the
    scheduled Oraons, are no longer scheduled and are placed among the caste
    communities. There have been demands to reexamine the list of STs to identify
    genuine Adivasis and to exclude the non-Adivasi communities who have been
    included' (Minority Rights Group International, 1998: 9).

8   While Adivasi communities are not homogenous, they are typically lumped together
    under uniform laws, which rarely address their needs. It is not surprising that they
    fail to address the historical, systemic marginalization, which they have been facing
    since the colonial era (Rao, 2018). Thus, in working towards overall tribal
    development and empowerment, the Adivasi's laws need to safeguard their
    fundamental rights, while acknowledging their diverse and complex identities locally
    developed and enforced.

9   https://dpe.gov.in/sites/default/files/Reservation_Brochure-2.pdf; accessed 1 June
    2021.

10 https://minorityrights.org/minorities/adivasis-2/; accessed 1 June 2021.

11 These measures include: The Scheduled Tribes and other Traditional Forest Dwellers
    (Recognition of Forest Rights) Act, 2006 (FRA); The Provision of the Panchayats
    (Extension to the Scheduled Areas) Act, 1996; Minor Forest Produce Act, 2005; and
    the Tribal Sub-Plan Strategy, which are all focused on the socio-economic
    empowerment of STs. The Land Acquisition Bill, which has been renamed as The
    Right to Fair Compensation and Transparency in Land Acquisition, Rehabilitation

and Resettlement Bill, 2012, has a separate chapter to protect the interests of SCs and STs. https://policy.asiapacificenergy.org/node/2511; accessed 22 November 2020.

12 https://policy.asiapacificenergy.org/sites/default/files/12fyp_vol1.pdf.

13 Moreover, in September 2013, the Parliament of India passed The Prohibition of Employment as Manual Scavengers and Their Rehabilitation Bill. This bill aims to eliminate the inhuman practice of manual scavenging and rehabilitation of liberated manual scavengers, all of whom belong to the Scheduled Castes. Furthermore, The Land Acquisition Bill, which has been renamed as The Right to Fair Compensation and Transparency in Land Acquisition, Rehabilitation and Resettlement Bill, 2012, has a separate chapter to protect the interests of SCs and STs.

14 This classification is ambiguous (at best), and often problematic because: 'The Indian Constitution only states that STs are specified by the President after consultation with the Governor; it does not specify specific criteria. According to the Ministry of Tribal Affairs, the criterion – while not spelled out in legislation – "is well established," and includes indication of "primitive" traits, distinctive culture, geographical isolation, "shyness of connect" with the community at large, and "backwardness." These general standards were established following the definitions of the 1931 Census, the reports of the First Backward Classes Commission 1955, Kalelkar Advisory Committee, and Revision of SC/ST lists by the Lokur Committee. However, more than a half-century later, these broad criteria leave a lot of discretion' (Dragomir, 2017, https://casi.sas.upenn.edu/iit/cristinaioanadragomir).

15 'Narikkoravar's constitutional struggle for dignity and representation', https://roundtableindia.co.in/index.php?option=com_content&view=article&id=8459:narikkoravar-s-constitutional-struggle-for-dignity-and-representation&catid=123&Itemid=139; accessed 5 February 2021.

16 For example, in 2016, Mr. Rajapandi remembers the contribution of Chief Minister Jayalalitha, who had written to the Central government to stress the need for including the Narikurava community in the ST list. 'On behalf of my community, I wholeheartedly thank the Central and the State governments for finally deciding to include the Narikuravas in the list of STs as that would open more windows of opportunities for our community people to join the mainstream and excel in their chosen careers', Mr. Rajapandi told *The Hindu*. A native of Vallimalai village near Uthangarai in Krishnagiri district, he is credited to be the first medical student from his community. 'Now our community youth will have a chance to enter government service that has so far eluded them. A Government job is a dream for many of us' (http://www.thehindu.com/news/national/tamil-nadu/narikurava-medico-happy/article8647516.ece; accessed 1 May 2018).

17 https://www.britannica.com/topic/Bharatiya-Janata-Party; accessed 17 February 2021.

18 https://swarajyamag.com/culture/tarun-vijay-only-continuing-a-historic-struggle-for-social-justice; accessed 28 May 2021.

19 On 8 November 2016, the Government of India announced the demonetization of all ₹500 and ₹1,000 banknotes of the Mahatma Gandhi Series. See Lahiri, 2020, https://pubs.aeaweb.org/doi/pdfplus/10.1257/jep.34.1.55.

20 https://www.ketto.org/fundraiser/help-to-feed-care-gypsy-people?fbclid=IwAR3hw kW2kFNLcvnx2w8qOJr71fPVCZvz2Sd84byBLJqPixwTRpzxi8PykUQ; accessed 28 May 2021.

21 Thomas Action, 'Migration and the Roma', https://www.romarchive.eu/en/roma-civil-rights-movement/migration-and-roma/.

22 These reservations in education were introduced slowly and painstakingly in Romanian legislation: 'First in higher education (since 1992) and then in high-school (since 1998), along with training programmes funded by international bodies' (Necula, 'Studiu de Diversitate', work in progress).

23 While this theory emphasizes the community's empowerment and self-identification, it is rather unclear how Necula could make this generalization over diverse communities, who have their different ways of self-identifying. This limitation becomes even more relevant when we see that not all those who were previously labelled as 'Gypsy' speak the same language, i.e. Romani (where the term Roma comes from). Thus, it is hard to see how this uniform labelling must have come from grassroots community level. Differently, I would suggest seeing the label of Roma as a product, like many other identity labels, of the people on the ground supported by the work of elites, who were able to push their agenda into recognition.

24 Necula's view is not accepted by all scholars in the field, who see Romaphobia as a process that, under various forms, has been in the making long before the Second World War (Dragomir, 2020).

25 http://www.errc.org/news/remembering-nicolae-gheorghe; accessed 28 May 2021.

26 https://www.economist.com/eastern-approaches/2010/12/08/ire-of-the-tigan.

27 http://www.romanicriss.org/statement%20osce%20summit%20rom-tigan.pdf; accessed 7 May 2021.

28 https://fxb.harvard.edu/2017/06/19/dear-gadje-non-romani-scholars/; accessed 7 May 2021.

29 https://www.mediafax.ro/social/antitiganismul-devine-infractiune-inchisoare-de-pana-la-zece-ani-pentru-discriminarea-romilor-19787072?fbclid=IwAR1x4w0uQo K1tpsvyFa48_R00jvHvlQD9ZIgNteLQNKMMZCmju2P9JP0sM; accessed 7 May 2021.

30 Moreover, 'they can be fined or imprisoned for taking forest produce which has traditionally been theirs. The ostensible reason for state intervention has been to stop the destruction of forest land which has continued throughout this century. There are a number of reasons for deforestation, although it is often blamed on the Adivasis' shifting cultivation practices; one has been the increase in demand for

firewood as fuel; another is the impact of commercial, sometimes illegal, logging' (https://minorityrights.org/minorities/adivasis-2/; accessed 20 January 2021).

31 For now, these are goals of economic and social empowerment, and not easy to reach. To overcome the limited financial support received from the government, the Narikuravars reach out to international donors to support their educational endeavours. To promote education within the community, the Narikuravars work with Christian organizations, who help them some time. However, this help comes with a history of supporting marginalized communities in India, while converting them to Christianity.

32 http://www.amnesty.org/en/documents/EUR01/007/2014/en/; accessed 7 May 2021.

33 https://citizenrights.euroalter.com/topics/roma-rights/; accessed 1 May 2021.

34 'Not only do the Roma form a large ethnic minority group, but due to its demographic characteristics, this group also accounts for an increasing share of new labor market entrants: currently, by using a population estimate of 1,800,000 Roma in Romania, the share of Roma among new labor market entrants reaches 20%. Hence, a large and growing share of new labor market entrants in Romania is coming from the Roma population. Creating the conditions for a productive inclusion of young Roma is critical for offsetting the steep projected decline in the country's working-age population (30% by 2050): in this respect, the labor contribution achieved through Roma inclusion should also be considered as an essential component of economic growth and contribution to financing of future pensions and social services' (https://www.worldbank.org/content/dam/Worldbank/document/eca/romania/OutputEN.pdf).

35 https://www.worldbank.org/content/dam/Worldbank/document/eca/romania/OutputEN.pdf; accessed 12 December 2020.

36 https://www.isj.tm.edu.ro/public/data_files/specializari/fisier-590.pdf; https://admitere.uvt.ro/procesul-de-admitere/categorii-de-candidati/candidati-de-etnie-roma-pe-locuri-special-alocate-acestora/; accessed 12 December 2020.

37 https://www.mediafax.ro/social/educatie-superioara-pentru-minoritati-romii-nu-isi-ocupa-locurile-speciale-17537130; accessed 12 December 2020.

38 https://nevoparudimos.ro/2020/05/25/tinerii-romi-au-locuri-speciale-rezervare-pentru-ei-in-licee-si-universitati-afla-care-sunt-acestea-si-cum-poti-beneficia-de-ele/; accessed 12 December 2020.

39 https://www.coe.int/t/commissioner/source/prems/RomaTravellersExtraits_ROM.pdf; accessed 16 December 2020.

40 https://mbq.ro/en/; accessed 10 August 2021.

41 These state programmes need to take into account the history of communities, and the larger political and legal systems. Moreover, in the Romanian case, this needs to include slavery reparations. For more, see 'Roma Slavery: The Case for Reparations' (Matache and Bhabha, 2016), where they argue that 'reparations for historical

injustices are an increasingly urgent topic of public discussion. It's time to include Roma in the conversation' (https://fpif.org/roma-slavery-case-reparations/; accessed 11 August 2021). Also see: 'It is time reparations are paid for Roma slavery' (Matache, 2020, https://www.aljazeera.com/opinions/2020/10/5/it-is-time-reparations-are-paid-for-roma-slavery; accessed 11 August 2021).

42 https://mronline.org/2009/05/16/interview-with-nancy-fraser-justice-as-redistribution-recognition-and-representation/; access 22 March 2018.

43 The Scheduled Districts Act XVI, 1874, was the first significant measure taken to deal with all Adivasi areas as a group, and envisaged these areas being outside the jurisdiction of the normal administration. By this Act, the executive could extend any enactment in force in any part of British India to a 'scheduled district', while also providing any necessary protection. The Montague-Chemsford Report, 1918, also addressed the question of the administration of the 'backward areas'. It considered that political reforms contemplated for India could not be applied in the same way to the 'primitive' peoples. The report suggested the demarcation of areas of such peoples and these areas' exclusion from the normal laws of the provinces. Consequently, the Government of India Act, 1919, was enacted to implement the report's recommendations (Minority Rights Group International, 1998: 6).

44 Minority Rights Group International (1998), https://moam.info/the-adivasis-of-india-citeseerx_59fc6f021723dd64b890104e.html; accessed 11 August 2021.

45 To address Adivasi-focused issues the Ministry of Tribal Affairs was established in 1999, and legislative action in the form of Scheduled Tribes (Recognition of Forest Rights Bill) was passed in 2005, but they have not secured more than a negligible impact in addressing the rights of the Adivasis: https://minorityrights.org/minorities/adivasis-2/; accessed 26 December 2020.

46 https://www.census2011.co.in/census/state/tamil+nadu.html; accessed 27 December 2020.

47 http://www.thehindu.com/news/cities/puducherry/narikurava-community-gets-a-feel-of-voting/article8559174.ece; accessed 4 June 2016.

48 https://uidai.gov.in/; accessed 2 January 2021.

49 Similarly, Kumar (2018) outlines the instability of community politics, as he argues that Adivasi politics is often depended on ambivalences found within community, which impact the political choices of the Adivasis.

50 https://timesofindia.indiatimes.com/city/chennai/amma-to-millions-she-lost-family-links/articleshow/55823979.cms; accessed 28 May 2021.

51 'Evaluarea Barierelor Participării Politice A Romilor Din România', September 2009, p. 31; https://www.ndi.org/sites/default/files/Evaluarea_Barierelor_Particparii_Politice_A_Romilor_Din_Romania.pdf (accessed 11 August 2021).

52 Also Necula, in 'Studiu de Diversitate' (work in progress), reproduces a quote from the Roma Ursari in Toflea who argued that 'politics means nothing: the politician is

voted only for the hope of economic change for the better, not out of ideological sympathies. Most people vote with whoever they are told. The leader is the one who decides for whom the vote is given: "At the time of the elections it was June. There are 240 people left. Personally, I showed them how to vote, how to do it. Exactly what I said. Not that they didn't want to, but 150 votes were canceled due to ignorance."' This is typically seen as the result of political discrimination: the most common dissatisfaction among Roma people is differential treatment – they are not seen as equal citizens, either by the authorities or by the majority: 'As bad state policies ... our disregard. He disregards everything. Discrimination, the perversity with which we are viewed' (Necula in 'Studiu de Diversitate', citing a Romanian Roma from Calafat).

53 https://ec.europa.eu/info/policies/justice-and-fundamental-rights/combatting-discrimination/roma-eu/roma-equality-inclusion-and-participation-eu_en; accessed 11 August 2021.

54 https://www.coe.int/t/commissioner/source/prems/RomaTravellersExtraits_ROM. pdf; accessed 28 January 2021.

55 Ibid.

56 https://www.dw.com/ro/romii-%C3%AEntre-statistici-%C5%9Fi-lumea-real%C4%83/a-17605757; accessed 28 January 2021.

57 To address this: 'Romania has introduced affirmative action measures in education, supports programmes of Roma health mediators and community nurses, promotes employment in communities with high numbers of Roma, and implements a pilot programme of social housing for Roma communities. However, most programmes are framed from a social perspective and do not sufficiently address the problem of ethnic discrimination', https://op.europa.eu/s/oBOK; accessed 28 May 2021.

58 Other MPs representing Roma in the Parliament were Gheorghe Răducanu (1990–1996), Mădălin Voicu (1996–2000), Nicolae Păun (2000–2016) and Daniel Vasile (2016–present). On other party lists, Roma were represented by Mădălin Voicu (Social Democratic Party, 2000–2016, Deputy Chamber), Damian Drăghici (UNPR, 2012–2014, Senate, 2012–present, European Parliament), Florin Manole (PSD, 2016–present). https://www.romarchive.eu/en/roma-civil-rights-movement/roma-movement-romania/#fn41; accessed 28 January 2021.

59 https://www.romarchive.eu/en/roma-civil-rights-movement/roma-movement-romania/; accessed 28 May 2021.

60 While in theory this accounts for a viable political success, in reality, due to the existing legislation – i.e. 'Because the law does not allow other organizations that are not public benefit organizations to compete. To become a public utility organization must approve ANR, which is the institution of the Roma Party' (Matache 2021, personal correspondence) – the Roma Party of Romania holds monopoly over political representation, which raises questions within the community about the fairness of Roma political representation.

61 3 April 1990 through the civil reference no. 1078, from 'Registrul Persoanelor Juridice al Judecătoriei', Sector no.1 Bucharest, 1111/03.04.199.

62 From 2004, the EU pre-accession funds (PHARE), and EU strategic funds (IPA), transformed most Roma NGOs into service providers: https://www.romarchive.eu/en/roma-civil-rights-movement/roma-movement-romania/#fn41.

63 https://www.changemakers.com/powerofsmall/entries/romano-cher-house-roma; accessed 28 May 2021.

64 http://udmr.ro/; accessed 28 May 2021.

65 https://www.romarchive.eu/en/collection/p/nicoleta-bitu/?fbclid=IwAR3ga_FoMYauBfpSsJp5nlgI229cSd8VAbx9qoeIynBNsZU1CHUV1rQvbOI; accessed 28 May 2021.

66 https://www.romarchive.eu/en/collection/p/nicoleta-bitu/; accessed 28 May 2021.

67 https://www.youtube.com/watch?v=WySzEXKUSZw; accessed 28 May 2021; Lin-Manuel Miranda, 'Hamilton: An American Musical'. In *Hamilton: The Revolution*, edited by Jeremy McCarter, New York: Grand Central Publishing, 2016.

68 The educational integration, as we have previously seen, during the communist era and after, has been problematic to say the least, with Roma often being assigned marginal roles and enduring systematic racism. The part that I would like to emphasize here is that under the efforts undertaken during communism to overcome analphabetism, the Roma were also (precariously) integrated into the mainstream educational system, which empowered an important Roma group/generation to further their education, to obtain higher education degrees and form a powerful and educated elite.

Chapter 8

1 http://delhitourism.gov.in/delhitourism/tourist_place/jantar_mantar.jsp; accessed 9 February 2021.

2 https://www.imdb.com/name/nm0707425/; accessed 4 October 2021.

3 'Push factors can include armed conflict, natural disasters, the lack of job opportunities, the possession of economic and cultural capital, a family break up or dissatisfaction with one's own life and surroundings. Pull factors can often be the polar opposites of the push factors, i.e. greater security, better job opportunities or the prospect of a more exciting life. But some pull factors have no immediate correlation with push factors, for example geographic proximity or the presence of family or community members in the destination country' (European Union Institute, https://www.futurelearn.com/info/courses/migration-theories/0/steps/35073, accessed 2 February 2021.

4 https://www.schengenvisainfo.com/schengen-visa-countries-list/; accessed 2 February 2021.

5 The situation of the Narikuravars is not unique, within the changing economy of India, where other Adivasi communities are pulled into migration practices and into becoming seasonal labourers: 'Seasonal labour migration has become an irreversible part of the livelihoods of rural adivasi communities in western India. This article examines the nature, experience and implications of such migration primarily to major urban centres for construction work. It goes on to suggest why those institutions mandated to protect vulnerable informal workers – labour departments, unions and the law – have largely failed to do so, and how in consequence adivasi migrants depend for their welfare upon agents, brokers and contractors who are also their most intimate exploiters' (Mosse et al., 2005: 3025).

6 'Migration from Central and Eastern Europe triggered policies towards Roma at the EU level and raised the issue to the international agenda more than any poverty level or discrimination that the Roma might suffer could have done' (Magazzini and Piemontese, 2019: 3).

7 While their migration patterns are not different from those of the Romanians or other migrants, the migration of the Roma is often racialized and linked to nomadic tropes: 'Different public debates discuss the position of Roma in Europe as if they were one of the most mobile populations in Europe. The position of mobile Romani individuals became especially visible after the 2004 and 2007 European Union (EU) Enlargements. However, only a certain type of mobility of intra EU Romani migrants became particularly highlighted by the headlines of European Media: the one that more or less corresponded to a stereotypical image of a "Roma nomad" and depicted Roma as a potential threat to the social welfare systems of host state' (Sardelić, 2019: 227).

8 http://migrom.humanities.manchester.ac.uk/project/romanian-roma-home-mobility-patterns-migration-experiences-networks-remittances/; accessed 27 December 2020.

9 'The weakness/ineffectiveness of state institutions and local authorities forces Roma to rely on non-state institutions, self-organisation and self-management' (László Fosztó, Stefánia Toma and Cătălina Tesăr, 2017: http://migrom.humanities.manchester.ac.uk/project/romanian-roma-home-mobility-patterns-migration-oexperiences-networks-remittances/; accessed 27 December 2020.

10 https://www.migrationpolicy.org/article/migration-factor-development-and-poverty-reduction; accessed 2 February 2021.

11 While it would be an arduous task, research on the begging practices of migrants within the EU needs to be undertaken. These studies need to be separate from ethnic studies, and therefore separated from the Roma communities. While begging is *not* a Roma practice, it is often associated with the community, due to the fact that many of the people in dire poverty who need to practice it are Roma. These studies would fit into labour studies, and need to follow the patterns suggested by Terry

Williams in 'Cocaine Kids' (1990), which reveals that labour practices from the formal economy are mirrored in the informal realm, with people having schedules, developing skills, incurring within group mobility, exercising influence, etc.

12 https://www.ihmiskauppa.fi/en/human_trafficking/forms_of_human_trafficking/ exploitation_in_begging#:~:text=Victims%20exploited%20in%20begging%20 do,come%20from%20a%20poor%20background; accessed 29 May 2021.

13 Of course, it is not wise or feasible to transform the Narikuravar and Roma communities into idealized communities with perfect labour track records. In other words, it is not to say that there aren't any people – as in every other community that ever existed – who refuse formal engagement in the labour market, and prefer finding more lucrative, often criminal, and criminalized practices to gain access to redistribution. However, in this study, the people I have worked with did not acknowledged being in these situations thus proving that criminalization of the Roma is part of structural racism rather than based on factual information.

14 The economic situation of the Adivasis affects the very life of the entire community. The World Bank study of 2011 found that Adivasi children have a lower risk of dying at birth, but a greater risk by age 5: 'Among STs and SCs (particularly STs in rural areas and SCs in urban areas), the change in child mortality has not kept pace with improvements in the other four mortality indicators. In fact, child mortality increased among the SC children in urban areas: with respect to 1991–95, SC children in cities or towns had a higher probability of dying between their first and fifth birthday' (p. 56): http://documents1.worldbank.org/curated/ en/857771468260645048/pdf/613140PUB0pove158344B09780821386903.pdf.

15 According to the World Bank, only 'a few elites among the STs had access to and benefited from reserved jobs, while a significant proportion [of Adivasis] served as manual labor in construction projects. (. . .) Only a little over 8 percent of Adivasi men are in nonfarm jobs to start with and that these are clearly people who may have acquired upward mobility over several generations of education and movement out of rural areas. In public employment, too, it is often not possible to find qualified ST candidates even to fill the reserved quotas' (World Bank, 2011: 45): http:// documents1.worldbank.org/curated/en/857771468260645048/pdf/613140PUB0pov e158344B09780821386903.pdf.

16 The Prevention of Cruelty to Animals Act came into effect in 1960. It has been articulated under various legal formats over the years, and in 1972 became India's Wildlife Protection Act (i.e. Act No. 52 of 1972), https://www.animallaw.info/statute/ wildlife-protection-act-1972; accessed 28 December 2020.

17 'Narikkoravar's constitutional struggle for dignity and representation': https:// roundtableindia.co.in/index.php?option=com_content&view=article&id=8459:nari kkoravar-s-constitutional-struggle-for-dignity-and-representation&catid=123&Item id=139; accessed 5 February 2021.

18 https://isha.sadhguru.org/us/en/wisdom/article/the-significance-of-rudraksha; accessed 1 February 2021.

19 As specified earlier, I invited Anuradha and Rajasekaran to the school near Coimbatore, where I was volunteering. Here they gave a talk for the children, faculty and staff of the school and then they set up their stands selling their 'fancy-beads'. In the meantime, they asked me to wear and pose with their beads and took photographs, which they later used to further market their products.

20 https://www.youtube.com/watch?v=GbPD6O4H35Y; accessed 29 May 2021.

21 https://www.vice.com/ro/article/xwbbnq/vrajitoare-din-romania; accessed 2 February 2021.

22 The Roma witches' endeavours are complex, and often engage a large PR machine that promotes their skill and service to the large population. See: http://www.vrajitoarero.com/; accessed 2 February 2021.

23 https://www.youtube.com/watch?v=DvpWI0V4od0; accessed 2 February 2021. https://www.youtube.com/watch?v=LDQRyzKBRpY; accessed 2 February 2021.

24 https://www.hindustantimes.com/india-news/gypsies-vs-pigeons-how-chennai-airport-deals-with-feathered-menace/story-VcH7xLOW6qWotUxnmBFQ5M.html; accessed 2 February 2021.

25 https://www.hindustantimes.com/india-news/gypsies-vs-pigeons-how-chennai-airport-deals-with-feathered-menace/story-VcH7xLOW6qWotUxnmBFQ5M.html; accessed 2 February 2021.

26 Stereotypes about Adivasi communities being knowledgeable about forest herbs and medicinal remedies extend beyond the Narikuravar community. For example, Chakma et al. (2017) look at different tribes in Odisha with high blood pressure, which is the result of their exposure to a non-traditional lifestyle and getting diseases otherwise unknown in tribal communities. Mukhopadhyay and Ray (2019) researched how eastern Indian tribes and show that they lack proper nutrition – poor health care practices among pregnant Bathudi women to poor accessibility to modern health care facilities.

27 Similarly, Silverman (2012) looks at how Roma musicians in south-eastern Europe address discrimination, and how they navigate the music business and bring into view how the Roma show adaptability, pragmatism, creativity, cultural hybridity and transnationalism to navigate the many constraints they face.

28 https://www.reuters.com/article/us-romania-discrimination-idUSKBN1ZL1YV; accessed 3 February 2021.

29 https://www.usnews.com/news/world/articles/2020-01-22/romanian-mayor-fined-for-speech-inciting-hatred-of-roma-minority; accessed 3 February 2021.

30 https://www.g4media.ro/video-protest-al-romilor-la-targu-mures-au-cerut-demisia-primarului-dorin-florea-pentru-declaratiile-acestuia-referitoare-la-conditiile-pe-care-ar-trebui-indeplinite-de-cei-care-vor-sa-aiba-copii.html; and https://adevarul.ro/locale/

targu-mures/video-protest-targu-mures-fata-declaratiile-dorin-florea-suta-persoane-iesit-strada-1_5e2225c85163ec42713702bc/index.html; accessed 3 February 2021.

31 https://www.bnr.ro/DocumentInformation.aspx?idInfoClass=13567&idDocument=17914&directLink=1; accessed 5 February 2021. The discrepancy between the acknowledged number of Roma and the estimated one by Ciprian Necula might be due to the fact that there might be a larger number of Roma living in the country's capital than in the overall country, and also due to the fact that as seen earlier some Roma do not identify as such in the census.

32 https://www.washingtonpost.com/archive/politics/1990/03/28/a-clash-of-cultures-in-romanian-province/5cabf7ed-dbf1-42bc-9d19-3525e6ccccdb/; accessed 5 February 2021.

33 https://www.usnews.com/news/world/articles/2020-01-22/romanian-mayor-fined-for-speech-inciting-hatred-of-roma-minority; accessed 3 February 2021.

34 'Narikkoravar's constitutional struggle for dignity and representation': https://roundtableindia.co.in/index.php?option=com_content&view=article&id=8459:narikkoravar-s-constitutional-struggle-for-dignity-and-representation&catid=123&Itemid=139; accessed 5 February 2021.

35 https://www.thenewsminute.com/article/st-status-now-reality-long-road-ahead-narikuravars-and-kuruvikarans-44178; accessed 5 February 2021.

36 'Resistance' has been used in critical social science since the 1980s. Uday Chandra analyses five articles acknowledging 'the inherent ambiguities and ambivalences of subaltern resistance in the face of hegemonic social formations, yet, shorn of exoticising and homogenising tendencies, resistance can be reconceptualised as the negotiation rather than negation of social power' (Chandra, 2015: 563).

Select Bibliography

Achim, Viorel. *The Roma in Romanian History*. Budapest: Central European University Press, 2005.

Allport, Gordon W. *The Nature of Prejudice*. New York: Basic Books, 2012 (1954).

Ambagudia, Jagannath. 'Scheduled Tribes, Reserved Constituencies and Political Reservation in India'. *Journal of Social Inclusion Studies* 5, 1 (June 2019): 44–58. https://doi.org/10.1177/2394481119847015.

Anan, K., S. Karacsony, S. Anton, M. Balica, F. Botonogu, A. Catana, A. Dan, et al. *Achieving Roma Inclusion in Romania: What Does It Take? (Vol. 2): Final Report*. Washington, D.C.: World Bank Group (2014). http://documents.worldbank.org/curated/en/149471468333037165/Final-report; accessed 23 December 2021.

Andrei, Tudorel, Alina Profiroiu, Marius Profiroiu and Andreea Iacob. 'School Dropout in Romania at the Level of Disadvantaged Groups'. *Procedia – Social and Behavioral Sciences* 28 (December 2011): 337–41. https://doi.org/10.1016/j.sbspro.2011.11.064.

Anton, S., M. Balica, F. Botonogou, A. Catan, A. Dan, P. Danchey, D. Farcasanu, et al. *Diagnostics and Policy Advice for Supporting Roma Inclusion in Romania*. Washington, D.C.: World Bank Group, 28 February 2014. https://documents.worldbank.org/en/publication/documents-reports/documentdetail/599081468094457693/diagnostics-and-policy-advice-for-supporting-roma-inclusion-in-romania.

Antonelli, Fulvia, and Mimmo Perrotta. 'Emancipation, Integration, or Marginality: The Romanian Roma in Bologna and the Scalo Internazionale Migranti', in *Migration, Squatting and Radical Autonomy*, eds Pierpaolo Mudu and Sutapa Chattopadhyay. New York: Routledge, 2017.

Aufschnaiter, Claudia Catherina. '"First You Push Them In, Then You Throw Them Out": The Land Rights Struggle of the ADIVASI Peoples in India with Special Reference to South India. Indigenous Strategies and the (Inter)National Law Context'. *Academia.edu*. Accessed 16 August 2021. https://www.academia.edu/27938787/_First_you_push_them_in_then_you_throw_them_out_The_Land_Rights_Struggle_of_the_Adivasi_Peoples_in_India_with_Special_Reference_to_South_India._Indigenous_Strategies_and_the_Inter_national_Law_Context.

Bancroft, Angus. *Roma and Gypsy-Travellers in Europe: Modernity, Race, Space, and Exclusion*. Burlington, VT: Ashgate, 2005.

Barany, Zoltan. *The East European Gypsies: Regime Change, Marginality, and Ethnopolitics*. Cambridge: Cambridge University Press, 2002.

Bates, Crispin, and Alpa Shah. *Savage Attack: TRIBAL Insurgency in India*. London: Routledge, Taylor & Francis Group, 2017.

Behera, M. C. *Tribe as Mode of Thought and Revisiting Contemporary Tribal Practices*. 2020.

Behera, Maguni Charan. 'Rethinking Perspectives in Tribal Studies: Anthropology and Beyond', in M. Behera (ed.), *Shifting Perspectives in Tribal Studies*. Singapore: Springer, 2019. https://doi.org/10.1007/978-981-13-8090-7_1.

Berland, Joseph C., and Aparna Rao. *Customary Strangers: New Perspectives on Peripatetic Peoples in the Middle East, Africa, and Asia*. Westport, Conn: Praeger, 2004. http://public.eblib.com/choice/publicfullrecord.aspx?p=3001130.

Bhabha, Jacqueline, Andrzej Mirga and Margareta Matache. *Realizing Roma Rights*. Philadelphia: University of Pennsylvania Press, 2017.

Boatcă, Manuela. 'Counter-Mapping as Method: Locating and Relating the (Semi) Peripheral Self'. *Historical Social Research / Historische Sozialforschung* 46, 2 (2021): 244–63. Accessed 14 August 2021. https://www.jstor.org/stable/27032980.

Bogdan, Maria, Jekatyerina Dunajeva, Tímea Junghaus, Angéla Kóczé, Iulius Rostas, Márton Rövid, and Marek Szilvasi. 'Introducing the New Journal Critical Romani Studies'. *Critical Romani Studies* 1, 1 (2018): 2–7. https://doi.org/10.29098/crs.v1i1.19.

Bogdán, Maria, Jekatyerina Dunajeva, Tímea Junghaus, Angéla Kóczé, Márton Rövid, Iulius Rostas, Andrew Ryder, Marek Szilvási and Marius Taba. 'Nothing about Us without Us?' *Journal of the European Roma Rights Centre*, 2 (2015): 3–6. https://doi.org/http://www.errc.org/uploads/upload_en/file/roma-rights-2-2015-nothing-about-us-without-us.pdf.

Borde, Radhika. 'Rallying Around Sacred Natural Sites: Adivasi Mobilisations in East-Central India' (2019): 167–82. https://doi.org/10.1007/978-981-13-8090-7_9.

Brayboy, Bryan McKinley Jones. 'Toward a Tribal Critical Race Theory in Education'. *The Urban Review* 37, 5 (2005): 425–46. https://doi.org/10.1007/s11256-005-0018-y.

Brooks, Roy. 'Critical Race Theory: A Proposed Structure and Application to Federal Pleading'. *Harvard Black Letter Law Journal* 11 (1994): 85ff. ISSN 0897-2761.

Bucken-Knapp, Gregg, Umut Korkut, Aidan McGarry, Jonas Hinnfors and Helen Drake, eds. *The Discourses and Politics of Migration in Europe*. London: Palgrave Macmillan, 2013.

Butera, Fabrizio and J. M. Levine. *Coping with Minority Status: Responses to Exclusion and Inclusion*. Cambridge University Press (2009). https://doi.org/10.1017/CBO9780511804465.

Carrera, Sergio, Lina Vosyliūtė and Iulius Rostas. 'Combating Institutional Anti-Gypsyism: Responses and Promising Practices in the EU and Selected Member States'. CEPS, 19 May 2017. https://www.ceps.eu/ceps-publications/combating-institutional-anti-gypsyism-responses-and-promising-practices-eu-and-selected/.

Chakma, T., A. Kavishwar, R. K. Sharma and P. V. Rao. 'High Prevalence of Hypertension and its Selected Risk Factors Among Adult Tribal Population in

Central India'. *Pathog Glob Health*. 111, 7 (2017): 343–50. doi:10.1080/20477724.2017 .1396411.

Chandra, Uday. 'Rethinking Subaltern Resistance'. *Journal of Contemporary Asia* 45, 4 (2015): 563–73. https://doi: org/10.1080/00472336.2015.1048415.

Chandru, S., and K. Thrimalaisamy. 'Status of Narikoravar (A Type of Gypsy Community) Women Entrepreneur in Coimbatore, Tamil Nadu', *Asian Review of Social Sciences* (2019): 150–5. Accessed 14 August 2021. https://www.trp.org.in/ issues/status-of-narikoravar-a-type-of-gypsy-community-women-entrepreneur-in-coimbatore-tamil-nadu.

Chang, Felix. 'Roma Integration "All the Way Down"'. *Critical Romani Studies* 1, 1 (2018): 62–85. doi: 10.29098/crs.v1i1.1.

Chatterjee, Partha. 'After Subaltern Studies'. *Economic and Political Weekly* 47, 35 (2012): 44–9.

Chatterjee, Partha. *Lineages of Political Society: Studies in Postcolonial Democracy.* New York, Chichester: Columbia University Press, 2011.

Chatterjee, Partha. *The Politics of the Governed: Reflections on Popular Politics in most of the World.* New York, Chichester: Columbia University Press, 2006.

Chaudary, S. N. 'In Between Inclusion and Exclusion: The changing face of health and disease management practices among Gonds in a central Indian village', in *Adivasi Rights and Exclusion in India*, ed. S.V. Rao. London: Routledge, 2018.

Chiriac, Bogdan. 'Mihail Kogălniceanu's Historical Inquiry into the Question of Roma Slavery in Mid-Nineteenth-Century Romanian Principalities'. *Critical Romani Studies* 2, 2 (2 December 2020): 24–41. https://doi.org/10.29098/crs.v2i2.64.

Cierco, Teresa. 'The Limits of Europeanization on Minority Rights in Serbia: The Roma Minority'. *International Journal on Minority and Group Rights* 24, 2 (2017): 123–49. doi: https://doi.org/10.1163/15685373-124021019.

Clegg, Stewart R. and Mark Haugaard. *The SAGE Handbook of Power*. London: Sage Publications, 2009.

Courthiade, Marcel. *Petite histoire du peuple rrom. Première diaspora historique de l'Inde,* Le Bord De L'eau Eds, 2017.

Collins, Patricia Hill. 'Gender, Black Feminism, and Black Political Economy'. *ANNALS of the American Academy of Political and Social Science* 568, 1 (March 2000): 41–53. https://doi.org/10.1177/000271620056800105.

Collins, Patricia Hill. *Black Feminist Thought: Knowledge, Consciousness, and the Politics of Empowerment*. London: Routledge, 2002.

Corradi, Laura. *Gypsy Feminism: Intersectional Politics, Alliances, Gender and Queer Activism*. London: Routledge, 2017.

Costache, Ioanida. 'Reclaiming Romani-Ness'. *Critical Romani Studies* 1, 1 (13 April 2018): 30–43. https://doi.org/10.29098/crs.v1i1.11.

Crenshaw, Kimberle. 'Mapping the Margins: Intersectionality, Identity Politics, and Violence against Women of Color'. *Stanford Law Review* 43, 6 (1991): 1241–99. Accessed 16 August 2021. doi:10.2307/1229039.

Crenshaw, Kimberle, Neil Gotanda, Gary Peller and Charles Inglis (1996). Critical Race Theory: The Key Writings that Formed the Movement. 106.

Crosby, F., S. Bromley and L. Saxe. 'Recent Unobtrusive Studies of Black and White Discrimination and Prejudice: A literature review'. *Psychological Bulletin*, 87, 3 (1980): 546–63. https://doi.org/10.1037/0033-2909.87.3.546.

Crosby, Faye. 'The Denial of Personal Discrimination'. *American Behavioral Scientist* 27, 3 (January 1984): 371–86. https://doi.org/10.1177/000276484027003008.

Crowe, David. *A History of the Gypsies of Eastern Europe and Russia*. New York: Palgrave Macmillan, 1996.

D'Agostino, Serena. '(In)Visible Mobilizations. Romani Women's Intersectional Activisms in Romania and Bulgaria'. *Politics, Groups, and Identities* 9, 1 (14 June 2019): 170–89. https://doi.org/10.1080/21565503.2019.1629307.

Das, Laponi. *Journal of Adivasi and Indigenous Studies* (JAIS) (A bi-annual peer-reviewed online journal posted on Academia.edu), vol. X, no. 1, February 2020: 87–96.

Das, Maitreyi Bordia, and Soumya Kapoor Mehta. *Poverty and Social Exclusion in India*. Washington, D.C.: World Bank Group, January 2012. https://openknowledge. worldbank.org/handle/10986/26335.

Das, Samarendra, and Felix Padel. *Out of This Earth: East India Adivasis and the Aluminium Cartel*. Hyderabad: Orient Black Swan, 2010.

Dasgupta, Sangeeta. 'Adivasi Studies: From a Historian's Perspective'. *History Compass* 16, 10 (11 September 2018). https://doi.org/10.1111/hic3.12486.

Das Gupta, Sanjukta, and Raj Sekhar Basu. *Narratives from the Margins: Aspects of Adivasi History in India*. New Delhi: Primus Books, 2012.

Delgado, Richard, Jean Stefancic and Angela Harris. *Critical Race Theory (Third Edition): An Introduction*. New York: New York University Press, 2017. Accessed 16 August 2021. doi:10.2307/j.ctt1ggjjn3.

Devy, G. N., Geoffrey V. Davis and K. K. Chakravarty, eds. *Narrating Nomadism: Tales of Recovery and Resistance*. New Delhi: Routledge, 2013.

Dragomir, Cristina-Ioana. 'Scheduled Tribe Status: The Need for Clarification', in *India in Transition*, University of Pennsylvania, 2017. https://casi.sas.upenn.edu/iit/ cristinaioanadragomir.

Dragomir, Cristina-Ioana. 'STs, and the Politics of Exclusion', *The Hindu Business Line* (12 January 2018). https://www.thehindubusinessline.com/opinion/sts-and-the-politics-of-exclusion/article9583825.ece.

Dragomir, Cristina-Ioana. 'Gender Practices as Rituals of Knowledge'. *International Feminist Journal of Politics* 21, 2 (2019): 326–33. doi: 10.1080/14616742.2019.1599296.

Dragomir, Cristina-Ioana and Mara Zafiu. 'Vulnerable Populations' Access to Health Care: a Study of the Nomadic "Gypsy" Narikuravars in Tamil Nadu, India'. *International Journal of Roma Studies* 1, 1 (2019): 58–83. doi: 10.17583/ ijrs.2019.3034.

Dragomir, Cristina-Ioana. (2020a) 'Destabilizing the Privilege of the Knower to Establish Forms of Solidarity: Reflections on Conducting Fieldwork with Vulnerable

Communities in India and Romania'. *Methodological Innovations* (September). https://doi.org/10.1177/2059799120968728.

Dragomir Cristina-Ioana. (2020b) 'The Narikuravars' Quest for Political Engagement in Perambalur During COVID-19', in *India in Transition*, University of Pennsylvania. https://casi.sas.upenn.edu/iit/cristinaioanadragomir2020.

Dube, S. C. *Tribal Heritage of India*. New Delhi: Vikas Pub. House, 1977.

Dubey, Amaresh. 'Exclusion and Persistence of Poverty Among Adivasis in India: A disaggregated analysis', in *Adivasi Rights and Exclusion in India*, ed. S.V. Rao. London: Routledge, 2018.

Dunajeva, Jekatyerina, Gopalakrishnan Karunanithi, Andrew Ryde and Nidhi Trehan. 'Collectivity and Empowerment in Addressing Marginality: The Roma and the Subaltern Communities of India'. *The Indian Journal of Social Work* 78, 1(1) (2017).

Dutta, Uttaran. 'Adivasi Media in India: Relevance in Representing Marginalized Voices'. *Intercultural Communication Studies* 35, 3 (2016): 213–31. https://web.uri.edu/iaics/files/Uttaran-DUTTA.pdf.

Eileraas, Karina. 'Reframing the Colonial Gaze: Photography, Ownership, and Feminist Resistance'. *MLN* 118, 4 (2003): 807–40. Accessed 16 August 2021. http://www.jstor.org/stable/3251988.

Few-Demo, April L. 'Intersectionality as the "New" Critical Approach in Feminist Family Studies: Evolving Racial/Ethnic Feminisms and Critical Race Theories'. *Journal of Family Theory & Review* 6, 2 (2014): 169–83. https://doi.org/10.1111/jftr.12039.

Firstpost. 'Land Pirates of Tamil Nadu History Forgot-India News', 2019. https://www.firstpost.com/india/land-pirates-of-tamil-nadu-that-history-forgot-6707351.html.

Foisneau, Lise. 'Dedicated Caravan Sites for French Gens du Voyage: Public Health Policy or Construction of Health and Environmental Inequalities?' *Health and Human Rights Journal* 19, 2 (2017). https://www.hhrjournal.org/2017/12/dedicated-caravan-sites-for-french-gens-du-voyage-public-health-policy-or-construction-of-health-and-environmental-inequalities/.

Földes, Maria Eva, and Alina Covaci. 'Research on Roma Health and Access to Healthcare: State of the Art and Future Challenges'. *International Journal of Public Health* 57, 1 (2012): 37–9. doi: 10.1007/s00038-011-0312-2.

Fonseca, Isabel. *Bury Me Standing: The Gypsies and Their Journey*. New York: Vintage, 1996.

Fraser, Nancy. 'Rethinking Recognition'. *New Left Review* 3 (2000). Accessed 22 March 2018. https://newleftreview.org/issues/ii3/articles/nancy-fraser-rethinking-recognition.

Fraser, Nancy. *Scales of Justice: Reimaging Political Space in a Globalizing World*. New York: Columbia University, 2010.

Fremlova, L. 'The experiences of Romani LGBTIQ people: queer(y)(ing)'. Student thesis: Doctoral thesis (2017). Accessed 14 August 2021. https://research.brighton.ac.uk/en/studentTheses/the-experiences-of-romani-lgbtiq-people-queerying-roma.

Gandhi, Malli. 'Developmental Challenges of Nomadic and Denotified Tribes of India with Special Reference to Andhra Pradesh', in *Adivasi Rights and Exclusion in India*, ed. S.V. Rao. London: Routledge, 2018.

Gandhi, Malli and K. H. S. S. Sundar. *Denotified Tribes of India: Discrimination, Development and Change*. London: Routledge (2019). https://doi.org/10.4324/9781003017622.

Gheorghe, Nicolae. *Nicolae Gheorghe: o viata dedicata romilor : culegere de texte, eseuri, dialoguri*. Bucharest: Centrul National de Cultura a Romilor, 2016.

Gómez-Carballa, A., J. Pardo-Seco, L. Fachal, A. Vega, M. Cebey, N. Martinón-Torres, et al. 'Indian Signatures in the Westernmost Edge of the European Romani Diaspora: New Insight from Mitogenomes'. *PLoS ONE* 8, 10 (2013): e75397. https://doi.org/10.1371/journal.pone.0075397.

Grigore, Delia. *Curs De Antropologie ŞI Folclor Rrom: Introducere În Studiul Elementelor De cultură tradiţională Ale identităţii Rrome Contemporane*. Bucharest: Credis, 2001.

Grigore, Delia, and Sarău Gheorghe. *Istorie şi tradiţii rrome*. Bucharest: Salvaţi Copiii, 2006.

Grigore, Delia, Mihai Neacsu and Adrian-Nicolae Furtuna. *Rromii . . . în căutarea stimei de sine: studiu introductiv*. Bucharest: Vanemonde, 2007.

Guimond, S., and L. Dubé-Simard. 'Relative Deprivation Theory and the Quebec Nationalist Movement: The cognition-emotion distinction and the personal-group deprivation issue'. *Journal of Personality and Social Psychology* 44 (1983): 526–35.

Gupta, Malvika, and Padel Felix. 'Indigenous Knowledge and Value Systems in India: Holistic Analysis of Tribal Education and the Challenge of Decentralising Control', in *Shifting Perspectives in Tribal Studies: From an Anthropological Approach to Interdisciplinarity and Consilience*, ed. M. C. Behara. Singapore: Springer, 2019, 67–86.

Hanchard, Michael. 'Contours of Black Political Thought: An Introduction and Perspective'. *Political Theory* 38, 4 (2010): 510–36. http://www.jstor.org/stable/25704831.

Hancock, Ian. 'The East European Roots of Romani Nationalism'. *Nationalities Papers*, 19, 3 (1991): 251–67. doi: 10.1080/00905999108408203.

Hancock, Ian. *We are the Romani People. Ame sam e Rromane džene*. Hatfield: Centre de recherches tsiganes/ University of Hertfordshire Press, 2002.

Heidegger, Patrizia, and Wiese Katy. *Pushed to the Wastelands: Environmental Racism Against Roma Communities in Central and Eastern Europe*. Brussels: European Environmental Bureau, 2020.

Jones, Camara Phyllis. 'Toward the Science and Practice of Anti-Racism: Launching a National Campaign against Racism'. *Ethnicity & Disease* 28, Supp 1 (8 August 2018): 231–4. https://doi.org/10.18865/ed.28.s1.231.

Kannabiran, Kalpana. 'Vulnerable Communities'. *Economic and Political Weekly*, 24 November 2017. https://www.epw.in/journal/2017/42-43/editorials/vulnerable-communities.html-0.

Kannabiran, Kalpana, Sujit Kumar Mishra, Soumya Vinayan and K. Jafar. 'Education and Its Discontents: Investigating Barriers to Schooling Among De-Notified and Nomadic Communities'. *Journal of Social Inclusion Studies* 4, 1 (2018): 80–103. https://doi.org/10.1177/2394481118774488.

Karlsson, Bengt G., and Dolly Kikon. 'Wayfinding: Indigenous Migrants in the Service Sector of Metropolitan India'. *South Asia: Journal of South Asian Studies* 40, 3 (2017): 447–62. https://doi.org/10.1080/00856401.2017.1319145.

Kaur, Ravinder. 'Mapping the Adverse Consequences of Sex Selection and Gender Imbalance in India and China'. *Economic and Political Weekly* 48, 35 (2013): 37–44. http://www.jstor.org/stable/23528753.

Kóczé, Angela and Raluca Maria Popa. 'Missing Intersectionality: Race/Ethnicity, Gender, and Class in Current Research and Policies on Romani Women in Europe'. *Digital Library on Democracy*, 2009. Accessed 16 August 2021. https://dld.omeka.net/items/show/3309.

Kóczé, Angéla, Violetta Zentai, Jelena Jovanovic and Magyari-Vincze Enikő, eds. *The Romani Women's Movement: Struggles and Debates in Central and Eastern Europe*. London: Routledge, 2018.

Kolekar, Sanjay. 'Violence Against Nomadic Tribes'. *Economic and Political Weekly* 43, 26/27 (2008): 569–71. Accessed 16 August 2021. http://www.jstor.org/stable/40278917.

Kumar, Sujit. 'Adivasis and the State Politics in Jharkhand'. *Studies in Indian Politics* 6, 1 (June 2018): 103–16. https://doi.org/10.1177/2321023018762821.

Lahiri, Amartya. 'The Great Indian Demonetization'. *Journal of Economic Perspectives* 34, 1 (2020): 55–74. https://doi.org/10.1257/jep.34.1.55.

Lal, Chaman. *Gipsies: Forgotten Children of India*. New Delhi: Publications Division, Ministry of Information and Broadcasting, 1962.

Lange, Barbara Rose. *Notes 69*, no. 4 (2013): 748–50. Accessed 16 August 2021. http://www.jstor.org/stable/43672653.

Lauritzen, Solvor. 'Nomadism in Research on Roma Education'. *Critical Romani Studies* 1, 2 (2018): 58–75. https://doi.org/10.29098/crs.v1i2.2.

Lee, Ken. 'Orientalism and Gypsylorism'. *Social Analysis: The International Journal of Social and Cultural Practice* 44, 2 (2000): 129–56. Accessed 14 August 2021. http://www.jstor.org/stable/23166537.

Lucassen, Jan, and Leo Lucassen. *Migration, Migration History, History: Old Paradigms and New Perspectives*. Bern: P. Lang, 1997/2005.

Lucassen, Leo, and Wim Willems, eds. *Living in the City: Urban Institutions in the Low Countries, 1200–2010*. New York: Routledge, 2012.

Lucassen, Leo, and Wim Willems. 'The Weakness of Well-Ordered Societies: Gypsies in Western Europe, the Ottoman Empire, and India, 1400–1914'. *Review (Fernand Braudel Center)* 26, 3 (2003): 283–313. http://www.jstor.org/stable/40241578; accessed 2 December 2021.

Magazzini, Tina, and Stefano Piemontese. *Constructing Roma Migrants: European Narratives and Local Governance.* Cham: Springer International Publishing, 2019. http://hdl.handle.net/1814/61904.

Mahi Pal. 'Panchayats in Fifth Scheduled Areas'. *Economic and Political Weekly* 35, 19 (2000): 1602–6. Accessed 16 August 2021. http://www.jstor.org/stable/4409256.

Majumdar, Dhirendra Nath. *A Tribe in Transition; a Study in Culture Pattern.* Calcutta: Longmans, Green & Co., 1937.

Majumdar, Dhirendra Nath. *Races and Culture of India.* Bombay: Asia Publishing House, 1961.

Maldonado-Torres, Nelson. 'On the Coloniality of Being'. *Cultural Studies* 21, 2 (2007): 240–70.

Malhotra, Rajiv and Satyanarayana Dasa Babaji. *Sanskrit Non-Translatables: The Importance of Sanskritizing English.* New Delhi: Amaryllis, 2020.

Martínez-Cruz, B., I. Mendizabal, C. Harmant, et al. 'Origins, Admixture and Founder Lineages in European Roma'. *Eur J Hum Genet* 24 (2016): 937–43. https://doi.org/10.1038/ejhg.2015.201.

Marushiakova, Elena, and Vesselin Popov, eds. *Roma Voices in History: A Sourcebook.* Brill, 2021. http://www.jstor.org/stable/10.1163/j.ctv1sr6k09.

Matache, Margareta. 'Dear Gadje (Non-Romani) Scholars …'. FXB Center for Health and Human Rights, Harvard University, 13 September 2018. https://fxb.harvard.edu/2017/06/19/dear-gadje-non-romani-scholars/.

Matras, Yaron. 'The Role of Language in Mystifying and De-mystifying Gypsy Identity', in *The Role of the Romanies*, ed. N. Saul and S. Tebbut. Liverpool: Liverpool University Press, 2004, 53–78.

Matras, Yaron. *I Met Lucky People: The Story of the Romani Gypsies.* London: Penguin, Random House UK, 2014.

Matras, Yaron. *The Romani Gypsies.* Cambridge, MA: The Belknap Press of Harvard University Press, 2015.

Mayall, David. *Gypsy-Travellers in Nineteenth-Century Society.* Cambridge: Cambridge University Press, 1988.

McDowell, Bart. *Gypsies, Wandered of the World.* National Geographic Society (1970).

McGarry, Aidan. *Romaphobia: The Last Acceptable Form of Racism.* London: Zed Books, 2017

McGonagle, Alyssa K. 'Testing a Model of Stigma Applied to Chronic Illness in the Workplace' (2011). Doctoral Dissertation. AAI3485412. https://opencommons.uconn.edu/dissertations/AAI3485412.

Mills, Aaron, Karen Drake and Tanya Muthusamipillai. 'An Anishinaabe Constitutional Order'. *Articles & Book Chapters* (2017): 2695. https://digitalcommons.osgoode.yorku.ca/scholarly_works/2695.

Mignolo, Walter. 'The Geopolitics of Knowledge and the Colonial Difference'. *South Atlantic Quarterly* 101 (2002): 57–96. doi: 10.1215/00382876-101-1-57.

Mignolo, Walter D. and Catherine E. Walsh. *On Decoloniality: Concepts, Analytics, Praxis*. Durham: Duke University Press, 2018.

Minority Rights Group International, *World Directory of Minorities and Indigenous Peoples – India: Adivasis* (2008), available at: https://www.refworld.org/docid/49749d14c.html [accessed 16 August 2021].

Mirga, Andrej. 'Roma Policy in Europe: Results and Challenges', in *Realizing Roma Rights*, eds Jacqueline Bhabha, Andrzej Mirga and Margareta Matache, Philadelphia: University of Pennsylvania Press, 'Critical Romani Studies' 2: 60–62. doi: 10.29098/crs.v2i2.108; 2017

Mirga, Andrej and Nicolae Gheorghe. *The Roma in the Twenty-first Century: a Policy Paper*. Princeton: Project on Ethnic Relations, 1997.

Mitchell, Lisa. 'Hailing the State: Political Arrival and Genealogies of Political Communication in Contemporary India'. University of Pennsylvania panel discussion: *The Technologized Call: Subjects of Responsibility in Mass-Mediated Religions and Cultures*, San Francisco, 15 November 2012.

Moisă, F., I. A. Rostas, D. Tarnovschi, I. Stoian, D. Rădulescu and T. S. Andersen. *Raportul societății civile asupra implementării Strategiei Naționale de Integrare a Romilor și a Planului de Acțiune al Deceniului în România în 2012*. Budapest: Decade of Roma Inclusion Secretariat Foundation, 2019.

Moorjani, Priya, Nick Patterson, Po-Ru Loh, Mark Lipson, Péter Kisfali, Bela I. Melegh, et al. 'Reconstructing Roma History from Genome-Wide Data'. *PLoS ONE* 8, 3 (2013): e58633. https://doi.org/10.1371/journal.pone.0058633.

Morar, Bharti, David Gresham, Dora Angelicheva, Ivailo Tournev, Rebecca Gooding, Velina Guergueltcheva, Carolin Schmidt, et al. 'Mutation History of the Roma/Gypsies'. *American Journal of Human Genetics* 75, 4 (2004): 596–609. https://doi.org/10.1086/424759.

Mosse, David, Sanjeev Gupta and Vidya Shah. 'On the Margins in the City: Adivasi Seasonal Labour Migration in Western India'. *Economic and Political Weekly* 40, 28 (2005): 3025-38. Accessed 22 August 2021. http://www.jstor.org/stable/4416873.

Mukhopadhyay, Sutapa, and Ray Ranjana. 'Mother Care Among Some Bathudi Tribal Women in Simplipal Reserve Forest Area in Eastern India', in *Shifting Perspectives in Tribal Studies: From an Anthropological Approach to Interdisciplinarity and Consilience*, ed. M. C. Behara. Singapore: Springer, 2019, 313–25.

Muralidhar, G. 'Livelihoods of Adivasis in India: Continuing Marginalization', in *Adivasi Rights and Exclusion in India*, ed. S.V. Rao. London: Routledge, 2018.

Murti, A. Mantra. 'Traditional Panchayat System of The Badagas of The Nilgiris'. *Indian Journal of Political Science* 42, 3 (1981): 48–61. Accessed 14 August 2021. http://www.jstor.org/stable/41855096.

Nagy, Melinda, Lotte Henke, Jürgen Henke, Prasanta K. Chatthopadhyay, Antónia Völgyi, Andrea Zalán, Orsolya Peterman, Jarmila Bernasovská, and Horolma Pamjav. 'Searching for the Origin of Romanies: Slovakian Romani, Jats of Haryana and Jat Sikhs Y-STR Data in Comparison with Different Romani

Populations'. *Forensic Science International* 169, 1 (2007): 19–26. https://doi. org/10.1016/j.forsciint.2006.07.020.

Naik, V. Sarveswara. 'Natal to Conjugal Household through Marriage: A Traditional Life Cycle of the Lambadi (Banjara) Women in Andhra Pradesh'. *Indian Anthropologist* 26, 1 (1996): 27–35. Accessed 16 August 2021. http://www.jstor.org/ stable/41919790.

Necula, Ciprian. 'Roma Sovieticus: Roma Experience under Communism'. European Roma Institute for Arts and Culture Panel Video. Viewed 13 October 2020. https://fb.watch/7y5H8aEi60.

Neela, N., and G. Ambrosia. 'The Reclamation of Criminal Tribes in Tamilnadu With Special Reference to Koravas'. *Shanlax International Journal of Arts, Science and Humanities* 3, 2 (2015): 44–9. http://www.shanlaxjournals.in/journals/index.php/ sijash/article/view/1229.

Nilsen, Alf Gunvald. 'Adivasi Mobilization in Contemporary India: Democratizing the Local State?' *Critical Sociology* 39, 4 (July 2013): 615–33. https://doi.org/10.1177/ 0896920512443574.

Oprea, Alexandra. 'Romani Feminism in Reactionary Times'. *Signs* 38 (2012): 11–21. doi: 10.1086/665945.

Oremus, Will. 'Did Obama Hug a Radical?' *Slate Magazine*, 9 March 2012. https://slate. com/news-and-politics/2012/03/derrick-bell-controversy-whats-critical-race-theory-and-is-it-radical.html.

Petcut, Petre. *Rromii, Sclavie si Liberate: Constituirea si emaniciparea unei noi categorii ethnice si sociale la nord de Dunare 1370–1914*. Bucharest: Centrului Național de Cultură a Romilor, 2016.

Picker, Giovanni. *Racial Cities: Governance and the Segregation of Romani People in Urban Europe*. London: Routledge, 2017.

Piliavsky, Anastasia. 'A Secret in the Oxford Sense: Thieves and the Rhetoric of Mystification in Western India'. *Comparative Studies in Society and History* 53, 2 (2011): 290–313. https://doi.org/10.1017/S0010417511000065.

Piliavsky, Anastasia. 'Please Don't Beat Me, Sir!' *American Anthropologist* 114, 2 (2012): 369–70. https://doi.org/10.1111/j.1548-1433.2012.01438.x.

Piliavsky, Anastasia. 'Secrets in the Field: The Antics of Researching Rajasthan's Banditry'. *Edinburgh Papers in South Asian Studies* 21, 1 (2006). Accessed 12 February 2015. https://scholar.google.co.uk/citations?view_op=view_citation&#hl=en&user=31z-eYcAAAAJ&citation_for_view=31z-eYcAAAAJ:9yKSN-GCB0IC.

Pons, Emmanuelle. *Les Tsiganes en Roumanie: Des Citoyens à Part Entière?* Paris: Éditions L'harmattan, 1995.

Pusca, Anca. *Eastern European Roma in the EU: Mobility, Discrimination, Solutions*. New York: International Debate Education Association, 2012.

Pusca, Anca. *Roma in Europe: Migration, Education, Representation*. New York: International Debate Education Association, 2012.

Quijano, Aníbal. 'Coloniality and Modernity/Rationality'. *Cultural Studies* 21, 2–3 (2007): 168–78. doi: 10.1080/09502380601164353.

Radhakrishna, Meena. 'Colonial Construction of a "Criminal" Tribe: Yerukulas of Madras Presidency'. *Economic and Political Weekly* 35, 28/29 (2000): 2553–63. http://www.jstor.org/stable/4409505 (accessed 1 December 2020).

Radhakrishna, Meena. *Dishonoured by History: 'Criminal Tribes' and British Colonial Policy*. New Delhi: Orient Longman, 2001.

Rai Niraj, Chaubey Gyaneshwer, Tamang Rakesh, Pathak Ajai Kumar, Singh Vipin Kumar, Karmin Monika, et al. 'The Phylogeography of Y-Chromosome Haplogroup H1a1a-M82 Reveals the Likely Indian Origin of the European Romani Populations'. *PLoS ONE* 7, 11 (2012): e48477. https://doi.org/10.1371/journal.pone.0048477.

Raile, Rocky Zilpao. 'Tribes and Tribal Studies in North East India: Deconstructing the Politics of Colonial Methodology'. https://www.academia.edu/6505077/Tribes_and_Tribal_Studies_in_North_East_India_Deconstructing_the_Politics_of_Colonial_Methodology (accessed 16 August 2021).

Ranendra. '"Subaltern" or the "Sovereign": Revisiting the History of Tribal State Formation in India'. *Journal of Adivasi and Indigenous Studies* 10, 1 (2020): 51–68. http://joais.in/Journal/4.%20Ranendra,%20Subalter%20or%20the%20Sovereign%2051-58@.pdf.

Rangarajan, Mahesh. 'Environmental Histories of South Asia: A Review Essay'. *Environment and History* 2, 2 (June, 1996), South Asia special issue: 129–43. doi:10.3197/096734096779522347.

Rao, V. Srinivasa (ed.). *Adivasi Rights and Exclusion in India* (1st edn). Delhi: Routledge India, 2018. https://doi.org/10.4324/9780429437076.

Rawat, Ramnarayan S., and K. Satyanarayana, eds. *Dalit Studies*. Duke University Press (April 2016).

Rawat, Ramnarayan S., and K. Satyanarayana. 'Introduction: Dalit Studies: New Perspectives on Indian History and Society', in *Dalit Studies*, eds Rawat, S. Ramnarayan and K. Satyanarayana, (April 2016). Duke University Press.

'Recovering the Archives of Adivasi Communities through Adivasi Studies'. Council for Social Development. http://www.csdhyd.org/adivasi_studies.html.

'Romani Women in Romani and Majority Societies'. European Roma Rights Centre, 12 April 2000. http://www.errc.org/roma-rights-journal/romani-women-in-romani-and-majority-societies.

Rostas, Iulius. 'The Romani Movement in Romania: Institutionalization and (De)Mobilization', in *Romani Politics in Contemporary Europe: Poverty, Ethnic Mobilization, and the Neoliberal Order*, eds Nidhi Trehan and Nando Sigona, 159–85. Basingstoke: Palgrave Macmillan, 2009.

Rostas, Iulius. *A Task for Sisyphus: Why Europe's Roma Policies Fail*. Budapest: Central European University Press, 2019. http://www.jstor.org/stable/10.7829/j.ctv1453hvp.

Rostas, Iulius and Anita Danka. 'Setting the Roma Policy Agenda: The Role of International Organizations in Combating School Segregation', in *Ten Years After: A History of Roma School Desegregation in Central and Eastern Europe*, ed. Iulius Rostas. Central European University Press, 2012. http://www.jstor.org/stable/10.7829/j.ctt128207.

Rostas, Iulius, and Andrew Ryder. 'The Roma in Europe: the Debate over the Possibilities for Empowerment to Seek Social Justice', in *Hearing the Voices of Gypsy, Roma and Traveller Communities: Inclusive Community Development*, eds Andrew Ryder, Sarah Cemlyn and T. A. Acton. Bristol: Policy Press, 2014.

Rostas, Iulius, and Rövid Márton. 'On Roma Civil Society, Roma Inclusion, and Roma Participation'. *Roma Rights* 2 (January 2015): 7–10. https://www.researchgate.net/publication/320445052_On_Roma_Civil_Society_Roma_Inclusion_and_Roma_Participation.

Rughiniş, Cosima. 'Quantitative Tales of Ethnic Differentiation: Measuring and Using Roma / Gypsy Ethnicity in Statistical Analyzes', in *Ethnic and Racial Studies*, 34, 4 (2011): 594–619.

Ruz, Tania Sordo. *Guide on Intersectional Discrimination: The Case of Roma Women*. Madrid: Fundación Secretariado Gitano, 2019.

Ryder, Andrew Richard, Iulius Rostas and Marius Taba. '"Nothing About Us Without Us": The Role of Inclusive Community Development in School Desegregation for Roma Communities'. *Race Ethnicity and Education* 17, 4 (2014): 518–39. https://doi.org/10.1080/13613324.2014.885426.

Schultz, Debra L. 'Translating Intersectionality Theory into Practice: A Tale of Romani-Gadže Feminist Alliance'. *Signs* 38, 1 (2012): 37–43. Accessed 19 March 2021. doi: 10.1086/665802.

Schultz, Debra, and Nicoleta Bitu. 'Missed Opportunity or Building Blocks of a Movement? History and Lessons from the Roma Women's Initiative's Efforts to Organize European Romani Women's Activism', in *The Romani Women's Movement: Struggles and Debates in Central and Eastern Europe*, eds Angéla Kóczé, Violetta Zentai, Jelena Jovanovic and Magyari-Vincze Enikő. London: Routledge, 2018.

Schwartz, Stephan A. 'Police Brutality and Racism in America'. *Explore (New York, N.Y.)* 16, 5 (2020): 280–2. doi: 10.1016/j.explore.2020.06.010.

Scott, James C. *Weapons of the Weak: Everyday Forms of Peasant Resistance*. New Haven: Yale University Press, 1985.

Sen, Asoka Kumar, and Sanjay Nath, eds. *Journal of Adivasi and Indigenous Studies* (February 2020). https://www.academia.edu/43969523/Journal_of_Adivasi_and_Indigenous_Studies.

Shah, A. M. 'Purity, Impurity, Untouchability: Then and Now'. *Sociological Bulletin* 56, 3 (2007): 355–68. Accessed 22 August 2021 http://www.jstor.org/stable/23620634.

Shashi, Shyam Singh. *Roma: The Gypsy World*. Delhi: Sandeep Prakashan, 1990.

Shattuck, John. *Ten Years After: A History of Roma School Desegregation in Central and Eastern Europe*, ed. Iulius Rostas. Central European University Press, 2012. http://www.jstor.org/stable/10.7829/j.ctt128207 (accessed 23 December 2021).

Shmidt, Victoria and Bernadette Nadya Jaworsky. *Historicizing Roma in Central Europe: Between Critical Whiteness and Epistemic Injustice* (1st edn). Routledge, 2020. https://doi.org/10.4324/9781003034094.

Sigona, Nando, and Nidhi Trehan. *Romani Politics in Contemporary Europe: Poverty, Ethnic Mobilization, and the Neoliberal Order*. Basingstoke: Palgrave Macmillan, 2009.

Silverman, Carol. *Romani Routes: Cultural Politics and Balkan Music in Diaspora*. Oxford: Oxford University Press, 2012.

Smith, David, and Margaret Greenfields. 'Housed Gypsies and Travellers in the UK: Work, Exclusion and Adaptation'. *Race & Class* 53, 3 (2012): 48–64. https://doi.org/10.1177/0306396811425985.

Smith, David M., and Margaret Greenfields. *Gypsies and Travellers in Housing: The Decline of Nomadism*. Bristol: Polity Press, 2013.

Soni-Sinha, Urvashi. 'Intersectionality, Subjectivity, Collectivity and the Union: A Study of the "Locked-out" Hotel Workers in Toronto'. *Organization* 20, 6 (27 August 2012): 775–93. https://doi.org/10.1177/1350508412453364.

Srivastava, V. K. *The Pahari Korwas: Socio-economic Conditions and their Development*. New Delhi: Sonali Publications, 2007.

Stewart, Michael. *The Time of the Gypsies*. New York: Routledge, 1997.

Surdu, Mihai. *Those Who Count: Expert Practices of Roma Classification*. Budapest: Central European University Press, 2016. http://www.jstor.org/stable/10.7829/j.ctt1ggjj08.

Swamy, Arun R. 'Sense, Sentiment and Populist Coalitions: The Strange Career of Cultural Nationalism in Tamil Nadu 1' (2019).

Trehan, Nidhi. 'The Contentious Politics of the Indo-Romani Relationship: Reflections on the "International Roma Conference and Cultural Festival" in New Delhi, February 2016 and its Antecedents'. *Indian Journal of Social Work* 78, 1 (January 2017): 11–26. https://journals.tiss.edu/ijsw/index.php/ijsw/article/view/88.

Tribune News Service. 'The Scourge of Untouchability Continues'. Tribuneindia News Service, 14 April 2020. https://www.tribuneindia.com/news/comment/the-scourge-of-untouchability-continues-70718.

Tsekos, Mary Ellen. 'Minority Rights: The Failure of International Law to Protect the Roma'. *The Human Rights Brief* 9 (2002): 7.

Van Baar, Huub. 'Travelling Activism and Knowledge Formation in the Romani Social and Civil Movement', in *Roma Education in Europe: Practices, Policies and Politics*, ed. M. Miskovic. London: Routledge, 2013. https://doi.org/10.4324/9780203111987.

Voiculescu, Cerasela. *European Social Integration and the Roma: Questioning Neoliberal Governmentality*, 2016. doi: 10.4324/9781315708737.

Wike, Richard, Jacob Poushter, Laura Silver, Kat Devlin, Janell Fetterolf, Alexandra Castillo and Christine Huang. 'European Public Opinion Three Decades after the Fall of Communism'. *Pew Research Center's Global Attitudes Project*. Pew Research Center, 10 December 2020. https://www.pewresearch.org/global/2019/10/15/european-public-opinion-three-decades-after-the-fall-of-communism/.

Williams, Terry M. *The Cocaine Kids: The Inside Story of a Teenage Drug Ring*. Boston: Da Capo Press, 1990.

World Bank, 2011. *Poverty and Social Exclusion in India*. Washington, D.C. © World Bank. https://openknowledge.worldbank.org/handle/10986/2289 License: CC BY 3.0 IGO.

Yengde, Suraj. *Caste Matters*. India: Penguin Viking, 2019.

Zuni-Cruz, Christine. 'The Indigenous Decade in Review (2020)'. *SMU Law Review* 73, (2020), UNM School of Law Research Paper No. 2020-02, available at SSRN: https://ssrn.com/abstract=3589492.

Index